SEEDS OF FORTUNE

SEEDS OF FORTUNE
A GARDENING DYNASTY

Sue Shephard

FOREWORD BY ROY LANCASTER

BLOOMSBURY

Published by Bloomsbury, New York and London
Distributed to the trade by Holtzbrinck Publishers

Library of Congress Cataloging-in-Publication Data has been applied for.

ISBN 1-58234-256-3

First U.S. Edition 2003

1 3 5 7 9 10 8 6 4 2

Typeset by Palimpsest Book Production Limited,
Polmont, Stirlingshire, Scotland
Printed in Great Britain by Clays Limited, St Ives plc

In memory of
William and Thomas Lobb
and all the plant collectors, nurserymen
and gardeners who have filled our
gardens

PICTURE CREDITS

William Boutcher's Frontispiece
Dr. Hope and the Gardener
Courtesy of the Trustees of the National Library of Scotland

An 18th century Kensington Nursery
Courtesy of the Kensington & Chelsea Reference Library

Portrait of Sir Thomas Dyke Acland by Sir Joshua Reynolds
Courtesy of the National Trust. Killerton.Devon

Painting of Killerton: An aquatint from a drawing by L. E. Reed 1819
" "

'The Beech Walk'
'The Lady Cot'
From W. W. J. Gendall's 'Fragments of Killerton (1830)'
Courtesy of The Devon Record Office. Exeter

Portrait of Sir William Hooker
Portrait of Dr. Joseph Hooker
Courtesy of the Picture Archives of the Royal Botanic Gardens, Kew.

From *Hortus Veitchii*:
Portraits of members of the Veitch family
Nursery plan
Cyprepidium villosum
Lealiocattleya dominiana langleyensis
Rhododendron balsiminoeflorum
Cypripedium curtisii
Gooseberry 'Golden Gem'
Meconopsis integrifolia
Cypripedium x 'James H. Veitch'

ALL
Courtesy of the London Library.

Bicton Monkey-puzzle Avenue
Veitch's *Manual of Coniferae*
'Crossing the River' Joseph Hooker's *Himalayan Journals*
'Ascending Mt Fuji'. R. Alcock. *Capital of the Tycoons.*
'Phalaenopsis in the wild' <u>and</u>
'Crossing the River'. F. Burbidge. *Gardens of the Sun*
Ernest Wilson in Birmingham Botanical Gardens.
" "

" "

E. H. Wilson's 'Chinese Collectors in China'
E. H. Wilson in China
Courtesy of Roy Briggs

Photo of Wilson's Veitch watch
Courtesy of Barbara Abbott

Veitch advertisement
Veitch Nursery photographs
Courtesy of St Bridget's Nursery, Exeter

Portrait of Sir Harry Veitch
Courtesy of Exeter City Museums and Art Gallery

Colour plates from *Curtis's Botanical Magazine*:
 Cantua buxifolia
 Berberis darwinii
 Hamamelis mollis
 Rhododendron vernicosum
 Davidia involucrata
 Viburnum farreri
 Begonia pearcei
 Lilium auratum
 Vanda caerulea
Cover *Lapageria rosea*
 Cattleya dominyii from: *Dictionaire des Orchidee*
 Alfred Goosens.
Courtesy of the Royal Horticultural Society, Lindley Library

" "

Colour illustrations from: Veitch Catalogues
Photo of Sir Harry Veitch and the Orchid Committee 1920
" "

Colour plates from *The Garden*:
 Primula obconica
 Cerasus pseudo-cerasus
 Aeschynanthus speciosus
All other B&W illustrations are taken from issues of the *Gardener's Chronicle*
Courtesy of the Bristol University Library of Biological Sciences

" "

CONTENTS

An abridged family tree showing members of the family actively engaged in running the two branches of the Veitch Nurseries.

JOHN
(1752–1839)
BUDLAKE (Killerton)

CHELSEA   EXETER

                              THOMAS   JAMES
                              (c1790–?)   (1792–1863)

        JAMES JUNIOR   ROBERT
         (1815–1869)   TOSSWILL
                                            (1823–1885)

JOHN   HARRY   ARTHUR   PETER
GOULD   (1840–1924) (1844–1880)   (1850–1929)
(1839–1870)

JAMES   JOHN   MILDRED
HERBERT   GOULD JNR   (1889–1971)
(1869–1907)   (1870–1914)

FOREWORD BY ROY LANCASTER

If . . . we could gather together a history of all the nurseries which have existed, and do exist; of the men who founded and possessed them . . . what an interesting volume it would make! Such a volume, after a fashion, might be got together by much painful research; but still it would be far from complete.

Cottage Gardener, 15 August 1845

One of my most treasured books was given to me by a dear old friend who had decided that it would be of greater use to an active explorer than it would be occupying a place on her bookshelf. It is a handsome bound copy of *Hortus Veitchii*, a celebratory account of the great Veitch nursery empire published in 1906 for private circulation. Complimentary copies were sent to all the most influential and important botanists and horticulturists of the time. What makes my copy all the more precious to me is the signature of its original owner on the title page: 'A. Henry, Kew 24th April 1906'.

Augustine Henry (1857–1930) was one of the most significant botanists and plant collectors of the late nineteenth century. His work was greatly admired by members of the Veitch family and it was his activities which helped alert that nursery, and other botanical establishments in Europe and America, to the wealth of potential garden plants in Central and South West China. Henry's discoveries in the provinces of Hubei and Sichuan, particularly in the vicinity of the famous Yangtze Gorges, were responsible in large part for a renaissance of Chinese plant introductions to British gardens. His activities were the prelude to a period commonly referred to by garden historians and plant enthusiasts as a Golden Age which saw nurserymen such as the Veitches, botanical institutions and private patrons employing some of the most successful plant collectors to seek out new ornamentals suitable for culivation in western gardens.

One of these plant collectors, arguably the most successful, was E. H. Wilson (1876–1930) who attracted the sobriquet 'Chinese' Wilson in recognition of his travels and exploits in that country. It was Wilson who coined the phrase 'China – Mother of Gardens' and he who introduced from four

expeditions there between 1899 and 1911 over a thousand plants apparently
new to the western world. He was engaged by the Veitch nursery's then
chief, Harry, later Sir Harry, Veitch, for his first two expeditions to China
that resulted in a wealth of plants being raised for sale to English gardeners
in the firm's nursery grounds at Coombe Wood near Kingston-upon-
Thames in Surrey. Wilson was undoubtedly the right man in the right
place at the right time, but had it not been for Augustine Henry's earlier
discoveries and the entrepreneurial skills of the famous nursery firm of
James Veitch & Son of Chelsea, Wilson's plant introductions might not have
graced our gardens when they did.

It must be one of the greatest ironies in horticultural history that this
pinnacle of the nursery's achievements and influence should have been so
soon followed by its demise. The story of Britain's most famous nursery
dynasty spans three centuries and there can be few gardens in Britain today
that do not contain a reminder of its achievements. Wilson might have been
the most successful and best-remembered Veitch collector, but he
was by no means the first, and the names of William and Thomas Lobb,
F. W. Burbidge, Charles Maries, Charles Curtis as well as John Gould Veitch
also played significant roles in the firm's success. Then there were the Veitch
hybridists, especially John Dominy, John Seden and John Heal, who did
what was previously considered the impossible in producing desirable hybrids
between species introduced by their plant collectors, especially orchids, streptocarpus, tender rhododendrons, begonias, hippeastrums and pitcher plants.

The influence of the Veitch nursery empire on the development of ornamental horticulture in nineteenth-century Britain cannot be stressed too
highly and I firmly believe that the lives of all who enjoy gardens and
ornamental plants wherever they are grown have been and continue to be
enriched as a result. It must have come as no surprise to the horticultural
world when Harry Veitch received a knighthood in 1912 for services to
horticulture, an honour enjoyed by no other nurseryman until the late Sir
Harold Hillier in 1983. In the opinion of some, Hilliers assumed the mantle
of Veitch's, especially in terms of the vast range of woody plants grown
and offered for sale. For eighteen years (1962–80), I worked for the Hillier
nurseries, most of this time as Curator of what is now known as the Sir
Harold Hillier Gardens and Arboretum. It is here that I became familiar
with so many Veitch plants, including clematis, peonies, magnolias, viburnums, conifers and rhododendrons.

The very first time I was made aware of the Veitch connection was in the early 1950s when, as a young apprentice, I was put to work in the walled garden of Moss Bank Park in my home town of Bolton in Lancashire. At the damp end of a long herbaceous border I was given to weed, grew a huge clump of *Senecio veitchianus* (now *Ligularia veitchiana*), a tall-spiked, yellow-flowered perennial with long-stalked, rounded leaves that had been introduced by E. H. Wilson from China in 1901 and subsequently named for his employer who distributed it from the Coombe Wood Nursery. Some thirty years later, I had the pleasure of seeing this plant in the wild in China's Sichuan province where it grows by streams and in damp ditches in the mountains bordering Tibet. Indeed, on a number of visits to China during the 1980s I was lucky enough on several occasions to follow in the footsteps of Wilson when he was collecting for Veitch and saw many of the plants made famous by both collector and nursery. I particularly remember finding *Meliosma veitchiorum, Davidia involucrata, Rhododendron augustinii, Lilium regale, Viburnum harryanum* (named for Harry Veitch) in Sichuan whilst in Hubei in 1983 I encountered two of Wilson's most popular introductions, *Kolkwitzia amabilis*, the Beauty bush, and *Acer griseum* or Chinese paper bark maple.

Likewise, in 1997 and 1999 when travelling in Chile I was privileged to visit areas explored by two other Veitch collectors, Richard Pearce in the early 1860s, and Cornishman William Lobb in the 1840s when he introduced so many new or little-known plants to the Veitch Nurseries at Exeter, including the Monkey-puzzle *Araucaria araucana, Crinodendron hookerianum, Desfontainia spinosa* and *Berberis darwinii*. Earlier, in 1957 as a National Serviceman with the army in Malaya I was reminded of Veitch when I found the curious pitcher plant, *Nepenthes ampullaria*, and the Lady's Slipper Orchid, *Cypripedium barbatum*, both of which were first collected and introduced from here to the Veitch's Exeter Nursery by Thomas Lobb in the 1840s. In Japan meanwhile I have admired the many splendid conifers and other trees first introduced to England from these islands by Charles Maries and before him John Gould Veitch in 1860, amongst which *Abies veitchii, Sciadopitys verticillata, Picea polita, Tsuga diversifolia* and *Larix kaempferi* particularly come to mind.

The name of Veitch and of James Veitch Junior in particular will forever be commemorated in the form of a medal awarded annually by the Royal Horticultural Society to those who have helped in the advancement of the science and practice of horticulture. The Veitch Memorial Medal is a prestigious award that by its very nature can be enjoyed only by a select few.

By contrast, many of the plants introduced, selected or bred by the Veitch nurseries are available to all who love gardens and gardening. As for *Hortus Veitchii*, this scarce work belongs to the world of the antiquarian bookseller and collector which is why this new account should be welcomed by all who recognise and appreciate the efforts of those who devoted and sometimes lost their lives to horticulture. Detailing, as it does, the rise and fall of Britain's most famous nursery, it is a timely reminder of a family and an age the likes of which we shall never see again.

Roy Lancaster, 2003

Disa veitchii. One of the finest Veitch hybrid orchids
first flowered June 1891.

INTRODUCTION

Not wholly in the busy world, nor quite
Beyond it, blooms the garden that I love.
Alfred, Lord Tennyson,
'The Gardener's Daughter', 1833

I AM SURE I AM not alone in my addiction to horticultural nurseries, or garden centres, as many are now called. Some people, who like to indulge in 'retail therapy' in the shopping malls, might think us rather eccentric but there are increasing numbers of gardeners and plant lovers who will happily forego a day's shopping for happier hours exploring a nursery garden in the company of keen fellow gardeners. In this seductive world there is the chance to discover new plants and find fresh ideas for the garden. I usually buy far more than I can afford or have room for. But much of the fun is in simply looking and marvelling at how all these beautiful and fascinating plants have found their way from every part of the world into the nursery and thus into our gardens.

Whilst specialist nurseries offer rare and choice trees and shrubs or collections of one species for the collector, the big nurseries stock plants for most tastes and for every kind of garden and gardener – old-fashioned, new fashions, common or garden, reliable old friends and exotic novelties. We can wander along row upon row of trays and pots of tantalising young plants, bushes and trees. Most plants are happy to colonise new territory and, with a bit of help, will flourish in suitable environments similar to their original homeland. Many nurseries helpfully display plants in groups, such as those for dry shade, woodland wet, chalky, well-drained or full-on-sun. How much more intriguing if we were told that they came from the steamy, equatorial jungles of Brazil or the hot, dry veldt of Africa, the sharp, cold mountain ranges of the Himalayas or the Andes, the boggy, insect-filled forests of Borneo, the cool, shady forests of Japan or the towering cliffs along the great gorges of Central China.

Most gardeners are aware that their gardens are home to a myriad of international plantlife. Nevertheless it is amazing to think that at the end of the last Ice Age, the British Isles were home to only a handful of indigenous plants. Slowly they have become host to a vast and varied collection of flowers, trees and shrubs from almost every corner of the world. The majority of these introductions occurred over two centuries, between 1735 and 1935, and produced such an extraordinary and rapid transformation of the landscape and garden that the Reverend Henry Hill wrote in 1838 that 'our island may be compared to a vase emerging from the ocean, in which the Sylvans of every region have set their favourite plants, and the Flora of every climate poured her choicest gifts'.

Their cultivation in European and American gardens has been going on for so long now that we take it for granted. Yet behind many of the thousands of now familiar trees, shrubs and flowers lies a human story of endeavour, enterprise, determination, skill and patience and, above all, a consuming passion for botany and horticulture. Most of us are familiar with the adventures of the more famous plant 'hunters' and botanists who found and brought home dried specimens, seed and living plants. Sir Joseph Banks, Francis Masson, David Douglas, Robert Fortune and Ernest Wilson are names that spring to mind – men who were driven by a burning passion and carried by extraordinary courage and luck to succeed where tragically many more did less well, were forgotten or died far from home. The plant collectors risked their lives, travelling thousands of miles for long, weary and lonely years in dangerous, difficult and unexplored territories, making huge collections of new plants and seed of which only a tiny proportion ever arrived home. Precious collections were lost or destroyed in every kind of disaster: robbery, shipwreck, careless ship's captains and the inability of delicate, living plants to survive being uprooted and carried through alien conditions and environments.

I have always wondered what happened to the seed and plants that, having survived, ended up in either the private garden of some rich collector, the botanic garden for study, or the grounds of a commercial nurseryman. How did these people know how to germinate the seed, cultivate and propagate the plant, identify and name it? In my search, I discovered that many of the forgotten heroes of the transformation of a plant from the wild to the garden were ordinary gardeners and nurserymen. It was they who had the task of trying to bring seeds of unidentified new plants to life and re-create the right conditions in which they could grow. It was nurserymen too who took huge financial risks in funding their own plant-collecting expeditions and investing years of labour in raising stocks, hoping that gardeners would desire their new introductions enough to bring them a profit. From seed to sale often took many years of patience and skilled work in the nursery seed beds and glasshouses, and nurserymen spent long hours at their bench trying to unlock the secrets of each new plant. Later, after they had mastered the art of hybridisation, they created entirely new forms and colours to feed the gardening world's insatiable appetite for novelty and for bigger, brighter, longer-lasting flowers for all seasons.

The early story of English gardening is one of immense wealth and privilege in which kings, noblemen and rich merchants created collections of rare and exotic new plants to show off their wealth and sophistication. But few of their introductions ever came over the garden wall into ordinary gardens. Only when commercial nurserymen developed the skills to cultivate and propagate their plants on a large scale for sale to the general public did new plants begin to flood in. By the mid-nineteenth century there was an explosion of hot-house exotics, novelties, ornamental trees, hardy shrubs and bedding plants. The tremendous progress made in horticultural and botanical discovery could never have occurred, however, without the continued support of enthusiastic and wealthy patrons. Their mania for orchids and tropical exotics set off a trend in glasshouses and conservatories, their mass-production made possible with new technologies.

The story of the Veitch family who, like so many horticultural names, came from Scotland, is in many ways typical of several late-eighteenth and nineteenth-century nursery establishments. They started by raising and planting trees for the landed gentry and later sold popular flowering plants to the burgeoning middle classes. With their newly introduced plants, they ignited and fed new fashions for plants and radical changes in garden design. Their botanical and horticultural achievements, their secrecy and cut-throat rivalry and, above all, their profits were typical of a number of family-run nurseries of the period. Several Scottish-born gardeners-made-good built up businesses with characteristic Victorian drive, energy and single-minded determination. The Veitch family and the empire they created was indisputably the most pioneering, most daring, most successful and, in its time, the biggest and best of them all.

The Veitches were the first nurserymen to send out commercial plant collectors, and over the course of three-quarters of a century, they despatched over twenty men to almost every continent. They were the first to collect in Japan and among the first to recognise the huge potential of botanical treasures in China. Their first collectors, the brothers William and Thomas Lobb, and the penultimate, E. H. 'Chinese' Wilson, were among the finest of all English plant collectors. From 1840 to 1913 an unprecedented 422 Veitch introductions were beautifully painted and published in *Curtis' Botanical Magazine* where only the finest and most interesting new plants were 'figured'. It was their leading nurseryman, John Dominy, who created the first ever hybrid orchid while others from their team produced the first hybrid begonias, pitcher plants, and rhododendrons. They gave us some of our most loved conifers, such as the Wellingtonia, *Sequoiadendron giganteum*, the Monkey-puzzle, *Araucaria araucana* and *Abies veitchii*. They produced hundreds of evergreen and flowering shrubs and ornamental trees such as the Dove or Handkerchief tree, *Davidia involucrata*, the Chilean fire bush, *Embothrium coccineum*, the Magic tree, *Cantua buxifolia* and *Eucryphia glutinosa*. They introduced several varieties of acers, including *Acer palmatum*, lace-cap hydrangeas, flowering cherries, magnolias, rhododendrons, berberis, escallonias, abutilons and ceanothus. They brought home the magnificent *Lilium auratum* and *L. regale, Clematis montana* and *Fremontodendron californicum*. They filled conservatories and houses with some of the finest new hothouse plants – fuchsias, amaryllis, hundreds of their famous rare orchids, fabulous nepenthes, exotic foliage plants and many fine fruits and vegetables, including the Kiwi fruit.

But it was not just the Veitches' huge achievements in the introduction and sale of new plants that keeps their name alive in the hundreds of plants which carry their name or that of their collectors and nurserymen. They also made a vital contribution through their longstanding involvement in the Royal Horticultural Society – its fruit and floral committees, its commitment to education, its magnificent floral hall and headquarters and the creation of the Chelsea Flower Show which has grown into such a major annual event.

Most of the Veitches were keen to encourage a love of gardening which they knew was a great social leveller. They were as happy to sell rare orchids to the richest millionaires as they were to provide fruit trees or cabbage seeds to a small gardener. Nevertheless, competition was always fierce and the Veitches and their rivals fought ferociously for the top position during the height of orchidomania. The result of such extensive plant collecting was the terrible devastation to indigenous environments that were systematically stripped of bulbs, seeds and living plants. Many of the plants introduced by Veitch have long since disappeared, lost to cultivation, and in some cases lost in the wild as well. It is now illegal to take plants from the wild without proper authority and it is shocking to realise that many plants now common in our gardens are threatened in their natural habitats: the Monkey-puzzle is becoming rare on the mountainsides of Chile, and the Monterey pine, so common in many parts of the world, is now confined to one small native population on the Monterey Peninsula in California.

Trees are a particular passion of mine and when I drive around the countryside, visiting historic gardens, the sight which never fails to give me delight are the relics of a pinetum towering above the native trees. I know immediately that there, in the mid- to late-nineteenth century, a family lived and gardened and bought and planted seedlings of some of the great trees introduced from around the world, especially by the Veitch nursery and its collectors – the towering, classic forms of the 'Wellingtonia', the huge heads of ancient Monkey-puzzle trees, tall, gaunt cedars and firs from California, the Cedar of Japan and, just occasionally, the rare whorled spines of the Japanese Umbrella pine. The great tradition of tree planting, started in the 1770s by the nursery's founder John Veitch, is still magnificently illustrated in his 'Clump' at Killerton in Devon, and in the gardens of stately homes across the country one can still see fine living examples of the first trees raised by the Veitch nurseries. In some gardens are elderly, original *Davidia involucrata*, massive and venerable varieties of rhododendrons and magnolias all reaching the end of their lives. But their offspring are flourishing in thousands of gardens. Conservatories have come into their own again and so, hopefully, will many of Veitch's exotic glasshouse and house-plants, such as the glorious Chilean Bell-flower, *Lapageria rosea* and the lovely varieties of hoyas and dipladenias and aeschynanthus. Perhaps some of the rare and magical Veitch orchids, and the weird, insectivorous plants which so excited the Victorian imagination, tender rhododendrons and the seeming infinite varieties of decorative foliage plants and delicate ferns will once again find a warm spot in which to show their unique beauty.

Gardening fashions have come and gone, and come round again. I suspect Harry Veitch would have enjoyed television garden programmes, though he might not have approved of so much concrete and decking taking up valuable plant space. Yet when fashions change and garden designs take a new turn, it is the plants that must take precedence. Plants, like gardens, evolve and our ideas and love for them evolve and change too. Like the Monkey-puzzle, they will always be there to go back to, if not, sadly, in the wild, then at least in the horticultural nurseries which continue to draw me and my fellow gardeners irresistibly through their doors to dream of the perfect garden among their rich, floral cornucopia.

CHAPTER ONE

A SCOTCH LAD

*The noblest prospect which a Scotchman ever sees, is the
high road that leads him to England.*

Dr Samuel Johnson, 6 July 1763

ONE DAY IN the late summer of 1768 a sixteen-year-old lad took leave of his father at the High Cross in Edinburgh. They had bought his ticket for the sea passage from Leith harbour. With ten shillings in his pocket and his father's blessing John Veitch was heading south, for London.

John was about to be taken on in one of the leading horticultural nurseries of London, having served two years as an apprentice in a tree nursery in Scotland. His family now hoped that, with a first-class training in London, the boy would be set up for a job in some fine English garden where he might have a real chance of bettering himself. But John was not the only young man to be travelling south in search of employment. He was joining a growing troupe of Scottish gardeners who, for some years, had been invading the great estates, gardens and horticultural nurseries in England – so many in fact that one Scottish minister, visiting England at the time, wrote that 'most of the head-gardeners of English noblemen were "Scotch", including the head gardener at Blenheim and another at Bulstrode who had charge of the whole park and of the estate around it'. By the time John Veitch was to travel to London, English gardeners were complaining that Scotsmen were usurping their places. The Chartered Company of Gardeners even published a pamphlet, *Adam armed*, declaring that 'no apprentice from the north should be employed'. The English garden designer Stephen Switzer had earlier complained that: 'There are several Northern Lads, which whether they have serv'd time in the Art, or not, very few of us know anything of; yet by the help of a little Learning, and a great deal of Impudence, they invade these Southern Provinces.'

But a powerful network of successful Scottish gardeners in England continued bringing men south with the lure of better pay and employment prospects. With their reputation for diligence, ambition and a willingness to grasp every opportunity to escape the still restricted world of Scotland, young men like John were irresistible. John Veitch, however, was not only about to become one of these 'impudent' lads whose invasion into English gardens, horticultural nurseries and the perilous world of plant collecting transformed the story of gardening; he would also give it one of its most famous names, that of the great gardening dynasty of Veitch.

Veitch is quite a common name in the Border regions of Scotland. There was once an ancient noble line including Sir John Veitch of Dawyck who represented the County of Peebleshire in the Scottish Assembly, but most Veitches were farmers, merchants, millers and gardeners scattered around the lowlands. John's grandfather was a miller who lived with his wife Bessie and their five sons in Bedrule near Hawick in the Border county of Roxburghshire. John's father, Thomas and his wife, Mary moved to the neigbouring village of Ancrum where he was employed by Sir William Scott as his gardener at Ancrum House. There were five children; John, the eldest son, was born in October 1752, and the second, Thomas, in January 1760. Both boys were to follow their father into gardening, but in very different directions.

Ancrum is one of the oldest villages in Scotland. It stands on the bank of the River Ale, a tributary of the Teviot, on the northward route of the endless waves of invading English and repelling Scottish armies. It had once been fortified, which did not protect it from being burned three times in the sixteenth century. The last of the Scottish victories was fought nearby on Ancrum Moor in 1545. Following the Act of Union in 1704, life in Ancrum had become considerably more peaceful and prosperous. The population had swelled to around 940 and when John was ten years old, a new church and parochial school were built. The Scottish education system, much envied by the English, offered even the poorest rural family a basic education. For a small payment, a bright boy like John could receive up to three hours a day of reading, writing and arithmetic as well as some Latin – an invaluable asset for someone entering the profession of horticulture. Schooling was not necessarily a daily event and boys were also required to work on the land during busy periods or to help in their father's trade. Even when quite small, John and Thomas were helping their father in the gardens at Ancrum House where village children and women were employed to do the weeding for around 4d a day. There were extensive woodland and deer parks where Thomas Veitch was sometimes required to work as forester. As John grew older, he often worked with his father in the woods and it was there that he began to acquire an early passion for trees and forestry work. John's father was not kept in regular work at Ancrum and was often away for long periods working on other estates, such as Newham Hall over the border in Northumberland.

Although work was not regular and money was often tight, John grew up in a close-knit and comparatively prosperous family with numerous relatives who lived and worked in and around the villages and outlying hamlets and mills along the Teviot and its tributaries. The 'softly picturesque' Border countryside offered endless childhood entertainment and John and his brother explored the richly wooded hills and red sandstone caves along the river banks and fished for salmon in the clear, fast-flowing water. But the place that most fascinated him was a short walk away along the River Ale where it joined the Teviot. On the wider, more fertile banks between Hawick and Hassendeanburn stood vast plantations of thousands upon thousands of young trees. Here, since 1728, Robert Dickson & Son, the first and at that time almost the only commercial horticultural nursery in Scotland, had set up a flourishing business raising and selling trees, plants and seed.

Through his extended family John could have chosen to train in a number of occupations but from early on, his mind was set on raising trees. So it was particularly fortuitous that the Dickson nursery was so close to his home. By the time he was fourteen years old, he was eager to start his training and he was taken on as an apprentice. As he worked among the rippling acres of saplings, John started to learn the nurseryman's skills and tricks of his trade.

Before nurseries such as Dickson set up in business, there had been little call for commercial nursery gardens in Scotland and the remoter parts of England. Most supplies of garden stock came from monastic orchards and gardens. For ordinary people a garden was more of an allotment or small-holding where only the essentials such as winter fodder, vegetables and fruit were grown. As the best vegetables were normally kept for the pot, only the weakest specimens were allowed to set seed and as a result most seed quality was rather poor. Few had space or time for flowers, though self-seeding annuals, such as ten-week stock, sweet peas and wallflowers became very popular. Gradually plant quality did improve, the sale of seed became a recognised trade, and one or two small seed businesses began advertising their wares in and around Edinburgh, mostly for fruit, vegetables and medicinal herbs. By 1700, quite large consignments of better-quality seeds were arriving from abroad, including flower seeds and bulbs brought over from Holland, where gardening was already quite sophisticated. A few early seedsmen started their own nursery gardens beside the seed shop. But the large landowners relied on their gardeners to produce what was needed on the estate.

MILLIONS OF TREES

Vast stretches of the Scottish countryside had become virtually treeless by the early eighteenth century as so much timber had been used for building and for fuel and little had been replaced. Travellers remarked on the absence of enclosures to the fields while much of the land itself was waterlogged and in need of proper drainage. Laws were passed to compel people to plant trees and hedges but progress was slow.

Only gradually did more enlightened agricultural and horticultural ideas begin to percolate through the country and some of the more progressive landowners embark on large-scale tree-planting. During the next two centuries the face of much of the Scottish countryside was completely altered by intensive reforestation and improved methods in agriculture. The wealthiest undertook vast schemes, the most renowned being the Duke of Atholl, known as the 'Planting Duke' for planting literally millions of trees on his land. The creation of forests on such a massive scale stimulated the infant nursery trade in Scotland and Robert Dickson was the first to grasp its potential.

Dickson had cleverly situated his nursery so that he could send his supplies both south and north. Like many successful horticultural nurseries, it was a family business which, over five generations, built up one of the biggest and most famous of all the Scottish nurseries with branches all over the country. But in its early days at Hassendeanburn, the nursery simply supplied agricultural products and services and raised quantities of tree saplings to supply the great explosion of new plantations. The Dickson 'Day' or account books dating from 1739 to 1766 give a fascinating glimpse of their business and customers. At first they sold mostly hay, honey, beer, oats, eggs, skins, sheep, hogs and wool and took contracts for agricultural work hiring out shepherds and farm workers. Gradually, though, the entries change to sales of seedbed and transplanted trees, including Scots pine, fir, oak, poplar, lime, laburnum, beech, ash, thorn, elm, and varieties of young fruit trees including apple, cherry, pear and plum. Several entries illustrate the range of sales and considerable tree-planting efforts of the nursery's wealthiest patrons – 4,000 seedbed firs for 12s. for Sir William Scott of Ancrum (who employed John Veitch's father), 30,000 seedbed firs sold to the Duke of Argyll for £5 and regular orders for plants and trees from the Dukes of Roxburgh and

Buccleuch, the Earls of Home and Bute and the Lords Minto and Carnworth. These entries are interspersed with orders from farmers, 'gardiners' and local people, including regular purchases of 'cabitch plants, purtates, onions and leeks', and seeds of 'hearbs'. There are regular orders from several of John's uncles, Robert the wheelwright from whom the Dicksons bought a barrow for 2s., and from James the miller. Large numbers of young apple and cherry trees, plus one-year transplanted firs, were delivered to John's father, Thomas, whilst he was employed in Northumberland.

The huge demand for seedling trees meant that the Dicksons' business grew quickly and so did their reputation. Their nursery dominated Scotland and the north of England, not just because they were the best quality nursery-men but also because they were fiercely competitive businessmen and undercut their English rivals. Large-scale production on plentiful cheap land and cheap labour meant tough price slashing. Robert Dickson's son Archibald adver-tised in the *Cumberland Pacquet* that he could supply two-year-old transplanted Scotch Firs at 10s. per thousand ('six score to the hundred given'), consid-erably undercutting the price in Yorkshire of 15s. per thousand, even apart from the advantage given by the Scottish 'long hundred'. The Dickson Nursery secured a foothold south of the Border and they were soon supplying and planting huge quantities of trees to many of the big estates as far afield as Haddington and Midlothian. By 1766 the Dicksons could afford to expand. They 'feued thirty-six acres of land at Hawick to open a new nursery' and hired in extra men and apprentices, including John Veitch.

A SCOTCH APPRENTICE

Scottish gardeners were comparatively badly paid. Dickson's, however, could afford to pay their workers between £5 and £6 per year, with allowances for shoes, oatmeal and beer for men and an apron, some wool and linen for women. They were generous in seeing to the needs of 'haiered pren-tices', including an allowance to buy single- or double-soled 'shoon'. In some contracts it was stipulated that young apprentices were to go to school for one month in the winter season. The work was tough, with long hours in all weathers, digging, carting and clearing. Gradually John learned about the art of propagating, cultivating, grafting, pruning and planting all kinds of trees. As well as work in the nursery, John was sent out with planting gangs to deliver trees and to plant up estates. At dawn a gang of men loaded up the huge, lumbering carts with hundreds of young trees, their roots well wrapped in sacking. They packed some spare clothing, tools, equipment

A *Treatise*

on

FOREST-TREES:

by

William Boutcher,

NURSERY-MAN, at *Comely-Garden*, EDINBURGH

Forbes
1778

and essential supplies and headed off. Two or three long wagons in a line, drawn by teams of heavy horses, travelled far afield where they planted out thousands of trees on estates all across Scotland as far north as Perth and south of the border into Cumbria and Cheshire, where a Nicholas Ashton Esq. employed men from Dickson's to plant nearly half a million trees during one bitterly cold November and December. These gangs were often away for months on end, living in temporary huts or 'bothies' through the autumn and winter, the best time for tree planting.

Though most of the tree planting was for timber, a few landowners were showing an interest in plantations with a picturesque look. They interspersed some ornamental trees for visual effect, especially new varieties from England and overseas. The anti-Unionist, Lord Belhaven, on one of his visits to London, brought back one of the first Cedars of Lebanon in a flower-pot tied on top of his baggage, while the ingenious landscape designer, Alexander Nasmyth, faced with a bare and inaccessible crag on the Dunkeld estate, decided it could be capped by a plantation of 'handsome ornamental' trees.

Unfortunately no one could reach it so Nasmyth used two old cannons which he charged with canisters of tree seeds and shot them across on to the crag where the seeds duly germinated.

The horticultural nursery trade had its share of unscrupulous dealers. William Boutcher, an Edinburgh nurseryman who wrote *A Treatise on Forest-Trees* in 1775, complained that as a result of the success of 'a few sensible judicious men' in the nursery profession, 'various imposters' had started up in business knowing little, or nothing, about gardening. They crammed too many trees into the smallest bit of ground and sold these 'crowded, half-suffocated' plants at the lowest possible price. According to the Dickson accounts, however, Boutcher was happy to receive large orders from them and the nursery continued to hold the lead as 'quality purveyors of tree stock'.

While John was working at Dickson's, Dr John Hope, the King's Botanist for Scotland and Professor of Botany at Edinburgh, was busy planning an important 'trip to London'. It was his job to fill the Botanic Gardens in Edinburgh, to keep abreast of horticultural and botanical progress and to keep up to date with the increasing numbers of new plants being discovered as the world opened up to trade and exploration. Having formed the first Scottish plant-collecting syndicate, the Society for Importation of Foreign Seeds, Dr Hope was keen to discover what plants were in cultivation in England that had not yet reached the less cosmopolitan world of Edinburgh. Setting out on his long journey, Dr Hope wrote in his journal that he first visited the 'celebrated nursery' of Dickson's at Hassendeanburn where he saw 'a white Spiroea wh. seems to be a different species from the *salicifolia*'. In the nursery the observant Doctor may also have seen a bright, keen and intelligent young lad and marked him for recommendation.

Dr John Hope and his gardener in the
Botanic Gardens, Edinburgh

His itinerary took in the best gardens in England, such as

Painshill Park in Surrey and Whitton Place in Middlesex, and meetings with
the most distinguished men of medicine and botany. Naturally, he made a
point of visiting his fellow Scotsmen who held important horticultural positions: William Aiton, head gardener at the royal gardens at Kew and a central
figure in the organised study of plants, and the veteran and influential Philip
Miller, author of the *Gardener's Dictionary* and curator at the Chelsea Physic
Garden. Miller, generally regarded as the greatest gardener of his time, was
notorious for his preference for employing his own countrymen. Boys from
the north were brought to London as apprentices and when trained, obtained
good positions in gardens through Miller's influence. If they reached the
post of head gardener, they in turn sent north for more apprentices.

As Dr Hope toured private and royal gardens and botanical collections,
he noted in his journal all the new plants he saw and observed that some
of the leading London nurseries were already offering these plants for sale
long before they were properly recorded by Aiton at Kew. The relationship between science and commercial horticulture, founded on inter-
dependency and rivalry, had already begun. One nursery where Dr Hope
noted some of the newest and rarest introductions was the Vineyard Nursery
in Hammersmith, owned by Lewis Kennedy and the doctor's old friend
and fellow Scot, the botanist and nurseryman, James Lee.

Dr Hope's trip was invaluable to the development of botany in Scotland.
It may also have been the turning point in the life of young John Veitch.
Whether it was through Dr Hope's recommendation is not known, but
arrangements were made for John Veitch's apprenticeship to be taken over
by James Lee at the Vineyard Nursery in London.

NURSERYMEN IN LONDON

There were always plenty of ships sailing in and out of Leith taking out wool,
iron and coal and returning with grain, hemp and tobacco. Most of these
coastal smacks also took a few passengers. While the better off could enjoy
'entertainment' below decks with tea and sing-songs at the piano, the steerage
passengers like John Veitch stayed on deck, hoping for fine weather and a fast
passage down the east coast of Britain. After a voyage of two or three days
they entered the Thames estuary and slowly headed upriver with the lookout
singing out the depths in the fog until they reached the Port of London at
Wapping. As he stood on the deck, John watched a riotous scene of hundreds
of sea-going ships of all sizes and nationalities swarming up and down river,
barely avoiding collisions with wherries, barges and river ferries passing and

re-passing under their bows. As his boat took its turn at the quayside, John got his first glimpse of the great capital. Although he had no doubt been warned about pickpockets and the press-gangs, the scene must have been an enormous shock to a boy used to the wild, empty Scottish countryside. He watched hundreds of dock labourers, carters, watermen, ships' crews and revenue officers busy with 'stowing away' and 'shoving ashore', loading and unloading bales, crates and barrels with all kinds of goods – sugar from the Caribbean, cotton and rum from the colonies, sacks of imported seeds, 'roots' (bulbs), bundles of young trees and pots of plants – and he could hear an endless and colourful stream of cries, shouts and oaths. Wapping was the heart of London life and all goods and passengers going to and from abroad or from other towns around the British coast came into the city through its docks. London nurserymen were often seen collecting and sending orders.

The Vineyard Nursery stood on about three acres of land in the village of Hammersmith (now the site of Olympia in Kensington). Nearby was the Bell and Anchor public house, conveniently situated just by the Turnpike Gate. Stage and mail coaches for Bath, Exeter and the west, flying by at regular intervals, had to stop at the tollgate to pay a fee for the upkeep of the still terrible roads. Their passengers alighted to stretch their legs and grab some quick refreshment. The road was always busy with huge, heavily laden, lumbering wagons drawn by up to eight horses crawling in convoys along the road passed by an endless stream of carriers' and tradesmen's carts, dung and scavengers' carts, horsemen and private coaches of all kinds that raced and rattled along past the nursery gate setting up dust or spewing mud and rainwater at passing pedestrians.

Behind the entrance, however, the nursery was a haven of calm and peaceful activity. It had formerly been a vineyard which had produced some 'very good Burgundy wine'. There had once been a number of small vineyards in the area but the introduction of cheap wines from France in the fourteenth century and the difficult climate had reduced them to only a few. In the nursery grounds was a thatched cottage known as the 'Vynehouse', the upper parts of which had been used as living space and for selling the wine, while below were the large cool cellars, now ideal for seed and storing bulbs and roots. The growing popularity of expensive exotics made intensive cultivation in heated houses more important than extensive grounds of trees and shrubs, so that the land held in 1768 was sufficient for the nursery's needs – quite a contrast to the vast tracts of land which Dickson & Sons

A typical 18th Century London Nursery

required at this time for their trees in Scotland.

By the time John Veitch took up his apprenticeship there were already a large number of successful nursery firms operating in and around the city of London, among them London & Wise, first established in 1681 by a group of gardeners in Brompton Park. They had the care of the royal gardens at Hampton Court, Kensington Palace, St James's and Windsor. George London and Henry Wise adapted the French and Dutch formal garden styles to suit English gardens and tastes so successfully that they travelled all over the country creating gardens for clients, selling them vast quantities of plants and hiring out the enormous amount of labour needed to keep these well-ordered gardens in shape. The sheer size and enormous profits of the Brompton Park Nursery meant that it dominated the garden scene for many years and its heavily advertised success encouraged rivalry from new nurseries which soon began to settle around London.

For enterprising nurserymen, the early eighteenth century was the beginning of real prosperity and with it, increasing competition. It was also a period when large numbers of plants were being discovered and introduced into the country. When the Vineyard Nursery was first established in 1745, there was already a lively trade and exchange of foreign plants arriving from many parts of the world and nurserymen could supply their 'special' patrons with a growing array of 'new things'. Philip Miller estimated that by the middle of the century the number of plants appearing in England had doubled to up to ten thousand new species with a steady stream of plants and seed coming in every year.

John Veitch arrived on the London horticultural scene at a particularly exciting time. As he sailed up the Thames, it is possible that he might even have passed the *Endeavour* carrying Captain Cook downriver on his three-year exploration in search of a southern continent, accompanied by the young botanist Joseph Banks. When Banks returned in 1771 to a hero's welcome, he had collected over 360 new plant specimens. James Lee, who was a central figure in the introduction and supply of new plants, was the first person to receive and raise seeds from Cook's second expedition, to Botany Bay. He had already established his name as an important botanist by publishing his *Introduction to Botany* in 1760, the first English translation and explanation of the Swedish naturalist Carl Linnaeus's *Philosophia Botanica* – a work that was to revolutionise the study and classification of plants. Its appearance in England ensured that Linnaeus's new binomial or two-word system, created in 1753, became widely known and accepted.

Lee corresponded regularly with the important figures in the natural sciences, including Banks and Linnaeus (whom he called the 'Father of Natural History'), exchanging plants, seeds and dried specimens and discussing botanical matters, including the description and naming of new plants. Linnaeus named an entire genus of tropical plants *Leea*, after James Lee. James Lee's reputation attracted visitors from all over the world to his nursery, '. . . the resort of all persons curious in botanical researches'. Thomas Jefferson, third President of the United States, and keen gardener, had Lee and Kennedy's catalogues.

A LONDON APPRENTICE

Life at the Vineyard Nursery must have been considerably more comfortable than it had been in Scotland. Apprentices slept in a bothy or dormitory on the nursery premises but were still worked hard at all hours. They were required to keep watch on the fires and flues in the hothouses throughout the night. There were 'Dry Stoves' which had heated pipes either in the floor or the back of the house, and 'Bark Stoves' which had a vast pit filled with fresh tanners' bark to make a hot-bed in which pots of tender and exotic trees and plants were plunged. They also had to guard against plant thieves; it was becoming common practice for 'thieving florists' to take the best bulbs and flowers for their own gardens and for less reputable nurserymen to order the theft of valuable rarities from other nurseries. A reward of thirty shillings was offered in an advertisement for the return of plants, including 'striped hollies of divers colours', stolen one night out of the Queen Dowager's gardens at Hammersmith. Plant theft became so rampant that in 1765 the theft of a plant or tree worth over 5 shillings was made a felony for which the punishment was death.

Apprentices were put to work in the hothouses and outdoor beds, doing the daily routine work of cleaning, weeding and sweeping. They spent long hours standing at benches sorting, treating and packing seeds of perennial, annual and biennial flowers, and filling sacks with seeds of clover, trefoil, flax and hemp which gardeners used to improve the soil. Training was intensive and they were expected to be able to recognise trees and plants and to pick out and name correctly varieties of plants even as seedlings or bare trees in winter. They began to learn how to propagate and raise hardy plants and shrubs, herbaceous plants for cool greenhouses and tender exotics in the heated stove houses. John's knowledge of pruning, grafting and culti-vating fruit and forest trees, learned in Scotland, improved as he worked in the nursery plantation of firs, pines and ornamental trees. He now also learned about the highly fashionable 'clipped' evergreens and 'foreign' trees, such as Lee's own introductions of the American beech and narrow-leaved Walnut cedar, and others such as cypress, catalpa and tulip trees.

Labour was cheap, but plants were not. James Lee could sell fuchsia plants at a guinea each whilst paying his gardeners less than 12s. per week. As an apprentice, John was paid only 8s, considerably more than he had received in Scotland. He said that 'he saved on it', presumably because his living was free. Lee was paying the standard rate for nurserymen who, as a contem-porary observer wrote, 'have their hands in general cheaper than common gardeners or farmers which can only be attributed to this, that their employ-ment is more constant, more to be depended on, and perhaps less severe'.

John's new master was always ready to befriend and help young gardeners and botanists – especially if they were 'Scotch'. Like John, Lee was a Border man and they spoke with the same soft brogue. Lee was also a canny busi-nessman and loved to regale people with colourful stories of his triumphs, one of which John always remembered and often repeated to his family in later life. A visitor, being shown Lee's fine collection of variegated fuchsia, declared that he had recently seen growing in a pot in a house in Wapping a far prettier flower. 'No! and pray what is this phoenix like?' enquired Lee. 'Why', said the visitor, 'the plant was elegant, and the flowers hung in rows like tasels from the pendant branches, their colour the richest crimson, in the centre a fold of deep purple.' Lee rushed to Wapping where he found the owner, a widow, and offered her over eight guineas for the plant. At first she refused, saying, 'I could not sell it for no money, for it was brought me from the West Indies by my husband . . . and I must keep it for his sake.' But the generous sum won her round and Lee left triumphantly with the fuchsia, promising to send the first seedling as replacement. As soon as his coach reached the Vineyard, Lee pulled off all the buds and flowers and divided the plant into cuttings which his gardeners set about forcing in the bark beds, dividing and sub-dividing them until there were 300 fuchsia plants ready to flower. Lee placed only two of these plants – possibly *Fuchsia coccinea*, a native of Chile – in his show house.

A lady customer, seeing them, asked: 'Why, my dear Mr Lee, where did you get this charming flower?'

'Hem, 'tis a new thing my lady – pretty! 'tis lovely . . . a guinea; thank your ladyship.'

The lady proudly showed off her new plant to a friend who admired it and demanded to know where it could be bought. 'A guinea, there is only another left.' Off rushed the friend to the nursery where she found 'only two plants available'. She too hurried home to display her rarity to more admiring friends. Carriages 'flew to the gates of the Vineyard nursery where *only* two beautiful young flowering fuchsias were always to be found'. The product of a single plant from Wapping – which Lee kept his promise to replace – soon brought in 300 golden guineas.

Lee was always ready to share his enthusiasm and knowledge with anyone, including his apprentices whom he took on his visits to customers' gardens and to other nurseries to carry plants and run errands for him. A great opportunity for a sharp-eyed, keen-eared lad eager to learn and curious about the horticultural world. John would have accompanied Lee on such visits to Christopher Gray's Fulham nursery which was famous for its plants from America. Gray's *Magnolia grandiflora* was said to be the first in England from which all others were propagated. It grew to a huge size over a hundred years and when it was in flower, it perfumed the whole neighbourhood.

Many plants changed hands through auctions or sales following the death of owners of notable gardens and it was often worth a visit to see if there was anything special. John would have seen how different nurserymen ran their businesses and how some specialised in just a few species. As well as cultivating on their own land, nursery stock was often bought from specialist growers for re-sale. The Shailors, a family of German nurserymen in Little Chelsea, specialised in moss roses and 'raised numerous varieties of roses from seed . . . and generally sold them to Messrs Lee, who sent them out under their own naming'. Knowing that the reputation of Lee and Kennedy would ensure big orders, they were content to receive a modest but certain profit, rather than concern themselves with sales. Some nurserymen would buy the entire stock of a desirable plant from its raiser to suppress competition.

Lee's partner, Lewis Kennedy, spent much of his time travelling all over the country and abroad collecting orders and debts. He was the favourite nurseryman to the Empress Josephine and, despite hostilities with France, was issued with a special passport to visit her garden at Malmaison. Lee and Kennedy's advice was regularly sought when trained gardeners were needed. Customers with both country and city gardens called on the expert attentions of the nursery's 'garden men' who planned, supplied and planted out borders, parterres and complete gardens if required. Plants could also be bought by mail order: a customer could send a messenger with his order which would be delivered to his door. Apprentices were sent into the city to work in a garden. Even quite small houses had gardens, with a few plants in pots and boxes and some trees and shrubs that could withstand the coal smoke. Larger gardens had a lawn which required regular rolling in the evening and scything in the morning before the dew dried. The Swedish botanist Per Kalm, on a visit to London, was fascinated by some of the curious methods for controlling pests. For example, earwigs 'may be destroyed by hanging hogs' hoofs, the bowls of tobacco pipes or lobster claws on the top of the sticks which support the flowers, and killing the vermin which will lodge in them every morning'.

In less than two years John Veitch had learned valuable lessons needed to establish a successful nursery business. He now understood the importance of knowing about different kinds of plant, how and where to cultivate them, and how they might be best used to 'ornament' a garden. He had also learned how to take orders from ladies and gentlemen, he knew about competition and secrecy and the 'Scotch' art in undercutting and profiting from all kinds of clever deals. He had acquired a useful fund of experience and a colourful collection of stories to pass on. His first love would always be for trees and the open landscape which he had discovered working with his father and at Dickson's. But James Lee needed men in London who had the dedication and skills to work in his fast-expanding speciality business of hothouse 'exotics'. He decided that John was ready to be sent out to work on a country estate.

CHAPTER TWO

COUNTRY LIFE

To build, to plant, whatever you intend,
To rear the column, or the arch to bend,
To swell the terrace or sink the grot,
In all, let nature never be forgot.
Alexander Pope, *Of Taste*, 1731

SIR THOMAS DYKE Acland, 7th Baronet, was a true West Country gentleman and 'sporting squire' who, through his marriage to Elizabeth Dyke, found himself the owner of numerous estates in Devon, Cornwall and Somerset. His houses and land extended into twenty-four parishes and legend had it that he could ride from the Bristol Channel to the English Channel without stepping off his own land. Lady Dyke Acland had died early in their marriage, leaving the Baronet with two young sons who, as they grew up, joined their father's pursuit of field sports, including shooting, fishing, cockfighting, fox and stag hunting. Although briefly a member of Parliament, once for Devon and once for Somerset, Sir Thomas had no taste for politics, nor for the fashionable life of London.

Throughout the year Sir Thomas kept himself constantly on the move, staying at his different houses or at those of his many friends across the West Country. Every day he 'dined' at one place and 'lay' in another, often many miles apart. Father and sons lived the life of typical

Sir Thomas Dyke Acland (1722–85)

eighteenth-century sporting aristocrats who had substantial property but were by no means the wealthiest or the noblest in the country.

Sir Thomas was planning to hand over most of his North Devon and Somerset properties to his son John and build himself a new home at Killerton, near Exeter in south Devon. The old house, which had lain neglected for many years, was too small. Towards the mid-1700s, when England was reaching the height of its powers, the greater prosperity and peace after the civil war allowed many old houses to be altered or rebuilt and whole landscapes to be changed. Even sporting country squires were becoming more sophisticated in their dress and life-style and Sir Thomas's endless social round gave him plenty of opportunities to observe the improvements his friends and neighbours were making to their properties. He decided it was time he kept up with his Devon neighbours. His new house, when it was built, would be just as grand and fashionable, set within a park to rival them in beauty. He hired James Wyatt, one of the leading architects, to design a house in the Palladian style which would stand, as was the current fashion, on an elevated position where the owner might look out over a splendid new 'landskip'.

Sir Thomas had an architect for the house but as yet, no man to create the new landscape. A visit to London in November 1769 turned out to be useful. In the course of the social round of visiting friends and acquaintances, he enquired about hiring a man who could transform his estate at Killerton. The Duke of Argyll once explained how he had first planted out his gardens and only later built the house: 'Nature must have its time; therefore he who intends to build a house, and lay out a garden round it, ought to make a beginning with planting trees to gain time.'

To find the right gardener Sir Thomas was recommended to visit James Lee at the Vineyard which stood on his route home to Devon. Lee had no hesitation in offering the services of John Veitch who, despite his youth, appeared to have the right qualities to set an estate in order and undertake some creative parkland planting.

Far from the influence of the London fashions, only the very largest and wealthiest country estates took on major landscape and garden designers. For landowners like the Aclands, who had always allowed nature up to their door, the new idea of using the existing landscape to create a fashionable garden had its attractions. Numerous country estates like Killerton were being improved in the 'best style' by enthusiastic landowners and their skilled and dedicated head gardeners, and dozens of new gardens were being created by amateurs who copied what they saw in neighbouring estates, making the most of the natural settings of their own homes.

FIRST YEARS AT KILLERTON

Fortunately for Sir Thomas Acland James Lee had made a wise recommendation in John Veitch. When John first arrived in Killerton in 1770 he found a house and grounds barely used or cared for. The old house was an H-shaped building set within an apron of peaceful sloping land and with a hill known as 'Killerton Clump' rising behind it. A deer park to the north-west ran down to the river's edge while close to the house was a small, formally laid-out garden and an orchard. Everything looked old-fashioned and neglected. The flower beds and paths were smothered in weeds, many shrubs and trees were broken and strangled with ivy, garden walls were crumbling and the orchard bowed with elderly, cankered trees. The bare hill behind the house, topped with the remains of a hill fort, made a bleak background to the house.

John Veitch (1752–1839)

The task of repair and renewal was enormous and presented a tough challenge for a twenty-year-old. Before John began, Sir Thomas was anxious for John to see the best of his friends' new garden 'make-overs'. He sent him off to meet Mr Henshaw, the head gardener at Saltram, to see how the top 'landskip' designer 'Capability' Brown was laying out the park. He looked over several other large Devon and Somerset estates, including Bicton, owned by Lord Rolle, Castle Hill, owned by the Earl of Fortescue, and Ugbrooke, seat of the Clifford family.

Records of John's early years at Killerton show that they were spent bringing the land back under control, planting the orchard with new fruit trees, digging a well, repairing walls, fencing the new park and creating new paths on the estate. As he directed his gang of gardeners and labourers, clearing, rebuilding and moving huge quantities of earth and stones, John grew familiar with the lie of the land, which was curiously similar to the

Border countryside of his childhood, and began to evolve a plan for planting the Great Park. He discovered that the Killerton grounds had a remarkable microclimate; the sloping land inclining to the sun contained few frost pockets and was sheltered from the cold north winds by the 'Clump'. The rich, lime-free soil also made the garden particularly suitable for shrubs such as camellias, magnolias and rhododendrons, while the mild climate was ideal for many kinds of less hardy trees and plants.

John's first task was to create several nursery areas on the estate where he could propagate and raise a variety of trees ready for planting out. He regularly made orders for firs, larch, pines and cedars from nurseries in Scotland, including his old masters at Dickson's, but managed to raise all the native English trees for Killerton Park himself. He grew from seed varieties of ash, beech, English elms, Spanish and horse-chestnuts, walnuts, mulberries, yews and hollies, white and black poplars, sycamores, hornbeams, planes and birch trees.

Although John had no training or experience in landscape design, his natural visual instinct, coupled with an understanding of how trees grew and shaped the landscape, resulted in landscape planting that was as sensitive and creative as that of many of the professional designers of the time. He decided to concentrate his plans on enhancing the landscape as he found it rather than trying to impose a pattern of his own. He planted trees so as to emphasise the height of the 'Clump' and create a woodland frame for the proposed new house. From the top would be views of the country below with, as the fashion of the time demanded, interesting objects to draw the eye. The sixteenth-century 'Somerset' spire of Broadclyst parish church provided one focus, while a new octagonal 'Folly' tower filled the gap looking towards the ruins of the old manor, Columb John.

Sir Thomas decided that the Exeter to Tiverton road which bordered the east side of his estate came too close to the house so he ordered the road to be diverted further away. Many landowners of the time thought nothing of shifting roads, cottages, even whole villages, if they spoilt the view or got in the way of their grand plan. Altogether about 500 acres would eventually be enclosed to form the new park, with the winding course of the River Culm flowing around the north and west. The home farm, the blacksmith's house, the linney and the old garden walls were all demolished to make way for a new walled garden, granary and stable block. Huge drains were tunnelled and bricked, while railings, grand gates and a lodge were erected for the new drive and a ha-ha was dug around the front of the house. The Deer Park was later enlarged and a herd of fallow deer bought from Sir Charles Bampfylde's neighbouring estate of Poltimore 'to complete the scene'.

Owners of city gardens and country estates were beginning to tire of the labour-intensive and costly formal layouts of the seventeenth and early eighteenth centuries. A new revolution in garden and landscape design had been gradually turning to the opposite extreme – to an idealised version of nature. This radical new style was partly influenced by English gentlemen returning from Grand Tours in Italy and France. There they had admired the works of Claude Lorrain and Gaspard Poussin whose paintings depicted romantic, allegorical visions of an ideal classical landscape.

A number of garden designers were responsible for the transition from formal layout to the landscape garden: the three most famous were Charles Bridgeman, William Kent and later, Lancelot 'Capability' Brown. They came from quite different backgrounds and worked in a wide variety of gardens but all spent part of their formative years at Stowe in Buckinghamshire, the vast and grandiose estate of Viscount Cobham. Bridgeman, who was gardener to Queen Anne, although trained as a formalist was, according to Horace Walpole, the first to set the garden 'free from its prim regularity, that it might assort with the wilder country outside'. He was said to have first used the ha-ha as a device to bring garden and countryside together without the unsightly use of a fence or wall. William Kent had trained as a painter in Italy and been influenced by Italian landscape painting, architecture and gardens. Kent created grand naturalistic landscapes with vistas and temples, shrines, grottos, statuary and lakes, often with classical allusions.

The trend towards more natural landscaping was developed most completely by Lancelot Brown, who came from Northumberland. He was appointed head gardener at Stowe where both Bridgeman and Kent had already worked and was probably influenced by their ideas, but went on to develop a much more radical style for designing and planting a landscape. Having moved to London and set up as a landscape architect, he acquired his nickname 'Capability' because he so often enthusiastically observed, on viewing a property, that it had 'great capabilities' for improvement: 'He had so quick and sure an eye for the country that after riding for an hour he would conceive the design for the whole park.' Within a day his team staked out the outline, followed by his gangs of men armed with shovels and barrows who dug huge lakes, flung up banks of turf and planted hundreds of trees.

The still familiar and distinctive features that mark Brown's work are the thick belts of beech trees which define the edge of the park and the skilful adaptation of natural features of the site to create a smooth, flowing effect such as a serpentine-shaped lake viewed from the house. He liked to create the effect of the house rising sheer from the park (with the use of the ha-ha ditch), surrounded by gently undulating, shaven lawns set about with clumps of beech, oak or chestnut trees. The whole creation was to be one of serene grandeur but Brown's critics complained that if it was Nature, it was a very dull and empty kind, without intricacy, variety or passionate wildness. Brown, who had great charm as well as boundless energy and enthusiasm, had more admirers than critics, and his landscape designs became the height of fashion among the wealthy and the aristocracy.

GARDENERS AND MASTERS

The relationship between the Acland and Veitch families which would endure through several generations, did not always run smoothly, as John was soon to discover. The Acland family had a wilful and unconventional streak which manifested itself in different ways in each generation. They would hurl themselves with equal passion into a political or religious cause or a pleasurable pursuit such as travel or hunting, their enthusiasms infecting those who lived with them and served them, throwing them around like leaves in a sudden squall. Over the years events in the lives of the Acland families would create fluctuating conditions at Killerton, affecting John's work there and indeed the direction of his own life. If he had been expecting regular interest and orders from his master, he was soon disappointed. After an initial flurry of excitement, John was left to his own devices to get on with creating the new Park and gardens as he thought best.

Six years after John's arrival at Killerton the 'rebellious war' of Independence in America was declared and in the following year, John Acland, as a Major of Grenadiers in the 20th Foot, went to Quebec where the British forces were struggling to hold off an American invasion of Canada. His wife, Harriet, insisted on accompanying him and when John was wounded and captured, she followed him. For several months, they were held by rebel leader General Horatio Gates who referred to John Acland as 'old Sir Thomas' son . . . a most confounded Tory'.

It was an uneasy time for John and the household at Killerton. News took weeks to arrive and Sir Thomas reached a state of frustration and ill-temper. He raced up to London and rushed round visiting friends who might have news of his son or could help secure his release. The small household at Killerton followed the unfolding drama, tension building up over the long months as Sir Thomas became increasingly anxious and taciturn, making life extremely difficult for John and the other servants.

When the young Aclands were at last safely returned to live at their Pixton estate, in North Somerset, and a son was born, Sir Thomas realised he could no longer delay in arranging a suitable home for himself. During the American drama, Wyatt's grandiose plans for the new house at Killerton had been put on hold. Many of the Aclands lived beyond their income and Sir Thomas no doubt realised, with judicious advice from his lawyer, that his dreams of a grand seat were beyond his purse or his current needs. More modest drawings, made by architect John Johnson, recommended as being 'exceedingly cheap and ingenious', were accepted. John Veitch later wrote that Johnson's house was 'only proposed to stand a few years, during the Building of a very large House then projected upon the top of the Hill'. In the event, no other house was ever built. The house went up in just one year, a year of further drama and tragedy for the Acland family. (This house, and the park and gardens created by John Veitch are now owned by the National Trust and open to the public.)

In July 1778 Mr Spring the builder was on site taking measurements, the old house was demolished and masons, labourers, stoneworkers and wood carvers quickly erected new walls. By October the plasterers were at work and in November the 'three Mahogany Doors' were hung in the Great Parlour. The following April Mr Spring wrote that 'The Carpenters have finished the Chamber Floor above stairs and are now putting in the skylights in the passage . . . finishing the Great Parlour below'. Sir Thomas meanwhile bided his time with his son and daughter-in-law and his new grandson at Pixton in Somerset. During this time, for a reason not recorded, John Acland was drawn into fighting a duel. He was not injured but afterwards rode home over Exmoor through a cold, damp winter dawn and caught a chill. This time his devoted wife was unable to help him and John died on 15 November 1778 aged thirty-four.

Sir Thomas's misery was compounded when, three months later, his beloved hunting lodge at Holnicote in North Devon was burned to the ground. The *Exeter Flying Post* reported that Sir Thomas was there amongst the ruins counting the losses, relieved that the precious Exeter Cup, which he had won at the races, was saved, but bitterly mourning the loss of his fine collection of stags' heads.

Sir Thomas was now impatient to move into Killerton and Mr Spring had to write and beg him not to 'send the Paper Hangers down before all the rest of the work is compleated'. John Veitch, garden hands, builders and decorators worked as hard and as fast as they could to finish the house, Park and gardens, and by July 1779 all was ready. Improvements to the estate continued: a new stable block was built for Sir Thomas's horses and he slowly recovered some of his old spirits. He was then only fifty-six and still in relatively good health. Harriet and his little grandson often came over for visits.

Sir Thomas began to show more interest in John's work on the estate and John reported to his master that the planting in the Park and on Killerton 'Clump' was completed. He had used mainly native trees such as beech, lime, horse-chestnut, sycamore and various oak, including *Quercus suber*, the local hybrid Luccombe oak, *Quercus hispanica 'Lucombeana'* and the Tulip tree, *Liriodendron tulipifera*, which was one of John's favourites. His tree nurseries around the estate were filled with a vast surplus of healthy young trees which were being profitably sold to Sir Thomas's friends and neighbours.

When he was an old man, John Veitch described to his grandson how one morning in the summer of 1779, Sir Thomas asked John to join him at breakfast. Sir Thomas appeared to be in relaxed good humour. His cravat was loosened, his boots unlaced and his wig was slung over the back of the chair. John stood waiting to be given his orders or to discuss some plan for the garden. With nine years' work on the estate, John felt confident that he had done well, his trees were growing to maturity, the gardens taking shape and Killerton beginning to look like a gentleman's home at last. Master and gardener's relationship had grown warm and mutually respectful. John's simple 'Scotch' manner and competence was like that of many gardeners who developed good working relationships with their masters whether they were squires, earls or monarchs. Sir Thomas always treated John, not as an equal, but as a man with whom he was at ease and could respect for his qualities and abilities. On that morning Sir Thomas told John that since he had proved to be skilful, intelligent and creative in laying out the park and in generally caring for Killerton, he was offering him the position of Head Steward or Agent on all his properties and estates which, John recalled, 'I of course gratefully accepted'.

Having noted that John was successfully producing prodigious quanti-ties of quality young trees in his tree nursery, Sir Thomas suggested to him that he might also try his hand at setting up a tree nursery business of his

Killerton in 1818

own: 'And now Mr Veitch, will you make a nursery here, and you may draw upon me for what money you may need.'

John replied that this 'made the undertaking an easy one'. Sir Thomas asked, 'Where would you have it?'

'At Budlake, Sir Thomas,' replied John.

'Well really, this is strange for I chose this place as the best on my estate and I will have a house built for you at once.'

Sir Thomas gave John a life tenure on land in the estate hamlet of Budlake to use for his own tree nursery business to run alongside John's duties as Estate Steward (an arrangement occasionally made by landowners). It was an extraordinarily generous reward and the vital first step towards the creation of one of the largest and most successful horticultural nurseries in the country.

Sir Thomas then suggested that it might be a good time for John to visit his family in Scotland and, despite the common practice of forbidding gardeners to marry, the liberal-minded Sir Thomas might even have hinted that it was time for John to turn his thoughts to marriage and a family. Sadly John had a more pressing reason to return to Scotland. In 1780, Betty, his mother, died aged only fifty after giving birth to a late baby boy. But it was an opportunity, after twelve years' absence, for John to see all his family again; his father, and brother Thomas who was now working as a gardener in Jedburgh, his sisters and baby brother Archibald, and all his numerous uncles, aunts and cousins. He also visited the Dickson nursery where he had served as apprentice twelve years previously, ordered Scotch pines for Killerton and discussed business deals for his own new nursery. He was now a successful and eligible young man with an important job and his own business. He met Anna Davidson, a young girl from a local family, to whom he took a fancy. After a long stay in Scotland, he was ready to go home to Devon, to his new house, new business prospects, and with his new wife Anna. The future looked secure and rosy.

Two girls, Mary and Margaret, were born at Budlake. Work on the new gardens at Killerton continued; a sundial was erected, the ha-ha was dug, banked and turfed, the huge walled garden was nearing completion and a new plantation and shrubbery were planned. As estate steward, John was also required to visit all the Acland estates, planning, reporting and improving, especially at Holnicote where a new lodge was being built 'in the cottage style'. Whenever he had the time, John was busy on his plot of land at Budlake, digging and planting, plotting and planning, and soon orders for his stocks of young trees began to pour in.

Meanwhile Sir Thomas hunted rather less and spent more time at Killerton. His restless energy finally ran out in February 1785 when he died. His infant grandson and heir survived him by only two months. The title passed to Sir Thomas's second son, another Thomas, whose huge debts had estranged him from his father. Some of the properties had to be sold to clear them. He and his wife, Henrietta Hoare, a daughter of the great banking family, remained in Somerset until he too died relatively young. His heir, yet another Thomas, who was then only seven, lived at Pixton until he came of age and inherited the baronetcy in 1808. During this long period of deaths and inheritances, Killerton was once again left empty and unwanted.

STARTING A BUSINESS

During this period, John dutifully carried out his many responsibilities as steward but he was also free to pursue his own business interests. Sir Thomas's death could have left John in a vulnerable position; with Killerton empty for so many years, he might have lost both his job and his new business. However, he was clearly both useful and reliable enough for the family to wish to retain his services and honour the terms of his contract for life.

Indeed, only one month after Sir Thomas Dyke had died, John felt confident enough to place an advertisement in the *Exeter Flying Post*:

Laying Out Ground in the Modern Taste.
John Veitch who has had the Management of the New Work for the late Sir Thomas Dyke Acland Bart. at Killerton, for Nine Years past, offers his Services to Noblemen and Gentlemen who choose to employ him in laying out their Gardens with Plantations and other Ground Works to beautify their Parks on the most reasonable Terms.

As he travelled round all the Acland estates, John took the opportunity to visit his own clients, often recommended to him by the Acland family; he carried out a number of important contracts in Devon and Somerset. He advised on garden and estate layout, on forest management, and sold ornamental and fruiting trees and hardy shrubs all of which he raised in his own nursery. His business increased and so too did his family as Mary and Margaret were followed by John, Thomas, Anna, and finally, in 1793, James. As they grew up the boys learnt to work with their father in the nursery, until John was able to leave them in charge for long periods while he was away on his business travels.

John and other nurserymen seeking business were not alone in travelling around the countryside visiting large gardens. Despite the appalling roads, visiting stately homes and gardens had become a popular activity in the eighteenth century. Jane Austen described the gentry who 'dropped in', sometimes by invitation but often unannounced. Many large estates allowed open hours and 'Garden Tours' became fashionable although many visitors were more keen on catching a look at 'Persons of Quality'. The head gardener was required to take visitors round, probably a tedious task if visitors were only half interested in the garden. In 1808, a Mrs Price of Chester toured several country houses and gardens, including Mamhead in Devon where she was 'miffed' to be refused entry to the house and had to be content with seeing the Countess Dowager and her daughter through the drawing-room window. A rebuff at Powderham Castle nearby was even greater; Mrs Price could not look round either house or grounds. As their carriage sat in the drive, Mrs Price and her companion saw Lord Courtenay cross the yard without looking at them which 'distressed them greatly' though they were pleased to note that 'His Lordship has a good figure and was dressed in a green jacket, with a black velvet collar and nankeen pantaloons'.

There were, however, more serious-minded 'professional' travellers who made tours of inspection, writing detailed and opinionated descriptions of the more interesting gardens. Their diaries and 'topographical journals' now give invaluable descriptive information, though they were not always so welcome at the time. The first accounts of John Veitch's work appeared around this time, usually with praise; in 1788, a young Fellow of Queen's College Cambridge, the Rev. Stebbing Shaw, described Killerton: 'a very neat white mansion, beautifully situated under a wood-crowned knoll, surrounded with a park of deer, and a fine vale in front, graced with the pleasing objects of a lofty village tower, and distant hills'. Local travelling clerics, such as the historian, the Rev. Richard Polwhele, and his friend, the Rev. John Swete, formed a literary circle in Exeter. They made tours of the British countryside visiting the 'seats' of important country families and wrote copious books or journals, often illustrated with their own water-colours of picturesque scenery, houses and gardens. These critics of gardens and 'good taste' recorded the names of designers and, since it was invariably the head gardeners whom they met, they too were often mentioned.

John came in for both praise and criticism: around 1790, Sir John Kennaway was rebuilding his house at Escot within a newly created landscape attributed to 'Capability' Brown, but John Veitch is also recorded as having given advice on the layout of the grounds and he planted the trees in the 'highly luxuriant wooded park'. Swete, a great admirer of Capability Brown, described how the house projected from groves of trees consisting of 'noblest elms', firs and beech 'with admirable effect'. But was much less pleased with John's work at Shute House where he had planted up and laid out a new drive; 'this new road I found to be a very bad one', Swete wrote. He disliked the hard flint surface, and described the roadside plants as being dead or dying among numerous thistles which were 'in the act of displaying its winged treasures in the neighbouring fields'. Construction work, which John was often obliged to do as part of landscape design, was probably not his forte. He was having to juggle his responsibilities as Acland's steward with his nursery business and was almost certainly taking on too many contracts at this time to be able to oversee all his workers properly.

But John was without doubt an expert forester who was in great demand by estate owners requiring management, assessment and advice with their woodland and in organising timber auctions. Constant wars with France meant an increasing need to build a larger navy and the demand for good timber rose and with it the price. The most profitable estates had vast 'standings' of trees grown for shipbuilding and heavy horses were specially bred to pull the huge wagons or 'tuggs', loaded with timber, to the naval dockyard at Plymouth. In 1792 John took on a contract to do work in the 'finely wooded' estate at Nutwell Court, owned by Major Eliott Drake, a relative of Sir Francis Drake. John's lengthy and detailed report describes the plantations of ornamental trees and the timber woods which required a great deal of attention. The trees, he wrote, were growing so 'thick in the stocks' which 'prevents circulation of air among them to promote their growth . . . The method therefore that I recommend to recover them and which I have done for many gentlemen and for many years with success' would be careful and judicious thinning and (his Scottish voice coming through in his spelling) 'prunning'.

MAPS OF INFLUENCE

Published praise ensured that a gardener's work became known beyond the confines of his world, but most contracts for work came through personal recommendation, and a really successful gardener and designer required social as well as gardening skills. The fashion for improvement and a 'new look' which Kent, Bridgeman and Brown had begun, blossomed with numerous imitators and reached its peak around 1792 with their self-proclaimed 'successor', Humphry Repton. Repton, born in the same year as John Veitch, rose not from the ranks of gardener but from the Norfolk gentry. He used his skills as a competent artist and clever salesman and his social and political connections to create a flourishing career, though he did not start landscape gardening until he was thirty-six years old, five years after the death of Capability Brown. His longing for social as well as professional acceptance turned him into a skilled social climber and he wrote that he benefited from his professional visits to the estates of society because it 'has been the society of those to whose notice I could not otherwise have aspired'. He even achieved some unusual publicity in Jane Austen's portrait of a country gentleman's seat in *Mansfield Park*:

'I never saw a place that wanted so much improvement in my life; and it is so forlorn that I do not know what can be done with it . . . I must try to do something with it, but I do not know what. I hope I shall have some good friend to help me.' 'Your best friend on such an occasion,' said Miss Bertram calmly, 'could be Mr Repton, I imagine.'
'That is what I was thinking of. As he has done so well by Smith,

I think I had better have him at once. His terms are five guineas a day.'

'Well, and if they were *ten*,' cried Mrs Norris, 'I am sure *you* need not regard it. The expense need not be an impediment. If I were you, I should not think of the expense. I would have everything done in the best style, and made as nice as possible . . .'

By the time Humphry Repton appeared people were beginning to realise the mistakes Brown and his imitators had made in the wholesale destruction of ancient gardens and historic buildings such as the churches which Brown had demolished. Repton developed a quite different pictorial or visual approach to landscape design, 'requiring house and grounds to be closely related to the character of the setting and to fit into the picture'. His designs were more integrated and he advocated natural moving water rather than large flat lakes, lusher planting with a softer, more detailed look including the use of bog or rock gardens, 'well-dressed' lawns, climbing plants trained over poles or hoops with borders and shrubs around the house. Most welcome of all for many people, he began to bring flowers back into their gardens.

As Repton built up his business based on social connections, he created what he called his 'Map of Influence'. In a much less conscious way, so did John Veitch who was fortunate to have found many admirers in the west country. One of his most important contracts at this time was obtained through the connection of Sir Thomas's widow Henrietta Hoare and her brother Charles who planned to build a seaside retreat for his delicate wife at Dawlish near Exeter: 'a delightful little place where the society is generally select'. Repton often worked with John Nash, the most fashionable architect of the time, and Hoare commissioned them to design the house and grounds. Repton always wrote up detailed plans and painted elaborate designs for each individual garden in his famous 'Red Books' which were bound in red Moroccan leather. But unlike 'Capability' Brown, Repton rarely stayed around to oversee his designs taking shape and left many of his clients to contract their own labourers and take from their 'Red Book' only the parts that took their fancy. John Veitch was contracted to do the work but it is not known whether he and Repton ever communicated. How much of Veitch's planting was true to Repton's plans for Luscombe is unclear but it is interesting that when the great Scottish landscape designer, horticulturist and prolific traveller and writer J. C. Loudon made his tour of Devon gardens thirty years later, he described the grounds at Luscombe as having been laid out by John Veitch, 'father of the present nurseryman of that name', and made no mention of Humphry Repton. Luscombe Castle lies in a magnificent natural setting at the head of a combe leading down to the sea and Loudon wrote in the *Gardener's Magazine* that 'The two sides of the valley are beautifully varied by trees which thicken into woods as they approach the summits of the two ridges, so that the house may be said to stand on the side of a valley surrounded by hanging woods.'

John planted vast quantities of beech, oak, sweet chestnut, elm, Scots pine, as well as laurels and holly along the drive and on woodland boundaries in the characteristic 'Picturesque' way, emphasising irregularity in the boundaries of the clumps and in the curious practice of planting several trees in one hole. Usually trees of one species were planted together, but often a timber tree was planted with a shrub or small tree such as holly, blackthorn, or hawthorn to create an interesting contrast. This huge undertaking earned John the magnificent sum of £1,312. 12s. 6d.

When the prime minister William Pitt declared war on France in 1793, times became increasingly difficult. It was the fifth war with France in a century and the English were by now used to the trade routes to the continent opening and shutting, and the warlike rhetoric bellowed from the Court and Parliament in London. But the following years were not good for the gardening business and according to Repton, it was a time which 'excited such alarm through all ranks of people that I felt as my profession was becoming extinct . . . the whole Nation was aroused to self defence . . . Nothing was heard but the dread of Buonaparte and the French invasion! Beacons, martello Towers, camps, Depots and every species of self-defence occupied all minds – and every-one trembled for the safety of old England.' The economic and social effects of the Napoleonic Wars, including heavy war taxes, forced many families to sell their estates and spelled the beginning of the decline of the old landed gentry and its replacement by wealthy merchants 'with neither pedigree nor taste, who saw their newly acquired land in terms of profit or scenery of country idyll'. Repton, the snob and social climber, feared the ascendancy of the new rich, the decline of traditional landed families and the growing power of urban interests. Others, however, were more concerned with the likelihood of French invasion.

When Napoleon threatened a seaborne invasion in 1798, wealthy coastal and southern-dwelling families packed up and fled to the safety of their London houses. For most ordinary country folk, it was business as usual. Young lads growing up in the countryside longed for travel and a taste of adventure and the rapidly expanding British navy seemed to offer all the excitement they could wish for. The newspapers were filled with sensational reports, from minor naval skirmishes to major sea battles, such as the Battle of the Nile in 1798 when Nelson nearly annihilated the French fleet. John Veitch's eldest son John, now a young man, was longing to join Nelson's great navy. As soon as he was old enough, he secured a post as a naval midshipman. Just as the Aclands had followed events in America thirty years before, the Veitch household now scoured the daily newspapers for reports about the war at sea. And on 21 October 1805, a great but terrible day, Britain celebrated the victory of Trafalgar, but mourned the death of Nelson and many thousands of mariners. Somewhere in that long drawn-out fight for naval supremacy, the young John Veitch was lost.

CHAPTER THREE

GARDENERS INTO NURSERYMEN

It has often struck us with surprise that the proprietors of
the finest residences in England, noblemen and gentlemen
of high education and refinement in other things . . . should
commit the laying out of their gardens to the gardeners.

J. C. Loudon,
The Gardener's Magazine 1828

B Y 1808, JOHN Veitch's tree business at Budlake had expanded so
much that his two surviving sons, Thomas, aged twenty-one, and
James, who was fifteen, were working full time. Both were skilled
and keen and John could now confidently leave them while he was away.
He was by then fifty-six years old and had become a respected landscape
consultant, forester and nurseryman. His small, stocky, cheerful figure was
a familiar sight in Devon, Cornwall and Somerset as he rode his pony
around the country lanes, visiting the Acland estates and drumming up
business for himself.

The Veitch family had become accustomed to living near a house that,
for twenty-three years, remained shuttered and empty, save for the occasional holiday visit from the Acland family who continued to reside in
Somerset. The Veitch children, who had never known the house be occupied, played and worked in the grounds and watched their father's park
grow to magnificent maturity.

In March 1808 Tom Acland celebrated his twenty-first birthday and
inherited the estates and responsibilities of the 10th Baronet. A month later
he married Lydia Hoare, his mother's second cousin. The couple decided
to make their home at Killerton: 'We came in our own carriage with four
horses and we were young people and we enjoyed it!' he wrote, full of
excitement. After its long sleep, the house was once again to be filled with
family life and laughter. The young baronet demanded John's undivided
attention with new plans for Killerton which, characteristically, were

required to be done immediately. John had to cancel contracts and leave the business in the care of his sons while he plunged into a frenzy of work, preparing Killerton House and gardens for the newly-weds.

As soon as they were married, Tom and Lydia were off on what became a life-time of travel and adventure. Killerton, though, remained their home to which they often returned for long, happy periods. John found himself in the role of wise retainer and sometimes stern adviser to his new master, whose 'impatient energy, reckless love of adventure and disregard of the advice of others' was tempered by his warm generosity to people in need, great intelligence and courage to speak his mind.

John was also pleased to discover that Lady Lydia was a keen gardener and began discussing plans with him for a new garden. By now John's original planting in the park and on the 'Clump' formed a mature and beautiful landscape, with deer grazing right up to the house. But the only real garden was a small, unexciting area on one side of the entrance. Lady Lydia wanted something grander with lawns, wide gravel paths, a shrubbery and fine ornamental trees.

John, always taking his responsibilities seriously, pursued Sir Tom on his travels with long detailed letters regarding estate matters, the poor of the parish and the progress of the gardens. Four of these letters survive, written between November 1808 and February 1809, while Sir Tom and Lydia were 'wintering' in Edinburgh.

Sir Thomas Dyke Acland Bart. Edinburgh. North Britain.
From Killerton 20 November 1808
'Honor'd Sir,
Thinking it my duty to inform you how things goes on at Killerton, I have now to inform you that the ground is planted & the walks formed and all the turf laid in the field between the Garden and the Crab Tree, now called Lady Acland's Shrubbery. The Grass Glades between the Thickets is thinly planted with Tulip Trees, to make a Tulip Tree Grove, when grown up. The Thickets is composed of different sorts of Forest Trees from 15ft. high down to 3ft, and a vast number of old thorns from Ashclist and different places intermixed in order to act as a Nursery to thin from & plant as single trees and thorns, to Forrest part of the Lawn for your Amusement for years to come as well as to make the plantation at once look like a rising wood . . . I have ventured to intrude upon your Patience with the

above observations about the Estate as thinking it my duty to inform you of anything respecting your Estates that I consider may in the least lead to the improvement of them & hopes I may soon see you & Lady Acland safe arrived in Devonshire.

A substantial part of the park was fenced off to keep out the deer. New tree-planting schemes described by John included a long Beech Walk, which would enhance the beauty of the existing views and create pleasant walks along mown grass glades, through a shrubbery, passing thickets of trees and groves of large Spanish sweet chestnuts, beech, Tulip trees '. . . finishing at the Large Cedar Tree on the side of the Hill, leaving room for the walk to pass through, but taking care to avoid the appearance of Belt by leaving a large opening between the Two Groves above mentioned to let the appearance of ground & single trees pass on in imagination before'.

John Veitch's Beech Walk. Killerton, 1830

Lydia later took John to see her half-brother Richard Colt Hoare who was constantly improving his estate at Stourhead in Wiltshire (originally laid out by his uncle, the banker Henry Hoare). John and Lydia no doubt picked up some ideas for their improvements to Killerton but John had by this time developed ideas of his own which seem to fall somewhere between the schools of Brown and Repton. His trick of planting clumps of forest trees is pure Brown with the 'walk' passing through them to give a subtle impression of more wood than there actually is, as well as the use of a 'large opening between the Two Groves' to 'coax the imagination' into expecting more sights still hidden from view. However, his subtle use of smaller flowering trees and bushes is more in keeping with Repton. He planted the shrubbery with some tender, but mostly hardy shrubs, including the local rhododendron,

'Cornish Red', and varieties of azaleas and magnolias. Around the edge he put 'Perreniel flower roots, some of which I had sent from Lord Eliot's garden, & some the Gardener got from other gardens in this neighbourhood'.

John's visual sense had become quite sophisticated and he understood just how his trees could create both shape and seasonal blends of colour and effect, giving a various 'tinge of colour in the Different seasons'. His plan to hide a neighbouring house with a 'Mass' of trees may be typical of Brown but leaving 'openings' for Killerton to be seen with a 'more perspective appearance from the road' is more suggestive of Repton. Overall, John's preferences (and probably Lady Acland's) seem to be more inclined towards Repton's gentler style.

Many years later, J. C. Loudon, who created his hugely popular *Gardener's Magazine* in 1826, published reports of his visits to gardens. Though usually sparing in his praise, Loudon found 'much to admire at Killerton, both of natural feature and artificial treatment . . . Nothing can be more judiciously disposed than the trees on the lower part of the slope, and in the level valley.' He described John's planting in the Park as 'at first thinly scattered and sparingly grouped, and then increased in number till the groups unite into masses, and the masses are lost in one grand valley of wood [which] forms a grand and effective contrast to the rest of the place.'

Meanwhile in Somerset, the new hunting lodge at Holnicote was ready for Sir Tom's mother to move into. John regularly visited her with supplies of trees and shrubs, and he wrote about his new plan for the garden and surrounding farm buildings, a little like Repton's style of *ferme ornée* 'which turns chiefly upon the principle of making the whole appear as an orna-mental Village, rather than covering any part with firs to conceal it'. Farm, stables, laundry and cottages would be planted around with beech 'thinly planted to form a Beech Grove with the Offices & Cottages intermixed as a village in a wood, or a wood in a village'.

These fascinating and very detailed gardening passages in John's letters to Sir Tom were no doubt intended to be read out to Lydia, as one sentence was clearly meant to provide her with a surprise: 'I have done a little thing for Lady Acland near Killerton House but I must not mention it now, it will soon be found out at your return.'

John was extremely fond of Lydia and had spent considerable time and care in creating his present for her – a curious little thatched wooden hut called 'Lady Cot' (now known as the 'Bear Hut') reminiscent of the hermitages popular in the previous century. It had lattice and stained-glass windows, the

floor was cobbled with
deer knuckles, the ceil-
ing covered with mat-
ting and pine cones, the
walls with bark and
skins, and all decorated
with fir cones and many
kinds of shells.

The changes and
improvement being
made at Killerton had
much to do with another
new development in
garden design. The more
relaxed, 'fun-loving' style
of Regency life – more
playful, more ornamental
and more feminine – was

'Lady Cot'. Killerton, 1830

extending into many people's gardens. The grand classical iconography of landscape gardens such as Stowe in Buckinghamshire and the vast sporting estates
such as Badminton in Gloucestershire, were giving way to smaller-scale gardens,
where owners could enjoy less rigid rules of fashion. With so many interesting changes being made there was plenty of tree-planting and garden work
to occupy John Veitch.

MATTERS OF ESTATE

But for Sir Tom and John there were many other pressing matters to be
dealt with. Sir Tom's lawyer was constantly at him to improve the income
from his estates. During the Napoleonic wars prices were high, and afterwards an agricultural depression brought lower wages and extensive unem-
ployment. Villagers' rights on common land had been removed in most
parishes by the Enclosures Acts and the cost of Poor Law relief was rising
fast. John Veitch and the parish vicar did their best to advise Sir Tom on
the fairest and most efficient ways to help his tenants and he agreed to
provide an annual sum of £100 to be spent on the poor, a large sum when
a hard-working labourer could not expect to save more than twenty pounds
in a short life-time. 'Poor old Sam Shepherd,' wrote John, 'is come nearly
to a shaddow. He can do but very little work now. Tyeing thorns about

the Trees and working a piece of a day at a time, but he has pay of the Parish. I let him have half a guinea last Saturday over his wages to help him over Christmas.' John wrote to Sir Tom, 'I have ordered 20 Blankets, to give those who have more than two Children, stockings and shoes to Old People & Hats to others, as they may want – To an old woman in Broadclist who has kept to her Bed for 7 years I have given a Flannel waistcoat to keep her warm in Bed.'

John complained that rabbits were barking thousands of new trees: 'I have often told the Keeper of it but he does not kill them fast enough,' while in the deer park the bucks were killing each other and in the stables the idle horses were eating too much. John, who loved to tease, enjoyed reporting to Sir Tom that 'The Coachman does not like your new Horse . . . He would make a famous Cart House and you want some Cart Horses.' The weather was, of course, a constant source of news: 'The late High-winds have nearly striped Culm John Chappel naked and Blow'd down 13 large Trees about the Ground and Farms.' John also supervised the building of a huge ice-house. Fortunately it was a particularly cold winter and the ponds were frozen hard. It took five days, five wagons and nearly thirty men to fill it.

Meanwhile John did not forget his own business interests, and when Sir Tom offered to do anything for him on a trip to Edinburgh, John asked him to place a large order for '25,000 2 years Larch & 25,000 one year Larch' from Mr Shade, 'a very nice Dealer'. He also suggested, for Sir Tom's own purposes, an even bigger order of larch and Scotch firs, to be sent in February 'when they are dry-packed and directed for me at Killerton to be forwarded from London by Russell's Exeter waggon'.

John also wrote to Sir Tom of serious troubles at home. His wife, Anna, who may have been suffering from tuberculosis, was in failing health: 'I was intending to go to London at Christmas but my wife is so very ill – I shall not go. I have had Doctor Daniel out to see her and he says her Constitution is almost broke down & he has little hopes of her getting better, but may be kept on a while by medicine.'

In a brief letter to Sir Tom dated early in January 1809, John closed with the words: 'I am sorry to add I have lost my wife, she died the first instant & was buried the 7th.' Anna was the first of several Veitches to be buried in the parish graveyard at Broadclyst. She was the first of many Veitch wives and mothers who left little or no record of themselves; but their love, hard work and dedication were vital support for their families and the growing business.

FAMILY MATTERS

In the following spring Lydia Acland gave birth to her first son. It was the beginning of eighteen years of childbearing, though it did not prevent her travelling with her husband. Ten children were born, and for every one, John Veitch planted a birthday wood near the lodge at Holnicote. John's own family were now all grown up; Thomas and James worked in the business; daughters Mary and Margaret had married into local families. A third daughter, Anna, went to work at Killerton to help Lydia with the new baby. In 1812 Anna, 'an earnest Christian with lovely long, soft hair and a sweet voice', married William Snow Betty, a surgeon from Hull where they went to live. But Anna became seriously ill after the birth of her second baby and decided to go home to her family. She got no further than an inn in Warwick where she died. Her younger brother James, then twenty-one years old, was at her deathbed and promised to care for her two sons. Anna was brought home and buried at Broadclyst beside her mother and the children were returned to their father in Hull.

Still grieving for his sister, James nevertheless was married within a month to Mary Tosswill, the daughter of a large farming family whose members were described as 'tough and with grit,' and who also owned a tannery in Bermondsey, London. In the following summer their first child, who would come to be know as James Junior, was born. The births of John, Thomas, William (his twin, Theresa Mary, died at birth), Robert and Anna followed closely. The nurseries at Killerton House and Budlake Farm were bursting at the seams with babies and young children.

The Acland and Veitch families, despite being master and servant, would continue to have a close relationship. A hundred years later, descendants of John Veitch and Sir Thomas Acland were still collaborating on matters concerning education, charities and religion. When he became the 10th Baronet, Sir Tom had drawn up a list of priorities; to improve his estates and to ease the state of the poor in Broadclyst. Another concern of his was the education of children. Until then the village children, including John Veitch's, were given their lessons in the parish room from a master who seems to have failed to teach them much. Sir Tom, always open to enlightened and progressive ideas, had heard of Dr Alan Bell's new teaching methods and he hired a 'Bell-trained' student from London to teach the village boys in the 'fine' new school that he built in the village in 1809. It was just too late for John's sons to have taken advantage of it; indeed James always seemed to have been self-conscious about his poor education. His sons, however, did benefit from a much improved schooling. Sir Tom also built a Dame school near Killerton where the village girls, dressed in red cloaks, learned suitable skills and received regular visits from Lady Acland who inspected their work.

Sir Tom spent most of his long life as an active MP despite it costing him a small fortune to retain his seat in parliament. He was enormously generous, spending far more than he could afford on charitable and worthy causes. Sir Tom was a committed Evangelical Christian, an admirer of Hannah More, 'high priestess' of the extreme Clapham Sect, and an advocate of religious tolerance. Despite considerable local opposition, he and his wife supported the emancipation of Catholics and often stayed in households of 'free-thinkers' where Protestant and Catholic servants knelt together for family prayers. Sir Tom insisted that his family, servants, estate workers and tenants attend Killerton chapel to hear the chaplain read the service. His religious principles were adopted by many of the Veitch family; Mary, for example, was well known in the community as 'a saintly & bountiful lady'. The simple Church of Scotland faith known to John was replaced with an ardent evangelicalism and a duty to charitable concerns.

JOHN VEITCH & SONS

As life settled down at Killerton, John and his sons were able to spend more time building up the nursery business at Budlake: its acres of young trees and plants were becoming a well-known landmark. John continued to advertise his services in local newspapers, and in 1826 *A Guide* written by 'A Devonian' informed the traveller that 'From the village of Broadclist . . . the nursery grounds of Mr Vetch commands a fine view of Killerton and the adjacent country'.

As the Veitch nursery business steadily grew, they hired an increasing number of men, wagons and horses 'taking up Trees; some sorting them; the large from the small; some counting them into hundreds and thousands; some laying them by the heels in little rows after they were counted.' In a good season the labourers would be kept busy packing up trees and loading them on to wagons from December to the middle of April for, despite the end of the war, demand for timber and forestry work continued. Veitch convoys jolted along poor, rutted roads all over the country, selling mostly ornamental, forest and orchard trees. John's 'prunning' account shows that they carried out regular contracts for coppicing, planting, felling, digging ponds, constructing fences and ha-ha's. At this period the nursery was run with only a few skilled men, plenty of cheap local labour, loads of horse manure, lime, primitive equipment and little scientific knowledge. Fertilisers were chiefly dung, seaweed and lime (much used for the garden, the fields and for the limewash on buildings) and bone manure – often, rather gruesomely, made from imported human bones.

The curious traveller could indeed stand near the Budlake road and look down over the large fields of row upon row of seedling trees, hedging, shrubs and young plants, and vegetables of numerous varieties. John Veitch, now an old man leaning on his stick, pipe between his teeth, would be skilfully grafting or pruning with his sharp, curved knife. Workmen were hoeing, digging and manuring while an apprentice boy and village women were weeding and sweeping. Thomas, who loved to care for the fruit trees, would be tying and staking orchard trees or training pleached branches of pears or peaches to the long south and west nursery walls. James, meanwhile, was most likely among the hot-beds and glass frames, sorting through sacks of seed and closely examining his boxes of emerging seedlings.

Even when he was quite small, John's youngest son, James, had shown that he was a born gardener. While Thomas happily raised forest and fruit trees like his father, James nurtured other, more ambitious ideas. Increasingly he took over the nursery business, his father happy to allow him to make radical changes and improvements. He began stocking a wide variety of annual and perennial flowering plants which were once again becoming

popular. James's real passion though was for growing varieties of unusual new plants arriving from overseas. James and his father often visited clients' gardens, but whilst John stood and admired the landscape or a well-kept plantation, James was peering into the shrubbery and flower beds, examining individual plants in the stove-house and cross-examining the gardener about the origins of his plants and ferreting out his secret methods of seed germination, plant propagation and cultivation.

James and his father could not have been more different. John's amiable, now aged figure had become rather paunchy, his hair silvery, his ruddy and weather-beaten cheeks folded into his chin. But his eyes were as alive and twinkling as ever, with a joke or quip ready on his tongue. James, on the other hand, was a tall, angular and rather uncoordinated figure. He seemed charged with tension, sometimes excited, sometimes irritable; he wore glasses from an early age which gave him an earnest, rather scholarly expression.

Unlike his father, James was not a servant of the gentry but an independent young businessman with no conflicting loyalties. The Aclands had been generous to his family and James regularly worked in the Killerton gardens and sold them seed and plants from the Veitch nursery. But he was his own man and even more so when his father handed him the reins of the nursery so that John could concentrate on his stewardship for the Aclands and his travels as salesman, which he clearly enjoyed.

James accompanied his father on several of his regular visits to London buying and selling stock at some of the largest, well-established London nurseries which were flourishing around the 1820s, such as Loddiges & Son, James Gordon & Co, William Rollison, Alfred Chandler and the already familiar Lee & Kennedy at the Vineyard Nursery. James listened enraptured to his father's stories of his apprenticeship to Lee in London: even as a boy he had loved to hear about Lee's famous plant introductions. He was fascinated by John's stories of great men in London who studied the natural sciences such as Joseph Banks who had made his botanical travels with Captain Cook. Old James Lee had died in 1795, and his son John in 1824, but John Veitch (and later James) kept in touch with the four grandsons who continued to run the nursery. J. C. Loudon, his opinions still much respected, noted that the Vineyard continued to be 'unquestionably the first nursery in Britain or rather the world', an accolade that no doubt set James Veitch's ambitious head spinning with his own dreams and plans.

At home in Budlake, James pored over the catalogues of some of the newer major British nurseries such as Peter Lawson of Edinburgh, John

Mackie of Norwich, the huge Caldwell nurseries of Knutsford in Cheshire which did business throughout the Midlands and northern England, the Handsworth nursery near Sheffield, celebrated for their fine collection of rhododendrons, and the Falla family of Gateshead & Newcastle, who ran one of the largest nurseries in the country. As the numbers of these nurseries outside London increased, so competition grew more fierce. Nurserymen regularly traded amongst themselves, but were almost cutthroat in their dealings. They worked in great secrecy behind their glasshouse doors and were quick to act on another's misfortune. Despite their advantages in having a financially secure arrangement and wealthy patrons to recommend them to new customers, James and his father could see that their nursery was also facing increasing local competition. There could be no let-up in the search for new customers and markets which would mean travelling farther afield on regular visits to clients, gardeners and nurseries throughout England. John Veitch, like James Lee, had long since taught his sons the importance of exclusivity and secrecy in the nursery business.

The Veitches' biggest local competitors were Lucombe & Son of Exeter who, like them, were not just nurserymen but also had a reputation for design and layout. The hybrid oak *Quercus hispanica 'Lucombeana'*, known as the Lucombe or Exeter oak, which became quite a fashion in parks and gardens in the western counties, was discovered by William Lucombe who had set up a nursery near Exeter as early as 1720. Lucombe, after introducing the Turkey oak from southern Europe, noticed among some seedlings that two of the plants grew very quickly and remained evergreen in the winter, pollinated possibly by a nearby Cork oak. In 1765 he planted two hybrids on either side of the entrance to his nursery and when the two original trees bore acorns, several distinct forms were planted in the nursery. The Lucombe oak proved very popular but Lucombe had failed to hold on to the exclusive rights and the hybrid that bore his name soon appeared in rival nursery catalogues.

When he was in his seventies, William Lucombe had one of the two oaks cut down to make boards for his coffin, which he stacked under his bed – but they perished before he did. He waited until he was ninety-eight before felling the other and was finally buried in a coffin made from the wood when he had reached one hundred and two years of age. After the venerable nurseryman's death, his son and later his great nephew Robert T. Pince, ran the family business well into the 1880s. The nursery, one of the oldest in the country, was noted for camellias and for the introduction of rare exotics, as well as for heaths, cinerarias and fuchsias. It would have many run-ins with the Veitches over the years.

James was heading in an entirely new direction. He started experimenting with new plants in the glasshouses and kept in regular contact with London nurseries, buying seed of their more interesting ranges of plants. Boxes of plants and sacks of seed began to arrive by boat into Topsham harbour at Exeter. The coaster *William the Fourth* entered in its log book: 'Goods sent to Killerton to James Veitch, nurseryman, two hampers, fourteen trees and a sack of seed.' The occasional cask of best Devon cider was sometimes sent back as part payment or gift.

James's education had been in the old parish school and his horticultural training restricted to his father's nursery business. He had nevertheless learned many of the necessary skills in propagating, pruning, grafting and cultivating plants and trees. Having worked with his father on contracts in gardens and estates around the county, he knew something of landscape and garden design. James was clearly highly intelligent and the extensive horticultural knowledge which he acquired came through long hours of reading the books and journals which were appearing around this time, such as J. C. Loudon's *Encyclopaedia of Gardening* published in 1822, *Exotic Botany* by Sir James Edward Smith and Charles McIntosh's *The Practical Gardener and Modern Horticulturist*. For regular news and information, James could subscribe to Loudon's *Gardener's Magazine* started in 1826, the *British Flower Garden*, which contained descriptions of the 'Most Ornamental and Curious Hardy Flowering Plants' (1823), Curtis's long-running monthly *Botanical Magazine*, price one shilling, and the *Transactions of the Horticultural Society*, first printed in 1807.

JAMES AND THE HORTICULTURAL SOCIETY

The most valued source of horticultural education, information and ideas for the provincial and rural nurseryman was the Horticultural Society, of which in 1825, James Veitch became a 'Fellow' (as members were known), the first of five generations of Veitch Fellows whose influence and participation were to be central to the Society's history. John Wedgwood, son of Josiah Wedgwood the great potter, had conceived of a plan for a society of horticulture, similar to the flourishing agricultural societies, which would give members information about new plants, new methods and new ideas 'for the culture and treatment of all plants and trees, culinary as well as ornamental'. William Forsyth, gardener to King George III, and Sir Joseph

Banks, then President of the Royal Society and Royal Advisor to the Gardens at Kew, gave the idea their wholehearted support.

On Wednesday, 7 March 1804 the Society held its inaugural meeting at Mr Hatchard's bookshop in Piccadilly. As well as Wedgwood, Forsyth and Banks, the meeting was attended by William Townsend Aiton, Royal gardener at Kew whose father, William Aiton, had compiled *Hortus Kewensis*, James Dickson, nurseryman and botanist, and two old friends, the Hon. Charles Greville and Richard Anthony Salisbury, Fellows of the Royal Society and keen amateur gardeners and naturalists. These seven distinguished gentlemen nominated and elected new members until by the end of the year there were approximately 250 members. (Despite there being many excellent women gardeners, women were not admitted to the Society until 1830.) For a small rural nurseryman such as James Veitch, the Horticultural Society offered not only news and information, but also a vital link to gardeners and nurserymen around the country. More attractive still was the prospect of acquiring new plant introductions from the Society's collectors which were raised and propagated in the Society's experimental gardens and regularly distributed to members who were gardeners and botanists both amateur and professional. During the 1830s, when James Veitch was beginning to formulate his own plans, the Society distributed over 350,000 packets of seed, 90,000 plants and nearly 50,000 parcels of cuttings that had been tried and tested in the gardens at Chiswick which rapidly became the hub of horticultural activity.

In the Society's gardens the most modern methods of cultivation were developed, large glasshouses were built to raise the fruits and new 'exotics' arriving from abroad, and extensive trials of fruits, vegetables and ornamental plants were carried out. Plants and seeds were also sent out to the British colonies where they might be useful and perhaps produce reciprocal exchange. Care was taken not to interfere with the interests of nurserymen and to avoid distributing plants and seeds that could be obtained from them. The education of gardeners was considered to be as important as the dissemination of information about methods, such as manuring or pruning, and every year twenty-six young gardeners received formal training in horticultural skills and knowledge. The formation of affiliated provincial societies soon followed with their own shows and competitions. Regular meetings were held where papers were read, lectures given and specimens of plants and vegetables scrutinised and discussed. No organisation or institution anywhere in the world during the first half of the nineteenth century

achieved as much as the Horticultural Society in distributing valuable horticultural plants.

As the Horticultural Society grew in size and importance the Council
created a series of awards. Medals, including the Large Gold and Large
Silver, were struck and the coveted Banksian Medal was created to commem-
orate the death of Sir Joseph Banks in 1820. From 1827 the Society held
an annual fête at its Chiswick gardens with floral, fruit and vegetable exhibits
sent from all over the country – an early forerunner of the Chelsea Flower
Show. Winning a prize became recognised as the hallmark of a successful
and skilful grower whether he was a nurseryman, head gardener or amateur
for, as the Gardener's Magazine observed, the popularity of the Horticultural
Society shows was a great social leveller: 'The principal part of the English
aristocracy are present and mix indiscriminately with the tradesman, the
mechanic and the gardener.'

Lee and Kennedy were regular prize-winners and, following their earlier
success with fuchsias, they began working on the newly popular genus of
dahlias. The current craze for brightly-coloured dahlias was almost as keen
as the mania for rare tulips of earlier years. A few dahlia roots had first
arrived in Europe from Mexico in 1789, when the French believed that
the roots would make a cheap alternative to the potato, but they did not
survive. The Empress Josephine later managed to obtain some roots and
successfully raised a wide range of dahlias in her garden at Malmaison in
France. She was extremely jealous of her collection which she weeded and
watered personally. But the Royal dahlias soon acquired a price on their
heads and, as the story goes, one of the ladies-in-waiting bribed a gardener
to steal some roots for her. Caught in the act, the gardener was sacked and
the lady dismissed. Enraged, the Empress ordered her entire collection to
be chopped up and dug in and refused ever to hear the name of the plant
again. But in Britain, dahlia mania was taking off and Lee & Kennedy, the
Empress's favourite nurserymen, were already propagating and selling roots
that they had acquired from Malmaison in happier times.

When James Veitch saw the French dahlias selling so well at the Vineyard
he too was hooked. He brought some roots home to Budlake where he
devoted many patient hours to cultivating his own perfect specimens of
the ball-type dahlias with their short, tubular florets and incurved margins.
These became all the rage in Victorian gardens where entire beds were
given over to late summer displays. Dahlia shows were held all around the
country with show benches filled with gorgeous exhibits of hundreds of

ball-type flowers – 'spotted, striped or bicoloured, laced, flaked, painted, striated, edged, clouded and picotees'. In 1826 James's double dahlia was shown at the Horticultural Society's autumn show in London and was awarded a Banksian Silver Medal, the first Veitch plant ever to receive an award. He returned home to Devon in triumph. The little Veitch nursery at Budlake was becoming known as a prime mover in the development of the dahlia, and the Exeter dahlia shows, where the nursery held regular exhibits, were particularly renowned.

FAMILY TROUBLES

Whilst James spent every day (except Sunday) absorbed in his plants, life at home in Budlake farm was not so happy. James's wife, Mary, ill for some time with tuberculosis, died aged only thirty-four. Her sister Rebecca came to live at Budlake to keep house and care for James's six young children. His eldest son James (who would always be known as James Junior) was then only twelve years old. Two years later Rebecca and James were married. Although some of the children resented their step-mother, the marriage seems to have been happy. Rebecca had no children of her own, but she proved to be a generous and kind step-mother. Her large new family was, however, about to be increased as a result of the behaviour of another step-mother. Disturbing news came from Hull concerning James's two nephews, William and Thomas Betty, whom he had promised his dying sister years ago that he would care for. Their widowed father had remarried a woman who turned into a cruel step-mother. She flogged the little boys with holly, rubbed the wounds with salt and locked them in the cellar with fearful tales of red-tailed monsters. Terrified and half-starved, Thomas had his legs held against the hot kitchen range until his screams brought the servants who broke down the door. The step-mother was tried and imprisoned and their father, who was by then bankrupt, soon died, leaving the boys destitute. John Veitch collected his wretched and battered grandsons and brought them home to Budlake. Not surprisingly, John was furious with his son-in-law for not having protected the boys and blamed his university education as the cause of his weakness. John believed in proper training in a trade and was deeply suspicious of 'University men'. Their arrival filled the house to the limit with Rebecca having to cope with seven rowdy young boys and one little girl. John, who was by then an old man, moved out to 'a place in the yard' for some peace and quiet.

Some letters by Thomas Beatty (he changed his name from Betty to that of an aunt in Ancrum) written when he was an old man, describe life with the Veitches at Budlake. Though much of the content is bitter and obsessed with money, he remembered his grandfather with considerable affection, despite many fights with him. Beatty often went on pony rides with the old man and spent long evenings reading to him. The walls of John's 'den' were covered in pages cut from old Almanacs and he loved to quote gems from them. He 'used to tell to me about all sorts of things when smoking his pipe in the little room & I enjoyed his bright talk'. John Veitch enjoyed his Dutch-cut tobacco which he smoked in long clay pipes 'by the Waggon load'. He was said to be a very temperate man but he took a regular liqueur glass of Scots whisky, 'his native beverage', immediately after his dinner before he rose from the table. He suffered terribly from gout and rheumatics and his knuckles had become painfully deformed, curtailing his pruning activities. He also became rather irascible, with occasional outbursts of temper when his gout troubled him.

Like a number of successful and elderly gardeners, John had reached the stage in life when he could indulge himself a little, terrorise his family and be welcomed at the table of many of the noble families whom he had served in his youth. In the village too, according to Thomas Beatty, old John Veitch was a well-known figure: 'He used to wear ribbed stockings drawn over his trousers and the School Boys . . . called out joyously when they saw him coming – "Hurrah – Here's Old Stockings" and well they might rejoice for his capacious pockets were filled with dozens of pocket knives which he bought wholesale at Sheffield or Birmingham on his rounds.' Despite being well into his seventies, John continued his extensive business travels and it was said that he visited customers and nurseries 'in every county in England except Rutland'. Records show that he was twice employed to oversee pruning and grafting work in the kitchen gardens at Stowe in Buckinghamshire even though he was then seventy-four years old. He was so punctual in his habits that innkeepers had his dinner on the table precisely when he was expected every six months. He was quite a favourite in the hotels he visited as he tipped everyone genially and generously. But he could also be difficult and demanding, bullying chambermaids if the room was not up to scratch and teasing the waiters. One night, in a regular inn, a new waiter who did not know John, told him that he could eat anything he could wish for. The obsequious servant was rewarded with a dose of John's sarcastic humour. 'Oh very well then, let me have a piece of broiled elephant,' John had replied. 'Oh, we can't get

that,' exclaimed the waiter nervously. 'Then a broiled monkey steak,' and
John roared with laughter, having 'roused the poor man'.

James Veitch was by now fully in charge of the nursery. He ran the business with tight discipline and, as an Evangelical Christian, allowed no one
to be admitted to the gardens on the Sabbath, instructing his foreman, Mr
Wooster, to be 'equally stringent'. Life at home was also strict. Having
received a poor education himself, James was particuarly fierce with the
boys over their schoolwork. Every evening and on Sundays the scriptures
were read by each member of the household in turn, which, recalled Thomas
Beatty, 'made the day a dreary one to us youngsters'.

   Despite being a strict Christian and a hard taskmaster, James did, however,
'have some fun in him, rather broad fun on rare occasions – and the old
GF [grandfather John] too could unbend'. Uncle James could even manage
to be a genial companion on occasions and he enjoyed fishing and shooting
despite his poor eyesight. According to Beatty he was a better shot than
most men: 'There was a certain Woodcock that used to laugh at their futile
efforts to bag it, so one morning Uncle James went out with us & it would
have been well for the bird it had not laughed at *him*!'

   But though his eyesight was poor, James's vision was not. He was already
nurturing ambitious dreams of discovering new plant species from distant
lands which he could profitably introduce into English gardens. And
knowing that when his father died, he would lose the tenure for the Budlake
nursery at Killerton, he began making new plans to move on.

CHAPTER FOUR

AN EXOTIC NURSERY

Read my little fable:
He that runs may read.
Most can raise the flowers now,
For all have got the seed.
Alfred, Lord Tennyson,
'The Flower' 1847

THE VEITCH NURSERY at Killerton was barely seven miles from the fast expanding city of Exeter, but for James that was now seven miles too many. Exeter was built on sea trade and the export of rough serge cloth which was woven in cottages scattered across the Devon countryside. When the cloth trade had been killed off by successive wars with France and trade barriers reduced shipping to a dribble, the enterprising merchants of Exeter quickly turned to finance and banking. A new, well-off population moved in, eager to buy substantial properties, and Exeter grew into a comparatively rich provincial city with a large, comfortable middle class which built 'superior cottages' or little Regency and Greek revival villas with trim front gardens. There were doctors, clergymen, lawyers and bankers as well as retired army and naval officers and sea captains. Between 1800 and 1840 the city doubled in size, growing outwards with suburbs of larger houses and more ample gardens. Some moved farther out and invaded the rich, fertile valley of the Exe, pushing between some of the old landed estates and building themselves large country houses and gardens which clustered on the hillside facing south to catch the sun. There were a number of good city architects to build their houses, skilled artisans to make fittings and furniture. And nurserymen and gardeners were needed to design and plant out their gardens. The wealthy new middle classes could build themselves grand houses but not large landed estates. Instead of landscapes they had to be content with large gardens where they could show off their wealth with extravagantly filled flower beds, manicured lawns, specimen trees and conservatories and stove-houses filled with the latest in exotics. It was the beginnings of the Victorian garden.

After lengthy discussions about their finances, which were very healthy thanks to the success of the Budlake nursery, the Veitch family decided to buy a substantial parcel of land at Mount Radford, near the centre of Exeter, where James would set up a new nursery selling garden and glasshouse plants.

James Veitch (1792–1863)

Meanwhile his father John and brother Thomas would continue to raise forest, fruit and ornamental trees at Killerton. In 1830, twenty-five acres of land were purchased for £200 an acre, quite a large sum even in those days. But the ability to buy land was important. Most large nurseries rented land on the outskirts of towns, and as the towns expanded they found themselves squeezed out or saddled with ever-increasing rents to pay.

As soon as James had acquired Mount Radford, he spent nearly two years in preparations, building green-houses and a conservatory, creating forcing beds, and laying out his nursery and stocking it to his satis-faction. He also rented a shop in the High Street where he planned to sell flower and vegetable seed, garden implements and sundries to the general public. It was beautifully fitted with walls lined with small mahogany drawers, each labelled with the variety of seed. Late in the evenings James rode his pony home to Budlake or, if he was too exhausted, stayed overnight with his mother-in-law nearer Exeter, lying awake at night anxiously considering how best to build up a new clientele.

Sir Tom Acland, himself spending more time in Exeter during his lengthy but intermittent career as MP for Devonshire, was always ready to recom-mend the Veitch services and, as his own social circles and spheres of influ-ence widened, so the Veitch business benefited. The city boasted a lively social scene of glittering balls, theatres, salons and a fashionable racecourse, all of which disguised the pressing need for reform, not just in Exeter, but throughout the land. Men were still hanged for poaching, the mad were locked up in chains, elections were won by bribery and corruption, and much of the population, including women, was still not able to vote. Acland, although deeply rooted in Tory tradition, was instinctively progressive and humane and always urged the liberal causes of religious tolerance, abolition of slavery, prison reform, and relief for agricultural workers. The Reform Bill was passed in June 1832.

Within six weeks, Exeter and Plymouth were plunged into a cholera epidemic. Exeter's claim to have become a centre of fashion and gaiety hid the uglier aspects of an overcrowded, medieval city with some brutalising slums where cholera crept in through the open drains and took hold of the city. As the weeks went by the streets became almost deserted and in the outlying villages such as Broadclyst, the tolling of church bells for the frequent funerals could be heard. Many people fled, business suffered and the entire Acland family escaped to Holnicote where they caught yachting fever instead. (For many years they sailed on their large yacht around the British Isles and the Mediterranean where Sir Tom painted and Lady Acland botanised and sent plants home for the Veitches to grow in the newly-built orangery at Killerton.)

The cholera epidemic was a serious setback for James whose business dreams would have to wait. Despite his air of anxiety, he was enormously patient and industrious and took most setbacks in his stride. He never hurried things and his attention to detail and preparedness to sit it out and wait for a new seed to germinate or a plant to be ready for sale was a vital part of his success. The increasingly long hours spent in the nursery were, however, making it difficult for him to continue living at Budlake and so James commissioned an architect, S. A. Grieg, to design a villa to be built in the nursery grounds in the 'Old English style'. Both the work and financial outlay must have been enormous but James had John's full support and, according to his nephew, James could not prevent his father from spending all his money on the new venture. Indeed the old man often visited Mount Radford on his pony, offering financial and moral support and, no doubt, plenty of lectures on how his son 'should be doing things'.

James was determined that his five sons, James Junior, John, Thomas, William and Robert, would have a good education and training to prepare them for their place in the family business. He had sent the eldest, James Junior, to London for his horticultural training, first at Alfred Chandler's nursery in Vauxhall where they specialised in raising camellias, and later, with William Rollison of Tooting, noted for its orchids, for which James Junior acquired a life-long passion. James made an arrangement with

Rollison to the effect that he paid them no fee for training his son but instead agreed to purchase from them his nursery stock of orchids: When James Junior returned to Devon his young head was full of new ideas; he also brought home many rare species of orchid which would later form part of the basis of the great Veitch orchid collection.

Meanwhile, to help him with the move to Exeter, James took on Thomas Lobb, a thirteen-year-old apprentice who, with his brother William, would make some of the most significant contributions to the future success and fame of the Veitch nurseries. Thomas and William were brought up in Cornwall; their father was gamekeeper at Carclew, the home of Sir Charles Lemon, a noted botanist, where the brothers helped in the stove-houses and Sir Charles encouraged their interest in plants and horticulture.

At the end of 1832, James was ready to announce the opening of his new Exeter nursery. He sent out a letter of advertisement headed:

Killerton & Mount Radford Nurseries, Exeter.
Having long felt the necessity of a place of reference, at or near Exeter, I take the liberty of informing you that I have now established a new Nursery adjoining Mount Radford on the Topsham Road, which I propose continuing, in connection with my present old and well known establishment at Killerton.

James sent this letter to all the nursery's patrons and to people country-wide who he hoped might be potential customers: 'As no expense has or will be spared in laying out, and ornamenting the Grounds, it is hoped they may prove an attraction not only to the immediate neighbourhood, but to Persons from a distance visiting.'

It was common practice for nurseries of the time to be laid out in a way that would appeal to the public, almost like mini pleasure grounds, where they could stroll and enjoy the plants in a garden setting. A contemporary description of Pontey's Nursery in Plymouth was typical: 'The grounds are exceedingly well laid out and remind us of Lucombe & Pince and Messrs Veitch of Exeter and like them are kept in excellent order. The houses were all heated by Corbet's open gutters, using hot water to create a moist heat, which all nurserymen and gardeners who have tried it, agree in most strongly recommending.' James also announced that he proposed to concentrate on a 'more *select* and *choice* collection of the *very best fruits*', and with a newly discovered flair for imaginative showmanship, he created an enclosed area

for fruiting trees and bushes where customers could not only see but also taste the various fruits 'in their seasons'.

Like some of his competitors, James planned to introduce into his nursery some attractive novelties and specialities and build for himself a reputation for selling 'Exotics and hardy American and other flowering shrubs'. Thus he decided to call his business the 'Exotic Nursery'. His first advertisement illustrates these early forays in stocking 'extensive and choice collections of stove plants' including 'various kinds of Orchidaceous, or Air Plants' bought wholesale by James Junior from Rollison's nursery in London, and displays of 'Geraniums, Ericas and other Cape Plants and New Holland plants'. Prominently placed were James's own prize-winning dahlias, including some 'beautiful new striped and shaded Varieties'.

James was a good businessman and always made sure that his nurseries were well stocked with the most popular and affordable standard perennial and annual plants, bulbs, shrubs and fruit trees with which to satisfy his customers for their 'usual requirements'. There were imported bulbs of hyacinths, narcissus, jonquils, English and Persian iris, Guernsey and other lilies, *double* and single tulips, crocus, Dutch anemones, ranunculus, fritillarias and tuberoses.

One local customer, Mr Westcott, bought for his orchard, 6 standard 'May Duke' cherries at 1/6 each, 3 Dwarf Greengage plums at 2/6 each,

2 'Moorpark' Apricots at 5/–each, 1 'Royal George' Peach for 2/6, plus 6 Giant Rhubarb at 1/– each. At his seed shop on the High Street James offered the general gardener an enlarged seed business including herbs and vegetables plus a wide choice of 'Hardy Perennials, rock Plants and Aquatics, Carnations, Picotees and Pinks'.

James also offered for sale stocks of forest and ornamental trees and hardy shrubs still being raised in the Budlake nursery which, he promised, 'would be kept up in every respect as before'. James was by now clearly in overall control of the burgeoning business. Thomas remained in charge at Budlake where he was raising an astonishing stock of young fruit, forest and ornamental trees of many varieties. An extensive list was supplied to Sir John Slade at Maunsel near Bridgewater including oaks, chestnuts, filberts, walnuts, maples, beech, willow, hornbeams, limes, conifers, acacias and mountain ash. Gradually however, the stock at Budlake was transferred to other areas of land around Broadclyst and south Exeter. 'Orchard trees, twenty five vines and gardening sundries' were sent out to Nynehead in Somerset from land rented at Poltimore.

Little is known of Thomas Veitch beyond his interest in his fruit trees. There is no record of his marrying or having a family and it seems unlikely that Thomas was still alive when his father died in 1839 as his name does not appear in John's will.

James continued to advertise the well-established Veitch services of laying out grounds as well as supplying experienced and trained gardeners to the gentry. When Miss Harriet Francis Smith bought Craddock Lodge in 1839, she made a massive order to Veitch's to supply and plant a new garden. The bill listed quantities of fruit trees including medlars, 'Red Filberts' and 'Baking Pears'. There were vegetables, fruit bushes, climbing roses, many varieties of ornamental and flowering trees such as 'Judas and Almond, Scarlet Arbutus, Tulip, silver Firs and Cedar of Lebanon', as well as numerous kinds of choice shrubs, rhododendrons and hardy heaths, all for a grand total of £95 3s. 9d. As often happened, however, payment was not made until five years after the work had started. (Trying to get customers to pay up in reasonable time was a problem commonly suffered by small businesses.)

Apart from his prize-winning dahlias, much of James's first advertised stock was similar to that offered in most nurseries; indeed much of his seed was purchased from them. He did, however, draw customers' particular attention to a new introduction of his own, the brilliant red-flowered Parrot's Bill, *Clianthus puniceus*, from New Zealand, which James claimed was a hardy evergreen, though in fact it was rather tender and only did well in a greenhouse. When it flowered in May, the bush was covered with a profusion of large, pendulous bunches of rich crimson flowers, 'one of the most beautiful plants introduced for many years', reported the *Gardener's Chronicle*.

Severe frosts in the winter of 1838 caused devastation in nurseries across the country, including the usually mild south-west coast. Fortunately James's new heated glasshouses saved most of his stock, including plenty of *clianthus*, and he was quick to take advantage of business lost by other nurseries.

For the discerning customer wishing to see something new and rare, an appointment with James Veitch and a guided tour of the glasshouses was essential. Indeed James's nursery garden was always open to the curious and he was happy to share his knowledge. The residents of Exeter flocked to see the new nursery and to admire the beautifully laid-out displays of trees and plants. They strolled down the pathways looking at the colourful beds of flowers, squeezed into the steamy stove-houses where they gasped at the perfumed and richly foliaged exotics and they tasted the soft and orchard fruits that grew on bushes and trees in weighty profusion. They asked questions, enquired about plans and plants for their gardens and placed their orders.

Although he was at his best working with his plants, James had learned from his father how to handle patrons and customers, and he attended to everyone, giving careful and patient advice to those who really cared and politely responding to the merely curious. The new Veitch Exotic Nursery was gradually breaking into the fashionable markets of the new middle classes and also, to James's great satisfaction, many customers were becoming more discerning, finding a new interest in an increasingly challenging kind of gardening. James Harrison of Bridehead House in Somerset, for example, bought a tree fuchsia from the Killerton nursery and wrote enthusiastically to the *Gardener's Magazine*:

The *Fuchsia arborescens* has attracted the observation of many scientific men here. It is 22ft high with a head 40 feet in circumference, the trunk at the surface of the soil 16 inches in girth. It had fifty trusses of flowers on it last August and continued flowering in successin until the end of December . . . I bought this plant of Mr Veitch of Killerton Nursery six years ago, and grow it in a mixture of loam and peat.

This extraordinarily huge plant has its origins in the mountains of Mexico and Guatemala. It is not clear how or where James first obtained this specimen – perhaps from another nursery, or possibly from some other new source – but James was beginning to explore every means of obtaining new plants for his nursery. Years of study, reading and networking had made him familiar with the numerous ways plants had been introduced in the past and now, more than ever, James was following exciting new events in the long story of plant collecting.

THE STORY OF PLANT COLLECTING

Many people contributed to the establishment of non-indigenous species in new places – pilgrims, sailors and armies on the move, merchants and travellers. Alexander the Great's soldiers returned home with the Lombardy poplar and Charlemagne's men brought new herbs from the Holy Land. Travellers carried seeds and occasionally live plants from place to place as curiosities, souvenirs of the lands they had visited. And merchants who journeyed along the ancient caravan routes traded in aromatic spices, herbs and flowering plants for medicinal and culinary uses, but also for decoration, flavour and fragrance. As the roads and newly discovered ocean routes became busier, the growing interchange of people and trade meant more plants and their products being taken from their natural habitats and grown in other parts of the world, wherever they found suitable conditions.

The emerging interest in the 'natural sciences' also played a role in the wider knowledge and distribution of previously unknown plants and the creation of herbaria for study and classification created a demand for dried specimens. In the Middle Ages, Albertus Magnus, the diminutive monk and botanist, walked all over Northern Europe botanising and was probably the first systematic plant collector.

From the seventeenth century onwards, imperial expansion, trade and private enterprise were to become the global driving force behind plant collecting. The rival British and Dutch East India Companies who operated the spice routes set up trading posts and established botanical gardens where they studied and cultivated commercial plants such as tea, rubber and sugar. Missionaries and clergy, settlers and merchants who moved into the colonised territories proved invaluable plant collectors. Naval and army officers who were keen amateur naturalists found foreign postings perfect opportunities to botanise and collect; Nathaniel Wallich, who was employed by the East India Company as an army surgeon, sent his trained native

collectors into regions inacessible to Europeans. Ambassadors and diplo-
mats used their priviledged positions to ship home many rare and valuable
plants. New plants continued to arrive from all quarters of the known
world and as more of it opened up, so a greater number and variety of
new plants came into the country; marigolds from Mexico, hyacinths from
Turkey, oriental plane trees from Persia, Madonna lilies from southern
Europe, the pomegranate from south-west Asia, the Italian cypress and the
Norway spruce.

A position of power was as useful as wealth in obtaining plants for the
increasingly fashionable floral gardens; in the seventeenth century Henry
Compton, Bishop of London, filled Fulham Palace Gardens with the largest
single collection of exotics in England, using his extensive army of strategically placed clergymen such as John Bannister who sent home the graceful
silver-leaved climber *Bannisteria argyrophylla* from Brazil, but broke his neck
collecting plants from a cliff-face. The Duke of Albermarle took Dr Hans
Sloane as his physician on a journey to Jamaica where the Duke promptly
died, leaving Sloane to return home with over 800 new plants. Sloane's
book *Voyage to Jamaica* was said to be the model for all the books of naturalists' voyages that were to follow. Sloane, who was later knighted, set up
his own syndicates of collectors, including Mark Catesby, the first full-time
professional plant collector and pioneer ornithologist who travelled in North
America and the Bahamas. Freelance collectors, working in all the five
continents, were financed by syndicates of rich enthusiasts such as Peter
Collinson, a wealthy Quaker merchant who formed a group of aristocratic
patrons to pay for boxes of plants shipped home by travelling botanists
hoping to make a bit of money. The most prolific was John Bartram, a
Quaker farmer and the first American botanist, who spent most of his life
hunting for plants along the eastern colonies of North America, penetrating
wild 'Indian country'. Bartram is credited with introducing more than 200
American 'discoveries' to the English garden such as *Magnolia grandiflora*
which became very fashionable in English shrubberies and was much planted
by John Veitch against the walls of many grand houses.

James Veitch was always on the lookout for anyone who might supply
him with seed and plants. As a Fellow of the Horticultural Society James was
entitled to receive seed and plants brought back by Society collectors and
raised in their trial garden at Chiswick. He was also finding new specimens
from increasingly wider sources. Over the years, James built up his own
network of travellers, enthusiasts and amateur collectors. He corresponded

with established collectors such as James Drummond in Australia, James Tweedie in Buenos Aires and Dr John Royle, a medical officer with the East India Company in the Punjab. By the 1830s, there were missionaries aplenty in India, the Far East, the West Indies and West Africa. Many of these clerics combined their religious faith with a passionate interest in flora and fauna. They were skilled amateur naturalists who happily spent almost as much time studying, collecting and writing about the wildlife around them as trying to bring God to the indigenous people. A large number of these missionaries were of the Evangelical movement and it was through his own church connections that James had access to a number of these men, sent out from Devon to remote and dangerous places from where, if they survived, James persuaded them to send him 'new things'. Among James's growing network of collectors and contacts was 'a gentleman going to Jerusalem as a superintendent of a medical college who was hoping to make a botanical collection'. Two of his most useful suppliers were Mr Freeman, a missionary in 'Ashantee' country in West Africa who 'gives a most interesting description of the splendid vegetation in those parts' and another, who went to a mission on the 'new Red river settlement' in north-west America who sent James seeds of native American trees such as a 'Silver Fir of that country growing 100 ft high'. There were also young gardeners sent out to work in foreign gardens, including a man whom James had trained 'who goes out as an emigrant, he promises to do what he can for us'.

One friend who had already emigrated to Australia was John Carne Bidwill, son of an Exeter merchant. Bidwill went on a trip to New Zealand, exploring and collecting, and claimed to be the first European to see Lake Taupo. He later became Director of the Sydney Botanic Gardens but was said to have been violent and disrespectful towards the indigenous peoples and their tribal taboos and traditions. He found the Australian Monkey-puzzle tree, *Araucaria bidwillii*, and wrote a book about his adventures, *Rambles in New Zealand*, which both James and his brother Thomas read with great excitement. Indeed James was by now deeply caught up in the feverish desire for new 'exotic' foreign plants. He did not want just to discover a new plant, he dreamed of successfully cultivating, propagating and selling it for profit.

CLIENTS OLD AND NEW
James was beginning to create his own global and exotic 'Map of Influence'. As his reputation and standing gained him social respectability, he also found that he needed to be able to join the learned societies whose members

could further his collecting and selling powers. When Queen Victoria was crowned in 1837, England was already embarking on an age of improvement and enlightenment. It was a rich and stimulating period for the amateur historian, naturalist and scientist, men with intellectual curiosity and the means to indulge their interests and tastes. Even small provincial towns such as Exeter had a small coterie of learned and cultivated people. The Devon and Exeter Institution included gentry mixing with the better-educated merchants who were keen to promote and extol the virtues of science, literature and the arts. Members could hear lectures on geology and mineralogy, botany, poetry and the 'natural history of the earth'. Gardening was becoming popular and was assured a respectable status. The Devon and Exeter Horticultural Society was launched in 1829 with Sir Tom Acland, doubtless with Lydia's encouragement, elected as president in its second year. Ladies, anxious about the proprieties, were reassured that for females, gardening was now 'an agreeable and rational occupation'.

In the late 1830s, Richard Ford, a traveller and writer, bought an Elizabethan cottage called Heavitree House close to the Veitch nursery in Exeter where he settled down to write the journals of his travels in Spain. Ford wrote that 'Exeter is quite a Capital, abounding in all that London has, except its fog and smoke'. He became a keen gardener and planned a Spanish garden 'with Moorish-patterned flower borders, and pines'. He grew so enthusiastic that he wrote: 'I have given up the pen for the hoe and spade all a-delving and digging.' He particularly loved myrtles and made a little summer house his 'myrtle Bower' to work in. James's Exotic Nursery supplied Ford with plants, advice and assistance and James loved to sit in Ford's garden on a warm evening, relaxing with his pipe and listening to descriptions of the romantic ruins of the Alhambra, the groves of olives and citrus, vineyards and orchards of peach and pomegranate. The serious-minded, hard-working, practical horticulturist and businessman also possessed a romantic streak and he dreamed of exciting new discoveries in remote parts of the world and sending men to find them, yet he himself never left the shores of England.

Like many Victorians who thrilled to exciting stories of exploration and adventure in the ever-widening world and its apparantly endless source of new natural wonders, James was becoming quite an armchair traveller. He pored over the journals and letters from the growing troupe of friends and correspondents who were sending him packets, sacks and boxes of new plants and seeds.

★   ★   ★

Despite trade with the new merchant class proving to be profitable, James knew that his father's aristocratic 'Map of Influence' still formed a vital part of the family business. The aristocracy still led the field and paid the largest bills. James wrote regular 'personal' letters to members of the nobility offering his services. He offered the Duke of Somerset at Stover 'a fine stock of forest trees, laurels, shrubs and ornamentals' and advised him to plant Veitch's new rhododendrons as a way to 'fill up space'. The nursery kept up regular contracts to service several large west-country estates, including an arboretum and new greenhouses for Baron Poltimore. James also took on an important new client.

The most powerful and richest family in the West Country were the Rolles, once the lords of forty-five manors, including Bicton House near the seaside resort of Budleigh Salterton, east of Exeter. In John and James Veitch's time, Bicton was lived in by Lord John Rolle and his much younger second wife, Lady Louisa, who, like Lydia Acland, was an enthusiastic gardener. Her doting husband spared no expense in improving the gardens at Bicton. The Aclands and Rolles were part of the elite circle of neigh-bours, friends and connections through profitable marriages, and the Veitches, naturally 'highly recommended' by Lady Acland, spent many years supervising work, supplying plants and laying out new gardens and pleasure grounds at Bicton.

James was contracted to create a new arboretum, a pinetum and a fash-ionable 'American garden' with new shrubs and trees from America. When Robert Glendinning, the Veitch-trained head gardener at Bicton, moved to another job, James Junior, who had recently returned from his training in London, took over the superintendence of the work. When J. C. Loudon made a visit to Bicton, it was James Junior who took him on a tour of the gardens. Loudon described a rather routine scene: 'Messrs. Veitch & Son having six men constantly employed mowing the grass, and mulching the dug circles round the plants with it . . . destroying weeds as soon as they appear; and removing dead leaves, suckers from grafted plants, insects, decayed blossoms etc.' For Loudon, though, one great beauty of the Bicton arboretum was that the name of a specimen could be read on its label by a person 'while sitting in a carriage, and driving through it along the green walk' and he praised Veitch for taking measures to have all the plants correctly named.

When Mr James Barnes, the new head gardener, arrived, he was not impressed and described 'six or seven men mowing a nobleman's flower-garden with each a short pipe in his mouth, blowing a cloud as if doing it for a wager'. It is not clear if he was referring to James Junior and his team, but Brown was appalled by the outdated techniques and poor standard of work from Glendinning's time at Bicton. He wrote a long tirade against slovenly gardeners who arrived later than 6 a.m. when 'the first thing they thought of was liquor to drink'. Good head gardeners had a fearsome reputation and Barnes was not afraid to crack down despite the resentment it initially caused: 'It was said that my long, ugly legs would not be walking Bicton Gardens long', but undeterred, he pinned up a list of rules with fines for shoddy workmanship, sloppy dress, swearing and intoxication. Apparently the men soon came to respect Barnes's new regime; he wrote 'the difference in the industry, cleanliness, happiness and contentment amongst my men is truly astonishing' with 'merry whistling' and singing to be heard as they went to work. However, the long relationship between the Bicton gardener and his mistress, Lady Rolle, ended unhappily when Barnes sued the ageing widow for libel because she had accused him of leaving the gardens 'in a disorderly condition' when he retired. It was a terrible slur, but it was unheard of for a gardener to sue his employer and the case became quite a *cause célèbre*. Barnes won and was awarded £200 – about £8,500 today.

Whether James Veitch, who ran his nursery along similarly strict lines, was in sympathy with Brown's regime is not known, but it is likely that he would have supported him and possibly exchanged a few sharp words with his son, for whom the routine work never had its attractions. What really excited James Junior at Bicton was the extraordinary Palm House being built there. The plan was to create rain-forest conditions where tropical and sub-tropical plants could thrive. Facing south, it was built of curved glazing bars in wrought iron, with gutters, pilasters and four slender internal columns of cast iron, all resting on a base of Bath stone. The central shell-like dome was self-supporting, held together by pressure from the thousands of scalloped panes of glass which overlapped like fish scales. It was one of the most beautiful the Veitches had ever seen. Happily the Veitches' long association with Sir Tom and Lady Lydia Acland and with Lady Louisa Rolle allowed them to use the Killerton and Bicton gardens and glasshouses as testing grounds for Veitch introductions.

The Rolle family filled the Bicton Palm House with a fabulous collection of orchids and James Junior, already a keen young orchidist, could hardly keep away. The finest of all was the 'Bicton Orchid', *Odontoglossum bictoniense* (*Lemboglossum bictoniense*), the first of its genus to reach England alive and to flower in cultivation. It was found by the Scottish trader and naturalist George Ure-Skinner who was later to become a close friend of James Junior. Ure-Skinner was hunting for orchids in the highland forests of Guatemala for his wealthy patron, John Bateman, a tropical plant enthusiast from Shropshire. Bateman shared part of this collection with his friend Lord Rolle, including some unidentified plants, one of which – the Bicton Orchid – turned out to be a particularly vigorous plant, its tall spikes bearing as many as twenty long-lasting pale olive blooms with brown bars and spots set off by a striking pink or white lip. It was lovely, new and fascinating and the Veitches guessed correctly that if the plant sold, it would be immensely profitable.

When John Veitch had worked at the Vineyard Nursery in London, orchids were almost unknown; there were only two North American orchids in cultivation in Europe – the Lady's Slipper from Virginia and the Canada Lady's Slipper. Some specialist gardens, including the Royal Gardens at Kew, possessed a few tropical orchids from Florida, China and the West Indies. Sir Joseph Banks later returned from his expeditions with the first three orchids from the East Indies and one from Australia. Royal patronage stimulated the growing interest in collecting orchids, a hobby in which only the wealthiest could indulge. Gradually, as Britain expanded her empire into the orchid-rich tropics and subtropics of India, South-east Asia, the West Indies, Guyana and Africa, new genera and species of orchids arrived home in mixed bags of plants with returning military, missionaries and colonial administrators – though the slow sea passage without suitable packing killed off all but a few plants.

In 1818 William Swainson, who was exploring the Organ Mountains of Brazil, sent home a consignment of plants which he had wrapped in what appeared to be dried plant material. William Cattley, a tropical plant enthusiast, was curious about the strange-looking wrapping and sought to bring some back to life. He was both amazed and thrilled to discover in only a few months that the plant had not only sent out shoots but produced huge, rose-coloured flowers with trumpet-like labellum. It was, he wrote, 'the most splendid, perhaps of all Orchidaceous plants, which blossomed for the first time in Britain in the stove of my garden in Suffolk'. The new genus was named Cattleya in his honour and the new species *Cattleya labiata* (from *labium*, meaning lip). News of this unique flower with its striking beauty and showiness caused an immediate sensation among horticulturists. Before the introduction of *Cattleya labiata*, the comparatively few species that had found their way into British glasshouses usually did so as 'curiosities'. Now orchid collecting and cultivation was turning into a sensational new branch of horticulture with amateur orchid growers building special orchid houses in which to grow them. The London nurseryman, Conrad Loddiges, began selling orchids and became recognised as the most influential and authoritative commercial nurseryman in the field of orchid culture. Others followed, such as Rollison of Tooting, where James Junior had trained. Hugh Low & Co of Clapton were among the first to receive orchids from abroad, whilst Lee & Kennedy were, as ever, already leaders in the field.

Far from London and the fashionable centre of the plant world, the Veitch nursery nevertheless were very aware of the growing demands for new orchids. Tucked away in their Exeter nursery, they watched bigger nurseries quickly moving into the orchid business. Father and son knew that the secret of success lay in their ability to improve techniques in germination and cultivation, skills that required patience and staff with special talent. When James heard that a promising young nurseryman called John Dominy had recently joined his rivals, Lucombe, Pince & Co., he quickly lured Dominy to the Veitch nursery, much to Lucombe's fury, and Dominy's skills as an excellent cultivator of stove and greenhouse plants soon became apparent. For several years James Junior and Dominy spent their days in the greenhouses absorbed in raising prize-winning specimens of rhododendrons, dahlias, fuchsias and camellias. Thanks to his father, James Junior had had a first-class horticultural training and was now proving himself to be a brilliant young nurseryman. He was as enthusiastic and ambitious as his father, but had less patience with the business side where he tended to look for quicker rewards and returns. James Junior was a curious combination of scientist and showman, deeply serious about the study and cultivation of plants but also revelling in showing them off. And he enjoyed the social approbation and success they brought him. Like his

John Dominy (1816–1891)

father, he was a prime mover in developing the increasingly popular varieties of dahlia and he exhibited Dominy's plants at some of the most prestigious horticultural events in London and the West Country, attracting considerable attention to himself and the Veitch nursery.

Veitch's were neither the first nor the only commercial horticultural nursery to advertise novelties and exotics but their reputation for selling newly introduced plants and hybrids was spreading. In 1835 a reporter from the *Exeter and Plymouth Gazette* visiting the nursery wrote, 'There are now in bloom in the new conservatory . . . several varieties of splendid hybrid Nepal rhododendrons of scarlet and crimson shades, beautifully spotted; with a variety of camellias; reticulata, imbricata, florida etc.' The Nepal rhododendrons were most likely raised from seed collected some years earlier by the East India Company surgeon, Nathaniel Wallich. The *Camellia reticulata* had arrived from Canton in 1820 with the captain of an East Indiaman. James, always on the lookout for new plants by whatever means they had arrived, heard on the network about the camellia and bought a specimen for the nursery.

James was always careful to ensure that quality was as evident as novelty. At the June show of the Devon and Exeter Botanical and Horticultural Society, the *Gazette* described the Veitch display of exhibits as 'of the most splendid' which must have required 'great labour and expense to produce'. On display were some 'very superior' pelargoniums, a beautiful collection of calceolarias and fifty different varieties of ericas, one of which was 'quite new'. There were pots of the now well-established *Clianthus puniceus*, some new yellow Scottish roses and *Phlox drummondii*, which had only recently been discovered in Texas by the Scottish collector Thomas Drummond just before his death. William Hooker, who was then Professor of Botany in Glasgow, hoped the plant would 'serve as a *frequent* memento of its unfortunate discoverer'. James, who had been communicating with Hooker for some time, obtained seeds as soon as he heard about the phlox; its richly-coloured, fragrant mounds were soon a popular selling plant for rockeries and sunny beds. James proudly showed a new 'very beautiful Chinese azalea with variegated flowers' at the Devon Floral Society's spring show where it was the centre of attraction as it had 'never before bloomed in this country'.

By 1837, James's new house, 'Graslawn', was finally ready to move into. Soon after, James Junior married Harriot Reynolds Gould, daughter of a local farmer, and they too left Budlake Farm to live near the Exeter nursery.

With no one in the family left to care for him, John Veitch, by then eighty-five years old, was moved to Hagli's cottage, close to Killerton House, where he had lived when he had first arrived nearly sixty-five years earlier. He was well looked after by the staff and visited by Lydia and Tom Acland whenever they were at home. Just before he died in 1839, John heard news of the birth of his first great-grandson, John Gould Veitch (he was always known as 'John Gould', using his mother's family name as was common practice at the time).

So much had changed in the world since the cheerful, reliable John first arrived in Devon and laid out his little tree business. His son and grandson, possessed with far greater imagination, drive and ambition, were pushing the nursery at Exeter into new and expanding markets. Yet again, however, the visions of father and son seemed set in different directions.

CHAPTER FIVE

FOR SCIENCE AND PROFIT

The silver lips of lilies virginal,
The full deep bosom of the enchanted rose,
Please less than flowers glass-hid from frosts and snows,
For whom an alien heat makes festival.

Theodore Wratislaw, 1890

WHILE HIS NURSERY business flourished, James Veitch took time off to make several trips to the Chiswick gardens of the Horticultural Society to see what was arriving from their expeditions, what they were able to cultivate, and to pick up the latest news and gossip. He read the Society's *Transactions* and *Curtis' Botanical Magazine* with its beautifully accurate and detailed illustrations of the more interesting new specimens by the best botanical artists. (These paintings were vital sources of information for identifying and naming new plants.) There were also accounts of collectors' travels, in particular David Douglas, the Society's finest and one of several famous Scots. Douglas introduced over 200 new species, his greatest achievement being the discovery and introduction of American conifers which ignited a passion for their planting in English shrubberies and pineta. Douglas made several dangerous expeditions and suffered appalling hardships before tragically being gored to death by a bull while collecting in Hawaii in 1834. Another collector whose discoveries attracted James's attention was Theodor Hartweg who was exploring the dangerous South American interior for the Horticultural Society and had already found nearly 200 species of orchids, various cacti and many species of other genera, including fuchsias, in particular *F. fulgens*, one of the main parents of modern hybrid fuchsias. By the late 1830s, the Chiswick glasshouses were bursting with interesting new plants and James Veitch had reached a peak of excitement and frustration. Despite being a small provincial nurseryman, James had become convinced of the value of sending out his own collectors and he was determined to do so as soon as possible before, as he feared, everything had been snapped up. But

James knew that if he was to pursue his dream he would need a lot of help.

For a commercial nurseryman planning to increase and improve his stock with new introductions, there were two men and two organisations to whom he looked for support, advice, supplies of new plants and, if he was introducing something of his own, the essential identification, description and naming without which the plant could not successfully be sold. William Jackson Hooker and John Lindley were, coincidentally, both born in Norfolk and educated at Norwich Grammar School. Hooker, whose family originated from Exeter, was older by fourteen years. He became a protégé of Sir Joseph Banks, who was then Director of the Botanic Gardens at Kew which, like the Horticultural Society, was also sending plant collectors abroad, among them three Scotsmen, Francis Masson and the Cunningham brothers, Allan and Richard. Banks helped Hooker get an appointment as Professor of Botany at Glasgow University where he taught medical students who at that time were expected to be able to identify and use medicinal plants.

Despite feeling isolated during his years in Scotland, Hooker became one of the leading botanists in the country, corresponding with thousands of scientists, botanists, gardeners and nurserymen, exchanging information, and borrowing and lending plant specimens. At a time when there were only a few scientific journals and books which carried news of new methods and theories, Hooker saw himself acting as a clearing house for the spread of botanical knowledge. He longed to be at the centre of the horticultural and botanical world and nurtured a dream of being Director of the Botanic Gardens of Kew

Sir William Hooker (1785–1865)

John Lindley, who was also highly ambitious, dreamed as a youth of travelling to Madagascar and the East Indies; in order to accustom himself to the hardships he imagined would have to be faced he slept on his bedroom floor. But he never went further than Belgium, Ireland and France. Lindley visited Hooker in London and became another protégé of Banks who made him an assistant in the Kew library. By the early age of only thirty-one, the precocious Lindley was Professor of

Botany at London University and of
the Society of Apothecaries at the
Chelsea Physic Garden.

He had been elected a Fellow of
both the Royal Society and the
Linnaean Society of London and
had completed his collaboration
with J. C. Loudon in preparing *An
Encyclopaedia of Plants*. He had also
taken over as editor of the *Botanical
Register* and, most importantly, was
appointed Assistant Secretary of the
Horticultural Society garden at
Chiswick.

Lindley's position there put him
in a perfect position to see every

Dr John Lindley (1799–1865)

new plant arriving in the country from correspondents and collectors
working for syndicates and amateur enthusiasts collecting in the field, as
well as the plants of Horticultural Society collectors. It became the practice for nurserymen and private collectors to send herbarium specimens
and live plants to Chiswick for Lindley to identify and name. The steady
stream arriving from around the world gave him unprecedented access to
new species and genera, especially the *Orchidacaea*, and he became captivated by this particular 'tribe of curious plants'. By the 1850s Dr Lindley
was the unchallenged expert of orchid taxonomy and the acknowledged
authority on plant nomenclature to whom all others deferred.

After Sir Joseph Banks's death in 1820, Kew lost its way as a botanical
garden; King William IV took little interest and there was no one to fight
for it. The Whig government drastically reduced Kew's budget and recalled
its plant collectors from around the world. For the next twenty years, the
future of Kew lay undecided. The garden failed to preserve its valuable
stock and lost many plants through carelessness and ignorance. John Smith,
a curator, was dismayed when he first went to Kew in 1822 and saw
Cunningham's collections of orchids from Brazil 'potted in common soil'
and left near unshaded glass. Cunningham himself had sent 500 packs of
seed to Kew, yet only a few had yielded useful plants. By 1826 the gardens
had declined so much that a German nurseryman, on a tour of London
gardens and nurseries, noted that the collections of nurserymen Loddiges

and Lee & Kennedy were superior to that at Kew. By the time the King died in 1837, Kew Gardens had been reduced to a sad and impoverished state. Perhaps the bleakest moment came when the Earl of Surrey, the Lord Steward of the Royal Household, decided without consulting anyone, to convert some of the glasshouses into a vinery. He instructed the kitchen gardener to empty the Botany and the Cape houses of their magnificent specimens. When the news leaked out, the newspapers condemned the scheme as a disgrace to the nation. The idea was quickly abandoned and the plants, exposed and dying in the winter cold, were rushed back into shelter, sadly too late for some to recover.

There was always some rivalry between Kew and the Horticultural Society – although they should have complemented each other since the Society's garden was intended to be horticultural as distinct from the botanic garden at Kew. Kew collectors were paid by the privy purse so that plants were Crown property and could not be sold. Only exchanges were permitted which put constraints on the distribution of Kew introductions into gardens generally and many thousands of specimens were subsequently lost. Private collections paid for by subscription did at least ensure a better distribution of plants, though many still ended up in only a few gardens of the wealthier members. It was commercial nurserymen who sold collector's plants and the Horticultural Society, with its policy of exchange among members, that finally ensured that large numbers of new species found their way into common cultivation.

In January 1838 John Lindley, aided by John Wilson, gardener to the Earl of Surrey, and Joseph Paxton, the Duke of Devonshire's remarkable head gardener at Chatsworth, conducted a 'forthright enquiry' which recommended that Kew should become a national Botanic Garden. Although he had been keen to take over the reins himself, it was Dr Lindley's friend, by then Sir William Hooker, who in 1841 finally achieved his ambition and was appointed Director of the Royal Botanic Gardens of Kew. Between them, they were the saviours of Kew while at the same time steering the Horticultural Society through its many difficulties. During their long and extraordinarily productive lives, gardeners, botanists, horticulturists, plant collectors and commercial nurserymen had much to thank them for.

It was characteristic of James Veitch to write immediately to Sir William Hooker and congratulate him on his new appointment, for James knew that his own interests would be considerably better served by Hooker's influential and important new position. Sir William, who had many relatives in Exeter, often visited Devon and was familiar with James's nursery at Mount Radford.

Their long relationship was a match of mutual benefit. Sir William represented the men of science, the botanists who created priceless herbarium collections and studied their dried specimens in a spirit of scientific enquiry, whilst Veitch was the horticulturist and businessman driven by a passion for raising new plants and a powerful profit motive. He knew that his association with Sir William would enable him to have his new introductions formally identified by Dr Lindley, and illustrated in *Curtis's Botanical Magazine* by the most brilliant botanical artists such as Walter Fitch. Hooker was then editor of the *Botanical Magazine* which also published brief accounts of new plants that were likely to interest professional and amateur gardeners.

James regularly wrote to Sir William that he was always 'hoping to get new things from our many correspondents in various parts of the world', sending him examples of specimens or descriptions of plants and asking for his help in identification. In return he offered dried specimens for Hooker's herbarium and live plants or viable seed for his private garden collection. But he knew that it was not a reliable method for building up a profitable stock of fashionable plants and exclusive new 'discoveries' for which the public were clamouring. In 1840 James's missionary friend in Western Africa had sent a 'Pod of the *Bignaceae*' which James had sent on to Hooker, still in Glasgow. 'I shall feel much obliged by a few lines at your convenience stating whether from the description and the Pod you know the plant and consider it to be a good thing, and whether it is new to you, as the seeds appear likely to vegetate, and if it be a new thing.'

James again wrote to Hooker about a beautiful 'clear-blue' *Leschenaultia* which he had raised from seed sent from Australia by James Drummond, younger brother of the more famous Thomas. 'From the seeds we raised 5 or 6 plants, 3 of which appear quite different and distinct in foliage'. Dr Lindley named and described the new *Leschenaultia* as *L. biloba* and in the spring of 1841 after successfully 'blooming' it, the Veitch *Leschenaultia* was awarded a prestigious Horticultural Society large Silver Medal when shown at the Society headquarters in Regent Street.

With a few exceptions, commercial horticultural nurseries had rarely been involved in plant-collecting expeditions. In 1790 James Lee sent his grandson, David Burton, out to Australia in search of new plants. Burton returned a 'useful collection' but after a shooting accident he was, Lee wrote, 'called to botanize in the celestial regions'. Between 1823 and 1832, William Baxter was sent to Australia on a couple of expeditions by a group of nurserymen, including Joseph Knight, who paid a subscription of £1,500

– an extraordinarily high sum for those days', which suggests how lucrative the nursery trade was becoming. The fortunes of current collecting expeditions were colourfully reported in the horticultural journals: some had proved successful but expensive and some had turned out disastrously.

TRIUMPHS AND TRAGEDIES

Only a few fabulously rich individuals could afford to finance their own expeditions. During James Veitch's lifetime there was one person, the Duke of Devonshire, who had the wealth, the driving passion and the perfect gardener. Rather late in his life, the Duke's eyes had been opened to the delights of horticulture and he became so engrossed that he agreed to become the next president of the Horticultural Society. Having let part of the grounds of his house in Chiswick to the Society, the Duke often walked around the garden examining the new plants. There he met the young Joseph Paxton, then employed by the Society, and took him as his head gardener to his country seat, Chatsworth in Derbyshire. The Duke first saw and fell in love with orchids at a Society exhibition in 1833 and the Chatsworth hothouses were soon filled with rare tropical plants and orchids. But the appetites of the Duke and his head gardener were insatiable. They decided that they would send 'their own man', John Gibson, to the remote mountains of Assam in India where numerous varieties of orchids and 'tropical novelties' were known to be abundant and, most importantly, where it was rumoured a new tree might also be found.

The distinguished horticulturalist Dr Nathaniel Wallich, head of the Botanic Garden at Calcutta, reported seeing an unknown and 'splendid' tree covered in large vermilion-coloured flowers in the garden of a ruined monastery in Burma. News of this extraordinary tree soon spread to England where it was named *Amherstia nobilis*, after the intrepid botanist Lady Amherst, wife of the Governor-General of India. However, no one had yet succeeded in bringing a live specimen back to England. The Duke of Devonshire desperately desired *Amherstia* and was determined to be the first to have it. The English horticultural world followed the story of the Duke's expedition with bated breath and no one was more fascinated by it than James Veitch.

In April 1835, Gibson started his long journey entirely funded by the Duke and organised with considerable ducal string-pulling. When Gibson arrived in Calcutta, he was taken to see the original *Amherstia* now flowering in the Botanic Garden and the young gardener ran round the tree 'clapping his hands like a boy who has got three runs in a cricket match'.

There were even more amazing sights for Gibson as he explored the Khasea Hills in search of new orchids for his master. His letters were filled with delight and excited surprise at what he found: 'I never saw, nor could I believe that there was such a fertile place under the Heavens, had I not the inexpressible pleasure of seeing it, and I think the whole of the plants are entirely new to the European collections'.

With literally hundred of orchids, 'some of them beyond description or comparison', safely packed up in cases, baskets, pots and bottles, Gibson sailed triumphantly home. Stowed on the poop deck were two huge glass cases, each housing a fine specimen of *Amherstia nobilis*, one for the Duke and a second for the East India Company. Disastrously, one of the specimens died en route and Gibson, being an honest soul, owned up that it had been the Duke's. When he heard the news, His Grace begged the Directors of the Company to give their tree to him, a request to which they graciously assented. On arrival, the precious little tree sat in its sealed case in the hall at Devonshire House where the Duke sat eating breakfast with Paxton and 'lavished their love upon the gem' while receiving early visits from Dr Lindley, Sir William Hooker, Mr Loddiges, Mr Rolleson, Mr John Lee and numerous other 'curious eminences'. Unfortunately the Chatsworth *Amherstia* refused to flower and twelve years later, to the Duke's great chagrin, Mrs Lawrence, an indomitable plantswoman, succeeded in producing the first flowers on a tree at her home in Ealing Park.

Acquiring the *Amherstia* and the fabulous collection of Indian orchids had cost the Duke enormous sums, but the success of the expedition infected him with a desire for yet more plants. He now planned to find and collect more of the increasingly fashionable hardy trees and conifers from the north-western coast of North America. This time, however, Paxton set up a co-operative expedition, to be funded with shares from noblemen with large estates, wealthy amateurs and the larger nurseries, including Knight, Loddiges, Rollison and Lee, who readily paid up their share of £50. Dr Lindley and Sir William Hooker, invited to assist in the identification and naming of new discoveries, would receive dried specimens for their herbaria, living plants for the botanic garden at Kew and the horticultural garden at Chiswick. Two young Paxton-trained gardeners, Robert Wallace and Peter Banks, were chosen to follow the routes first taken by David Douglas in the remote and perilous Pacific slopes of the Rockies. Despite opposition from Hooker and Lindley, Paxton insisted on sending his collectors on a long and dangerous route across Canada, apparently to toughen them up.

After signing an agreement for their usual wages of twenty-four shillings a week, a promise not to spend more than £1,600 and a warning to beware of bears and women, the two men were launched into the unknown. They joined an overland despatch being sent by the Hudson Bay Company to the headwaters of the Columbia river. The party struggled along icy rivers, across dangerous portages, threaded their frail craft through boiling rapids in thunder, and rain wind until one day in October 1839 their boat struck a rock and all, including Banks and Wallace, were drowned. Shattered by the deaths of his two gardeners, the Duke took no further part in sending collectors in search of plants.

News of the expedition's fate spread like wildfire amongst plantsmen and commercial nurserymen, especially those who had lost their subscriptions. For James Veitch, it must have clearly brought home to him that plant collecting was a seriously dangerous and financially risky business. But he astounded everyone by refusing to abandon his dreams, despite some of his friends and colleagues laughing at him, and others fearing for his common sense. Less than a year after the Chatsworth disaster James had come to the conclusion that despite all the risks, there was only one way of getting sufficient quantities of the plants that he wanted. He would go ahead with his plans and send out his own collector.

In August 1840 James wrote to Hooker that 'we have had an application from a young man desirous of going out as a Collector but he declines the Coast of Africa, he is desirous of going either to Guatemala, Mexico, Chile or Peru'. He added that he was 'rather inclined to send him', but needed first to ascertain something of the expense and the best location to send the man, 'as we are growers of orchidaceous plants . . . Guatemala would present the finest field'. The Horticultural Society's collector, Theodore Hartweg, was already in Mexico and although Chile was considered expensive, James believed it would eventually prove to be the best area for a nurseryman to find plants such as penstemons, hardy annuals, fuchsias and salvias. James conceded that in the world of plant collecting he was as yet a novice, but wrote that, as he wished to be well informed on the subject, 'your advice will be very acceptable'. Of course, James wanted to send someone he could trust, who had a knowledge and love of plants but, he pointed out, the man had to understand 'what to collect for a nurseryman rather than one who only appraised plants with a Botanist's ego'. James was the first nurseryman to send a commercial collector and his description was of a quite new breed of collector who would be under orders to send back specific species of plant in commercial quantities.

James continued to ply Hooker with questions and requests for advice on a wide range of questions: 'What are the usual things required as expected by the outfit of a Botanical Collector?' 'Are there any particular Botanical books or works desirable to supply the collector with?' 'What description of paper would be best for dried specimens?' 'What would be the best season to arrive there in?' and, with an eye to selling to customers abroad, he also enquired: 'Do you think there are any kinds of seeds we could send out with a prospect of profit?' and what about presents to give to 'Persons in Official situations to smooth the collector's way?'

Getting plants home alive and in good condition was a major undertaking. Tender plants carried overland could pass through several different temperatures and be exposed to excessive moisture, heat and disturbance. Boxes of plants sent on the long sea voyage home were usually stacked on deck where they faced storms, salt spray and uncaring seamen, as well as rats who made their nests among the plants and ate the seeds and roots. Plants were often housed in fetid, dark cabins where they soon succumbed. There were exceptions: captains who had become quite keen shippers of botanical specimens included Captain Richard Rawes who brought home *Camellia reticulata* and live plants of *Primula sinensis* on his ship the *Warren Hastings* and Captain Robert Wellbank nursed a plant of *Wisteria sinensis*, one of the most beautiful of all climbing plants sent from China by the East India Company tea inspector, John Reeves.

James would no doubt also have read advice published by both Dr John Lindley and Dr John Livingstone, chief surgeon of the East India Company in China and one of the Horticultural Society's overseas Corresponding Members. Their directions were fairly similar: plants should be collected in proper time, so as to enable them to be firmly rooted in the appropriate soil in robustly made chests or boxes in which they were to be transported to England. When stowed on ship the covers should be kept closed to protect them from salt spray, but opened during fine weather and carefully watered. Bearing in mind the dramatic changes in climate the plants would experience, Livingstone suggested that particular attention be paid to them from the time of the ship's arrival in the Thames until they were unloaded – a critical period when many collections were lost. Livingstone estimated that for every plant successfully brought home from China, a thousand were being lost, making the cost and waste unendurable. 'If the English horticulturist and botanist is to be gratified then more certain methods must be found.' He suggested having a trained gardener to prepare, pack and escort the plants home, thus avoiding the risks of careless ships' captains. Unfortunately this good advice was not fully taken up for many years and millions of rare plants would be destroyed in the meantime.

Transporting seed was almost as hazardous. Poorly packed seed rotted or sprouted while ships' rats and cockroaches could speedily chomp through an unprotected sackful. Sand was most commonly used and John Bartram packed his seed in sealed bottles of sand or dry soil. The plantsman Dr John Ellis recommended sealing them in wax, even dripping. Linnaeus had a complex theory of packing seed to keep it cool in tropical conditions, by putting it within a small glass container which was put inside a larger bottle and the space between filled with a mix of nitre and small amounts of salt and sal ammoniac. Dr Livingstone suggested that, for damp conditions, large seeds be held over concentrated sulphuric acid to dry the air around them. Whether or not either idea worked, they were hardly practical suggestions for the collector working alone in the steaming jungle. Salt and sugar, both absorbers of moisture, were also proposed. Nathaniel Wallich successfully sent back enormous quantities of seed, including the first rhododendron seeds, packed in brown sugar. He also recommended that paper used for wrapping plants should be impregnated with arsenic to kill off would-be attackers. Later collectors solved some of the problems by germinating seed straight into cases before putting them on the ship.

Fortunately for James Veitch, a revolutionary change in transporting plants

The Cask for sowing East-India seeds with the openings defended by Wire.

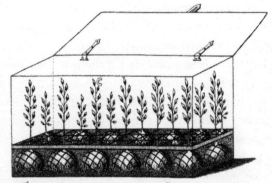

The Inside of the box shewing the manner of securing the roots of W. Florida and W. India plants surrounded with earth & moss tied with packthread and fastend cross & cross with laths or packthread to keep them steady.

Two methods of transporting plants. They were rarely successful had been introduced just in time to give his expedition a good chance of success. James, who was always up to the minute with information about the latest techniques, wrote to Kew that 'there is now a new patent glass case, very strong, would it be desirable to have a few cases with glass tops to grow seeds in to vegetate on the journey?' He was referring to the new 'Wardian' case first used by Joseph Paxton. Dr Nathaniel Ward, an amateur naturalist, had discovered in 1827 that a sealed jar in which he had placed a caterpillar to pupate had also grown a tiny fern and some miniature blades of grass. The plants were living in a permanent state of humidity as the moisture condensed by day and returned to the plants at night. The protected environment excluded polluting air and moisture and kept the plants clean and undisturbed. By 1834 Ward had proved conclusively that plants stood the best chance of surviving if they were transported in sealed, glazed cases modelled on his caterpillar jar. He experimented by sending some English ferns to New South Wales. After a six-month voyage, the plants arrived in perfect condition. The cases were then planted up with especially tender and difficult native Australian plants, and returned home through storm-tossed seas undergoing temperatures ranging from F20° to F120°.

When Ward opened the cases in London, the plants were secure, fresh and green. Collectors all around the world realised that their troubles with

The Wardian case

transportation were largely over although care still had to be taken not to 'drown' or 'boil' the plants in the cases under very hot sun. Glass, wood and nails were often sent out to collectors in 'kits', to be made up, though the joinery had to be perfect to prevent salt or bacteria getting in. Wardian cases were made in all sizes and shapes to suit requirements, from a shoebox to huge cases weighing nearly three cwt in which to transport young trees. Their reliability now made future plant-collecting expeditions viable propositions.

Considering how keen he was to know what everyone else was up to, James was cannily secretive about his own plans and he wrote to Hooker, 'Having decided on sending out a Collector, we would thank you not to name him'. However, he was happy to come to a mutually agreeable under-standing with Hooker: 'If we send him, it will be solely on our own account as regards plants and seeds, but we shall be most happy to afford every facility for his collecting for you such dried specimens as you require.' The collector would be instructed to make not less than six herbarium sets of which two were to go to Kew. Hooker replied generously with advice on routes, places to search in, plants to collect and, on the basis of expeditions he had sent, an idea of the costs. He also offered to help with letters of introduction, applications for passports and information about necessary equipment and supplies. Once James had finally made his 'bold and radical decision' to send a collector to South America, he wasted no more time and wrote to Hooker telling him that he had booked 'Mr Lobb' on the packet *Seagull* leaving for Rio de Janeiro on Saturday, 7 November 1840.

Thomas Lobb had been working at Veitch's nursery for ten years and had become a valuable member of the Exeter nursery. His older brother, William, was employed as a gardener to the Williams family at Scorrier House near the port of Falmouth. There William watched the packet boats setting out and returning from long voyages, befriended some of the captains and listened eagerly to their colourful tales of voyages to the West Indies, Brazil and other far-flung places. He longed to travel and to discover for himself foreign countries and unknown 'vegetation'. He was already a keen amateur botanist and had made a fine collection of dried speci-mens of British plants, particularly Cornish ferns. James Veitch no doubt discussed his ideas with Thomas Lobb who told James of his brother's dreams. James immediately sent for William, then thirty-one years old, and was impressed with his 'keen manner' and his horticultural and botan-ical knowledge. James decided that, despite not being a trained botanist, William would prove a steady, industrious, and dependable collector.

One week before his departure William made a final visit to Exeter to collect his equipment, passport, maps, money and tickets. James, concerned that Lobb should not be 'cramped for funds', arranged for an allowance of around £400 per annum which was available to draw on in the large cities along his route. James was now well aware that he faced a huge and potentially costly gamble. Although much was left to William's discretion, he was given instructions about routes and where in particular to obtain certain plants. James had seen a few rare specimens of very young Monkey-puzzle trees, *Araucaria imbricata* (now *A. araucana*) growing at Kew from seed brought back by the Horticultural Society's collector, James McRae, but first discovered by Archibald Menzies in 1795. James was convinced that this tree would be hugely popular and he instructed Lobb to collect substantial quantities of seed. Lobb was contracted to be in the field for at least one full year so that plants in flower could be located and noted and later revisited to harvest the seed. James himself had little interest in dried specimens, but he was happy for Lobb to make sets to send as sweeteners to Hooker at Kew and Dr Lindley at the Horticultural Society. Lobb visited Kew where he was shown how to make herbarium specimens by placing plant material between special papers. It was a job that most collectors loathed as it usually took up half the night, squatting tired and sweating over delicate petals and leaves in the guttering flare of a lamp. In later years, James would sell his collectors' herbarium sets at auction, allowing the collectors the proceeds after deducting his expenses. For his spiritual nourishment, James presented William with a small leatherbound book, *Daily Food for Christians*, one of the few items which, after many disasters and difficulties, he managed to hang on to and return home with.

JAMES AND SONS

No Veitch archives have survived, and so it is difficult to gauge how much James's plant-collecting expeditions cost, or indeed how he paid for them. If successful, the returns could be large and, in the case of some plants, fairly quick. Other plants, however, might take years before they were in a saleable state. Characteristically, James chose to go it alone in order to assure himself of secrecy and exclusive control over every living plant, root and seed that was sent back to Exeter. He knew that it would be many months before he heard from William Lobb and before any plants reached Exeter. Resigned to a long wait, he continued to write to Hooker with queries about other possible sources of plants, the address of a collector going on a Kew expedition to Africa and the name of a botanical collector going to the Niger so he could 'enter into correspondence'.

He also had other pressing matters at home to worry about. When James and Rebecca moved into Graslawn in 1837, their extended family of five sons, one daughter and two orphaned nephews were almost grown up. These were times when fathers ruled over their large families with an unquestioned authority. Religion, discipline and industry were James's orders of the day and his conviction that his sons should train for and enter the family business was no more than the prevailing notion of the time. Although James apparently helped pay for one of his Beatty nephews to go to university, the other, Thomas, always complained bitterly of his uncle James's meanness and harsh behaviour. He alleged that his uncle would not allow him to train for the profession of surgeon. 'lest it might encourage insubordination among his own boys'.

Justifiably proud of the great achievement that he and his father had already made, James never made a secret of the fact that he wished his sons to follow him into his profession as he and his brother Thomas had done. But James knew that his ambitions for the future of the nursery would require enormous energy and dedication from every male member of his family. As James observed in a letter to Sir William Hooker, he had 'been much harassed of late by family cares and perplexities of which I believe all persons who have families and are connected with business are more or less subjected too'.

James was not particularly concerned when his second son John decided to study medicine at Edinburgh University as many of the great botanists of the time had received medical training. But when John graduated in 1841, he announced his plan to take up an appointment as assistant surgeon on HMS *Melville*, flagship of the China Seas squadron 'where I think probably he may remain several years'. If James was disappointed that John would not be joining the business, he hoped that he would at least make a useful collector since it was not uncommon for naval surgeons to include botanical collecting among their interests and skills. Indeed, Hooker's own son Joseph was already sailing with the *Erebus* as assistant surgeon and unofficial ship's botanist. James wrote to Hooker that John was on board ship off Plymouth waiting for orders, 'due to sail at a days notice . . . he will no doubt touch at many islands and I think we may get some good things through him'. But John's interests were in travel and medicine, not travel and botany, and the only useful plant he ever sent home was a feathery tropical fern, *Stenoloma chusanum* var. *veitchiana*, which he found in Malaya.

In the same letter to Hooker, James mentioned that another of his boys was talking of going to Australia or New Zealand: 'He talks of leaving in the Autumn so I shall have plenty of Collectors,' he wrote optimistically. Thomas was soon packed off to train in the Edinburgh branch of Dickson & Co., the nursery where his grandfather had first learned his trade more than seventy years before. But after two years Thomas went his own way and sailed out to the Cape of Good Hope where he became a partner on a farm in the Somerset East district.

James again wrote to Hooker about more family 'cares': 'You will be surprised to hear that I have another son likely to go abroad.' This time it was Robert, aged twenty, keen to travel and like his brother, become a farmer. Having done agricultural training at Slough and gained some experience in farm management, Robert was offered a post in Turkey teaching the 'English system of husbandry' on a large farm jointly owned by Admiral Walker in the Turkish Services and a merchant at Constantinople. 'A gentleman of London, a Mr Brown from the House of Reckitt Brothers, goes out as acting resident partner and my son would go with him,' James wrote to Hooker. But he held out little hope that Robert would be able to supply him with anything of great interest from Turkey: 'I am not at all aware of what sort of plants he will find there.'

And so, out of five sons, only the eldest, James Junior, was working in the Veitch nursery business. With two now farming abroad and one in the navy, this left only William, happily training with S. A. Grieg, the Exeter architect who had designed Graslawn. Desperate to ensure that Veitch & Sons was what it said, James made the wretched William leave architecture to train in horticulture, about which he neither knew nor cared. For a year William trailed around the nursery at Mount Radford, getting under people's feet and causing his impatient brother to fight with him. James Junior worked hard and with great dedication but he did not suffer fools gladly. He had a quick temper and 'was not loathe to put forward his own views on any matter in an emphatic way'. In a letter to Hooker, James described the brothers' row as 'a misunderstanding' which did not 'blow over' and 'as a consequence it places him [William] under many disadvantages in acquiring the knowledge he otherwise would have done'. James planned instead to send William to a horticultural nursery or botanical garden where he could gain experience and attend lectures. But the Edinburgh Botanical Gardens turned him down. James enquired if Sir William knew of anywhere either in England or on the Continent that would take William. He was, he wrote, so desperate he was prepared to pay. James's finances, however, were clearly beginning to cause him some concern: 'After the expense I have incurred in the formation of this place and the expense of Collectors – it grieves me to speak of other establishments being preferred and the advantages lost and I [would not] have thought of such an outlay but for my intention of having two sons in it [the business].'

William was sent to train with Low of Clapton which did not please James at all:

I feel this is a serious matter because I see in it the seeds of a breach in the establishment, but if my son leaves home for say 6 months and if he acquires a botanical knowledge of plants . . . he will stand in a different position than he does at present. If all goes well, by 1845, he will have a place in the business in which his knowledge of archi- tecture will be very useful.

Meanwhile, news in March 1841 of a package awaiting collection at Topsham dock brought thrilling distraction from family strife. It must have been one of the most exciting days of his life when James received his first letter and consignment of plants and seed from William Lobb who had spent some weeks 'collecting a few things' in the Organ Mountains near Rio. Happily they had arrived 'in excellent order'. One was a new alstroe- meria, another was an echites which Lobb described in his letter as having 'the colour of a Tuscany rose', plus an oncidium, *O. curtum*, with yellow flowers and cinammon-brown markings, and a new red salvia. There were several species of dipladenia, beautiful pink or crimson-flowered climbers, of which *D. splendens* would become the most sought after for cultivation. There was also the small Brazilian shrub *Hindsia violacea*, with its clusters of ultramarine flowers, which quickly became a hugely popular addition to Victorian greenhouses. Of William Lobb's achievements James wrote that 'we are so far pleased with him' but, secretive as ever, he cautioned that 'of course we shall say nothing about these things till we raise them'.

A second consignment sent from Brazil in May was more disappointing. The shipping agent in Rio failed to get the cases on board the right ship and the hold-up proved disastrous. 'From the delay the plants much dead, many taken from their Box before it reached us as only about half full,' James wailed to Hooker. Only a few seeds were viable, a fuchsia and two escallonias were 'vegetated'. As was often the fate with delayed packages, many living plants perished but the dried specimens survived in good condition and were sent on to Kew and other herbarium collections.

James Veitch did not hear again from William Lobb until January 1842. In the meantime Lobb had apparently left the 'fine field' around Rio with some reluctance and sailed south to Buenos Aires in Argentina where he had spent the winter exploring and collecting. In his letter, which he failed to date, William wrote that he had sent five cases of plants, seeds and dried specimens on the Packet. Unfortunately the ship had sailed past Falmouth without docking and gone straight on to Leith in Scotland. In great alarm, James sent a message to friends in Edinburgh requesting they obtain the packages 'but not open them' and return them 'post-haste' to Exeter. In his letter, Lobb explained that rather than face the perilous sea journey around Cape Horn, he had hired mules and headed west inland towards Mendoza where he had made the gruelling but beautiful and dramatic crossing over the Andes via the Upsallata Pass into Chile. 'On the fourth day from Upsallata,' James wrote to Hooker, quoting from Lobb, 'the snow was five feet deep, frozen so hard that the mules made no impression and the cold was intense.' The only shelter were crudely built trackside huts and William was beginning to feel the strain and collapsed ill with fever on several occasions.

Following his instructions to obtain quantities of seeds of the Chilean Pine or Monkey-puzzle, *Araucaria araucana* (see the colour plate section), William continued south to the region of La Araucana in southern Chile where the forests of these strange-looking trees grew on the exposed ridges below the snow-capped volcanic peaks of the southern Andes. Known locally as '*paragua*', they stood like huge umbrellas with their tough, arching branches of hard, pointed leaves. The Araucaria Indians used the kernels as a fruit or ground them into flour. Lobb collected over 3,000 seeds by shooting cones from the trees while his porters gathered nuts from the ground. This precious cargo was nearly lost when he entrusted the seeds to a man to take down to the coast who promptly died. After rescuing the seeds, William then personally carried the sacks down to Valparaiso and saw them on to a ship bound for England. He also sent seeds of a beautiful purple-blue nasturtium climber, *Tropaeolum azureum*, which he had found and collected from 'Cuesta Dormeda, about sixteen leagues from Valparaiso'. From this area he also sent the still popular pale-blue mallow, *Abutilon vitifolium*, and the snow-white, rosemary-scented *Calceolaria alba*, the first of many calceolarias to become popular Victorian plants for summer bedding as well as famous Veitch introductions.

According to James in his letter to Hooker, William continued travelling

Abutilon vitifolium

'by steamer to Talcahuano, from there to Los Angeles, a village 40 leagues from Concepción towards the Cordillera. After making preparations at this place, he followed the course of the River Laja to the volcano of Antuco; from thence to Santa Barbara, taking various elevations along the western side of the Andes, intending to go back to the snow line, but such was the timidity of his guide respecting the Indians that he would not proceed with him . . .' Collectors and their teams of guides and porters were often known to fall out, even to come to blows and James had earlier discussed with Hooker whether William understood about the 'importance of conciliating manners to the natives . . . he says he is quite aware of it but I am *told* he is sometimes a little quick in temper' – hardly surprising after such a gruelling period of travelling and collecting. By now William was exhausted and often ill and his next shipment was rather a disappointment, containing only one plant of interest – the dazzling, magenta-crimson flowering perennial *Calandrinia umbellata* which he discovered among dry rocky places near Concepción. William wrote that he hoped to sail from Chile to Lima in Peru. Disappointed, James enquired of Hooker whether other collectors already in South America, such as Theodore Hartweg, were doing any better. He was worried that William might be trailing in Hartweg's footsteps, although the two never actually met: 'Of course if there is anything confidential . . . I would not for a moment ask a question, but perhaps you could offer information as to prevent Lobb taking the same plants.'

Nothing more was heard from William Lobb for many months and James ranged between expressions of concern and irritation. Both Veitch's and Lobb's families were becoming increasingly anxious for news. But James was already deeply absorbed in the challenging business of germinating thousands of different seeds and raising new, sometimes quite unknown, plants that had been sent by William Lobb.

CHAPTER SIX

ADVENTURES IN THE GREENHOUSE

*There is a fashion in all things, and novelty as respects
flowers is now a complete mania.*

Joseph Paxton,
Gardener's Chronicle, 1842

1842 WAS THE first full year of promise and reward and each day in the Veitch nursery began with a sense of excitement. As the sun rose and slowly warmed the glazed roofs, a nurseryman entered the stove-house and found that a plant, grown from a handful of unpromising-looking seeds of a barely known plant, brought from a country and climate thousands of miles away, had produced its first tight little bud or two. Every day James Veitch and his sons, James Junior and the reluctant William, toured the glasshouses, the heated 'stoves' and the cool greenhouses to check on the progress of their carefully nurtured plants putting out new foliage and slowly opening their buds to reveal astonishing colours and forms. A fuchsia had produced a truss with fifty flower buds, the colours yet to reveal themselves; 'I like the appearance of the Fuchsia more and more every day,' James wrote, and in one glasshouse he noted 'a most curious columbine in bloom, one flower which has dropped but there are other buds showing'. There were even occasional surprises to be found such as a 'curious little plant' which had arrived from overseas hidden among the roots of another plant. James wrote to Sir William Hooker that the mystery plant had produced 'very small flowers on the underside of the leaves . . . it came up in one of our orchidaceae'.

One can only imagine the nervous anticipation James experienced when he first prised open Lobb's boxes, searched through the packages of seed and read Lobb's descriptions and lists of plants. If James seemed rather dour in daily life, it was in the glasshouses that he showed his true passion. It was not just the courage and determination to take a risk, nor was it simply Lobb's undoubted abilities to find new plants that put James and his nursery at the forefront. It was his own remarkable horticultural skills in dealing with the seeds and plants that were sent to him. He had a marvellous talent for growing plants, wherever they originated, and in 1842 *The Cottage Gardener* noted that: 'All new introductions are on their arrival taken under Mr Veitch's care. He sows all seeds with his own hands, watches and tends them, and it is not until they are beyond all danger that they are committed to the management of others.' Or, as was sometimes the case, rejected as being of no commercial use.

One glasshouse was reserved entirely for raising William Lobb's plants and seed and it was soon home to a growing collection of wonderful-looking exotics which James was confident would be very profitable. Among Lobb's most gorgeous introductions were varieties of trumpet-shaped *Cantua* flowers found growing in Bolivia, Chile and the Peruvian Andes. *Cantua*, meaning 'Magic Tree', is its Indian name and the first species to flower at Exeter in May 1848 was *C. buxifolia* (see the colour-plate section) and later, the shrubby *C. bicolor* producing large golden-red trumpet flowers. Lobb also introduced four attractive nasturtiums: the brilliant scarlet Flame Flower, *Tropaeolum speciosum*, found in the mountainous areas of Ecuador and southern Colombia; *T crenatiflorum* had pale orange blooms while *T. umbellatum* was more showy, having orange-tipped red flowers; as one of William's *tropaeolium* was thought to be a new one, James asked Hooker to name it after Lobb. Hooker obligingly named it *T. lobbianum*, but when it was exhibited it was clearly too similar to Hartweg's *T. peltophorum*, already described by another botanist, George Bentham, and '*lobbianum*', on this occasion, was dropped. Naming a plant after someone had always been much sought after and was regarded as a great honour and reward. But with so many collectors from different countries travelling around the world sending back new plants to different botanists and no central system to regulate them, there was inevitably some confusion and 'double-naming'.

At the beginning of 1842, one of the nursery's most important early introductions, the drumstick primula, *Primula denticulata*, displayed its delicate, purple globular flower-heads in the cool greenhouse for the first time in England. It had been sent to James from the Himalayas by his friend Dr John Royle and when it was later exhibited before the Horticultural Society it attracted much appreciative attention. At first regarded as tender, Hooker later commented that 'when it shall be more increased and planted in the open air it will succeed there as well as our European primulas'. By early spring, seeds of a new alstroemeria from William Lobb's first package revealed its delicate flowers. Hanging on loose clusters at the ends of long stems, the yellow flowers were edged red, with dark markings on the three inner petals.

It was sent to Dr Lindley who named it *Alstroemeria nemorosa*. By March, excitement was reaching fever pitch as James Junior coaxed Lobb's first orchid into flower, the unusual *Cynoches pentadactylon* or Swan Orchid from Brazil.

A garden journalist who visited the nursery that spring reported that they were already cultivating some fine heaths, camellias and new pelargoniums which 'give promise of blooming abundantly in a few months', and they now had many new species of orchid with several 'grown in rustic baskets suspended from the roof which give quite a unique appearance to the house'.

Patience was essential and progress slow. There were many disappointments as seed pans remained empty and some seeds stubbornly refused to reveal their secrets. Many plants either failed or died. 'One plant is alive but remains obstinately much as when we received it,' James wrote to Hooker, and some species of plants did not come into flower for up to five years. (One plant, *Cordia decandra*, which James grew from seed sent by William Lobb in 1849, did not flower until 1875, twenty-six years later and long after James had died.) But there were unexpected rewards: *Cuphea cordata*, one of the few plants raised from seed sent in William's disastrous consignment from Peru, amazed everyone by producing its first scarlet tubular flowers in June.

Other plants seemed happy to get on without help, James wrote to Hooker about a 'Bulbous plant from Peru, flowering without foliage on a dry shelf where it has been a long time without water or care, it flowers generally in threes – will cultivate well. I think it will be very beautiful particularly if hardy.' Not all plants passed James's taste and high standard. In the same letter to Kew he noted that several dozen bulbs of *Ruellia*

The Orchid House. Chelsea

spectabilis sent from Peru had produced a 'bluish shade' of flower; 'I did not think much of this,' he commented and it lost its place on the shelf. James was quite ruthless with plants that he did not consider would sell and despite his success with the *Leschenaultia*, he appeared to see little future in other plants from Australia. The increasing need for more house-room for his South American introductions meant other Australian species were left to 'dwindle away as not being the sort of plants likely to sell with us'.

James often complained about William Lobb's handwriting. He sometimes found it difficult to make out names of plants and descriptions of where Lobb had found them, essential information to understanding plant characteristics and growing conditions. He spent many hours trying to raise unknown plants from unidentified or poorly labelled seeds. It was the practice for plants to be given numbers and James would, for example, write to Hooker about problems with Lobb's 'Number 181'. Cases of plants were often disturbed during shipment or in customs offices and arrived with labels jumbled up and seeds spilled. One correspondent's case from New Zealand arrived quite empty, the captain of the ship having thrown the collection of dried specimens overboard because he said 'they were quite dead'. Delayed, partially lost or damaged consignments of packages meant confusing information about exactly where seeds had been collected, conditions of climate, altitude and soil type, which led to errors in germinating and cultivating plants. Unless the plant was already known, James was entirely reliant on the collector's descriptions of plants seen in the wild. Although usually careful with detail, William's observations were occasionally more romantic than scientific, his only words about a primrose he found were that 'the whole air for a considerable distance was perfumed with it'. On the other hand, it would seem that he was sometimes more accurate in his description than the experts at home; an evergreen *Ceratostema longiflorum* was described by Dr Lindley as one of the prettiest of greenhouse shrubs, 'its long trumpet-shaped flowers are of a rich purple'. James, however, noted that 'Mr Lobb' more correctly 'says scarlet'.

From Ecuador, Lobb sent seeds of the passion flower *Passiflora tacsonia* (now *P. mollissima*) which caused a few problems for James. 'We have cultivated it here in the stove,' he wrote, 'but there the flowers invariably drop off before they have expanded. In a cool greenhouse it blooms freely and from what Mr Lobb has said respecting it, and from our experience, I am inclined to think it might survive our winters here on a sheltered wall . . . As a conservatory climber it is eminently beautiful, and is best cultivated in a mixture of loam and peat with decayed leaves and a little sharp sand.'

Here again William Lobb was right; *P. mollissima* proved that, in the right conditions, it could be a vigorous outdoor climber. One satisfied customer later wrote to the *Gardener's Chronicle* that his three-year-old plant had already reached the top of his house, with seventy-foot branches bearing from fifty to a hundred 'fully expanded flowers' each day from May to the middle of October: 'We are of the opinion that [the blossoms] are better formed and of a richer colour each successive year.'

James continued to train up his team of hand-picked and highly trained specialist propagators and nurserymen who could work to his most exacting standards. He was an autocrat and allowed no one else to say which plant would be developed, exhibited, promoted and sold. But it was a great blow when John Dominy, his best nurseryman, left to work as head gardener to J. P. Magor of Redruth. Dominy's skills as a hybridiser had already made him one of the most priceless of all nurserymen.

James Junior was as ardent a worker at the benches as his father, at least when he was not travelling around exhibitions, for he could never resist those 'most tempting arenas for the display of horticultural prowess'. Growing plants for competitions was time-consuming and a labour of love, but the prestige was highly important to a nursery, giving it national recognition, and the coveted First Class Certificate for a plant from the Horticultural Society was certain to guarantee its commercial success.

By early May of 1842 the Veitch nursery was ready to advertise a selection of newly flowered introductions which included William Lobb's *Begonia coccinea* from Brazil, the orchid *Cycnoches maculata*, James Tweedie's large frilly-leaved greenhouse climber *Stigmaphyllon aristatum* from the Argentine, Dr Royle's *Primula denticulata* from the Himalayas, and *Triptilion spinosum*, an azure-blue daisy from China. To James's immense satisfaction, the begonia, orchid and primula were awarded a Banksian medal when they were exhibited as a group of new arrivals at the London Horticultural Society.

While many of Lobb's introductions are still grown in gardens, a large number of his collections from South America have not survived in common cultivation, being only suitable for large heated greenhouses. (In 1845 it was calculated that of the 238 new plant species introduced to this country, only thirty-five were hardy enough for cultivation in the outside garden. All the rest, including fifty-five new orchids, were greenhouse, conservatory or stove plants.) In James Veitch's time, exotics and giant novelties were enormously popular, though rather a challenge to the head gardeners who had to grow them and very large plants were always popular as dramatic centrepieces in conservatories such as Chatsworth. The enormous South American *Victoria regia*, the vast *Ampelopsis veitchii* and the huge, scary and strange nepenthes, flourished in artificial environments created by British engineering and industry and their vigorous growth symbolised the confidence, energy and expansionist ambitions of the early Victorian years.

William Lobb also brought back with him the tall *Fuchsia simplicicaulis*, described as 'a magnificent ornament in a large conservatory', however a number of his smaller, more manageable new fuchsias became enduring popular favourites; *F. spectabilis* was found in shady woods from the Cuenca area in Ecuador, and *F. dependens*, which both Lobb and Hartweg discovered near Quito. One fuchsia in particular, *F. serratifolia*, which Lobb described as 'very beautiful, the flowers resembling a mass of purple wax', was much admired and later exhibited in London where it was awarded a Silver Gilt Medal by the Horticultural Society.

That summer James also sent up for exhibition in London two of Lobb's new species of *Dipladenia*. One, a beautiful evergreen climber, *Dipladenia splendens*, was described by Hooker as 'one of the handsomest novelties in the exhibition, bearing large blush-pink blossoms with a darker throat'. James was reluctant to release new plants until he had propagated a sufficient quantity for exclusive sale from his own nurseries. While his stocks increased, he allowed interest in his new introductions to build until he had taken advance orders for all the plants raised. (In June 1846, Paxton wrote in the *Magazine of Botany* about a fuchsia which had attracted attention, the curious dwarf *F. macrantha* of which 'We understand Messrs. Veitch will let it out this month'.)

James Veitch's business strategies were canny: he knew the importance of creating the right image and appeal for a new plant and the best way of promoting it to the public. The nursery was quite advanced in its advertising and promotion with special offers and inducements. For example, their trailing *Cantua buxifolia*, beautifully painted for the botanical magazine, was included in an advertisement for 'Messrs. Veitch's New and Rare Plants' in the *Gardener's Chronicle* at 21s a plant, together with the offer of a free gift of a 'beautiful coloured plate to persons purchasing a plant and to persons forwarding six postage stamps'.

By the middle of 1842 there were so many young plants competing for greenhouse space and sale that James Veitch found it necessary to choose only the best for promotion and propagation and reject many that he felt were not competitive. In August the bright blue tubular flowers of the

Brazilian *Hindsia longiflora* appeared in the hothouse and it was much admired, but a few months later it was eclipsed by another, *H. violacea*, which produced even larger, gorgeous porcelain deep-violet flowers. It was chosen for large-scale development, and won a Silver Medal from the Horticultural Society the following year. James was so anxious for *H. violacea* to be described that he sent Hooker three flowers for his artists to see the colour and wrote at the same time, 'Dr Lindley particularly wished to figure it [in his *Botanical Register*] and we left with him a branch'. Joseph Paxton was also asked to 'figure' it in *Paxton's Magazine of Botany*.

In late September, the stunning blue *Tropaeolum azureum*, a discovery of Lobb's from Chile, was 'finally in bloom' and one plant was shown at the Horticultural Society's Regent Street rooms and was awarded a Silver Medal. This time, instead of waiting for stocks to build up, James Junior showed the plant to Dr Lindley and then rushed it by hansom cab to the home of the successful gardener and plantswoman, Mrs Lawrence in Ealing Park, who wished to be the first to own an original plant. (*T. azureum*, however, proved difficult to grow and rarely kept the deep blue of its wild state.)

Last in that year, but by no means least, *Stigmaphyllon aristatum*, James Tweedie's climber from Argentina, finally revealed its yellow flowers in December after long and careful nurturing in the stove-house. By the end of 1842 James was very satisfied with a fine productive year and was confident enough to state that 'we have enough eventually to clear our first year's outlay'. Despite the failure of some of William's collections to arrive in good shape, the nursery overall was beginning to amass a large profit and a widening reputation.

Although a large proportion of the plants being introduced into Britain were tender exotics needing a great deal of care and protection, there was also a growing interest in hardy plants, shrubs and trees, especially conifers. James needed large areas of suitable grounds for 'trying' his hardy introductions and he was fortunate that estate gardens with suitable soils and climate such as Killerton and Bicton were available to him. In the winter of 1843, Lady Rolle asked James's advice on planting an avenue of Monkey-puzzle trees between two lodges at Bicton. But she would not be using Veitch seedlings because, since 1839, James Barnes, the head gardener, had been quietly raising trees from precious seed he had purchased from Loddiges of London especially for this grand and rather eccentric scheme.

Barnes described in his journal how he first raised the seedling trees in 60-sized pots which he then shifted into 32-sized pots and placed for the

winter in a cold pit, fully exposing them to sun and air in early spring
when they made a 'free, healthy and vigorous growth'. They were put
through the same process for another winter when they were ready for
planting. The 500-yard avenue was planted with twenty-five pairs of trees,
which James suggested should be placed opposite each other on raised
mounds of earth and covered with a little wire cage for protection. But
Barnes' men planted them straight into the ground and, five years later,
when the trees had made such a vigorous growth that their branches began
to graze the Rolle carriages, they had to be replanted further apart. (Today
despite its rather gaunt appearance, much of this avenue still survives.)

James was pleased with his own collection of *Araucaria* grown from William
Lobb's seeds and it must have been galling for him not to have had his own
trees ready in time to supply the Bicton avenue. James Barnes believed that
earlier collections of seeds had failed to germinate because they had been
grow on hotbeds and in stoves which were entirely unsuitable for mountain trees. The extraordinary attention given to this unique (and some people
thought ugly) avenue at Bicton was a perfect advertisement and James was
soon selling his own Monkey-puzzles in huge numbers. Sir Tom Acland gave
a Veitch-grown seedling to all his tenants in Broadclyst while many hundreds
more were planted in estates in England and in city and municipal gardens
where they thrived; some ancient specimens are still living. They became
enormously popular and were often planted in front of houses and in school
playgrounds where they grew to enormous size, dwarfing tiny front gardens
and dominating buildings with their strange whorled branches and rigid

spiny leaves. The trees often became untidy-looking as they aged and the erect bole spread into heavy folds until it resembled an elephant's foot.

A NEW COLLECTOR

The 'Exotic Nursery' of Messrs. James Veitch & Son of Exeter was at last making its name as a supplier of new, rare and exclusively introduced choice plants, in particular greenhouse plants from South America 'sent by that nurseryman's own collector'. As the cost of William Lobb's expedition was now more than covered, James was eager to send out another collector, this time to quite a different part of the world, to concentrate on what he knew was by far the richest seam of horticultural gold – orchids.

William Lobb's brother Thomas, who was by then twenty-six years old, had been working and training with the Veitch nursery for thirteen years. He had never travelled beyond Devon and Cornwall, spoke no foreign languages and had only a faint idea of other parts of the world, their climates, terrain and customs of the people. But he did know about orchids. He had spent many years with James Junior and John Dominy poring over different species of orchids, studying, learning and observing all he could. Thomas had been keenly following his brother's journeys along the edge of the Brazilian highlands, through the primaeval rain forests, across the Argentine pampas, over the high snow-capped Andes and into the temperate forests of Chile. He too longed for travel and adventure, particularly to discover new orchids growing wild in their homelands.

Once again, James wrote to Sir William Hooker at Kew enquiring about the best places to visit, asking Hooker to favour him 'with your opinion of Java as a place for a collector . . . what description of plants are likely to be procured?' Plants from South-east Asia had never been well represented at Kew and Hooker replied with great enthusiasm that Java (then in Dutch hands), Malaya and possibly even China would be valuable areas in which to collect new species of *Orchidaceae*, tropical rhododendrons and hothouse novelties such as the extraordinary insect-eating nepenthes or pitcher plants. Hooker went to considerable lengths to help with letters of introduction, a passage on the East Indiaman *Samarang* and a passport from the Dutch ambassador in London. He suggested that James accept offers of subscription to Thomas's expedition but James replied, 'I would rather pay for his trip to send him out in some comfort . . . as he is a young man of very respectable manners and appearance.' What he really meant was that he preferred to fund expeditions himself for the sole benefit of his nursery.

He did, however, gratefully receive letters of introduction from his friend Dr Royle in India, which would help smooth Thomas's way.

In 1843 Thomas Lobb signed a lengthy and exclusive three-year contract with Veitch:

> Thomas Lobb agrees to proceed to the British settlement of Singapore, in the employ of James Veitch & Son, as botanical collector, to make collections of living plants, seeds and dried specimens of plants, and to collect for the said James Veitch & Son and for no other person.

It is possible that William had been quietly sending a few things direct to his old employer and amanuensis Sir Charles Lemon and Thomas's old employer John Williams of Scorrier House was another enthusiastic buyer of Lobb introductions. But Veitch's were always very strict about not allowing anything at all to be sent to anyone other than the nursery.

> The understanding of this agreement is that the said Thomas Lobb's destination is China, should that country be open to admit a botanical collector, and in the absence of any definite instructions from James Veitch & Son, Thomas Lobb is to use his own discretion and be guided by existing circumstances as to what part of China he proceeds to, he shall be at liberty to proceed to such of the oriental islands as may appear to him most desirable; but next to China, the island of Java appearing to offer the greatest advantages to a botanical collector (if facilities offer for exploring the same with safety) he is directed to proceed thither, but it is left to his own discretion.

Thomas said his farewells to his family in Perran Wharf in Cornwall and sailed from Portsmouth in January 1843, his brother William meanwhile was struggling in South America with agents, illness and difficulties of his own.

Thomas was not allowed to enter China, which was not then 'ready to receive a botanical collector'. To nineteenth-century Europeans, China was a remote and inaccessible place of 'oriental mystery', a country that, since 1755, had been virtually closed to foreigners. Long before that, botanists and gardeners had been casting covetous eyes to China, and longing to obtain the magnificent flowers seen in Chinese paintings, textiles and ceramics. Travellers were pestered for plants to be sent home with captains of the fast tea-clippers. The Horticultural Society and Sir Joseph Banks were able to receive a number of plants from employees of the East India Company, including the first seeds of the shrubs *Daphne odora, Osmanthus fragrans* and the greenhouse plant *Cordyline terminalis*. But restrictions made it extremely difficult to travel. Kew did send a few collectors, including William Kerr, and, after the Opium Wars of 1840–42, some areas were partially opened to trade in what were known as the treaty-ports. A year after the Treaty of Nankin, the Horticultural Society were able to send one of their best collectors, Robert Fortune, who arrived only six months after Thomas Lobb was refused entry, though on this first trip he was never allowed to go more than thirty miles from a treaty-port.

Plant collectors tended to be extremely single-minded and perhaps rather politically naive. Many seemed unaware of or indifferent to the conflicts or troubles they wandered into, unless these difficulties prevented their movement or threatened their own safety. Thomas Lobb was of this type. He sailed on to Java where, finding that his Dutch passport had still not arrived, he was forced to land in Singapore, where he plunged straight into the steamy forests, exploring and collecting around the Malay peninsula, Malacca and on the island of Penang. What he found there kept him happily occupied. Speaking to no one but his native porters and seemingly impervious to the daily torments of insects, heat and disease, he emerged intact nearly a year later with his first collection of living plants 'in their ancestral forms'.

With his 'pair of Collectors' in the field James was more anxious than usual; every day he waited for mail and news of ships returning from two continents. Sometimes, though, he seemed resigned, almost humorous about it: '. . . another Mexican Packet has just arrived . . .' he wrote to Hooker, 'no news however is said to be good news, it is easier to antici- pate more'.

Perhaps the troubles experienced by his Exeter rivals, Luccombe & Pince, who had also sent out a collector, were cheering him up: 'I am told Mr Pince has not yet received a single article from his Collector, neither heard for a long time.' When

Nepenthes rafflesiana. One of many nepenthes sent by Thomas Lobb from Borneo and Java

Robert Pince joined his uncle's firm in the 1820s, it was among the earliest English nurseries to introduce new plants from abroad, such as the fragrant shrub *Luculia pinceana* from Nepal. Competition between nurseries to introduce new exotics was becoming increasingly fierce and Luccombe & Pince obtained plants and seed from collectors in Central and South America, West Africa and Australia. Like Veitch, Pince corresponded with Sir William Hooker and described his experiences with his collector, a 'Mr Barclay', which had been far from successful; indeed, they seem to have been disastrous.

Pince's collector was most likely George Barclay, a young Kew gardener who had just returned from five years collecting for Kew and the British Museum herbarium during a survey of South America by HMS *Sulphur*. Barclay had failed to produce any seeds or plants of worth and was not re-employed by Kew. It is possible that Hooker had sent him on to Pince who complained that 'His letter like everything connected to him is rambling, unsatisfactory and incomprehensible. He talks of his plants and collections but gives us not the least idea what he has collected.' Pince finally lost patience entirely and wrote, 'We have lost confidence in one of the greatest scoundrels in existence and I am deeply mortified – surely he must have collected something or other.'

Pince was also paying James Drummond in Australia, but complained that 'Drummond sends the same old thing over and over again, mixing the good things with a vast quantity of trash which costs us much in room and time to raise and then throw away'.

James Veitch, who had also used Drummond's services for many years, was similarly fed up with him. Drummond, by now quite an old man, had nevertheless achieved a great deal, travelling thousands of miles with his son John and introducing many good plants, including over forty species of banksias and dryandras as well as Veitch's lovely *Leschenaultia biloba*.

WILLIAM LOBB'S COLLECTING ADVENTURES
Meanwhile, at the end of April 1843, a long letter arrived from William Lobb in South America explaining his movements between reaching Lima and eventually Panama. He had taken four cases of plants collected on the slopes of the Peruvian Andes, by sea to Guayaquil, on the coast of Ecuador. Unfortunately yellow fever broke out as he arrived in the port and, along with other British residents, he had moved to the island of Puna until the scare was over, leaving his cases with an agent in the port for shipment. He then hired mules and guides and continued inland, travelling north to Quito and across into southern

Colombia. Descending to the port of Tumaco with a fresh collection, William sailed with his friend, a Devon sea captain, and reached Panama with the intention of getting himself and his cases on the first ship home.

But in Panama William received news from James that the cases of Peruvian plants which he had left in Guayaquil had not arrived (his letters had not even been posted because apparently he had not paid enough postage). William despatched his collection from Panama which arrived safely at Exeter. James wrote to Hooker:

> Seeds, specimens, bulbs and part of the orchids are in good order – one like *Oncidium ampliatum* collected near Panama is quite fresh but others are rotten . . . Lobb also sends a *clitoria* with beautiful azure blue flowers and *Centropogon coccineus* which he described as 'a lobelia' growing 'in shady places on the banks of the River Chagres' . . . He says he likes the appearance of the country around Panama and will remain there till he gets instructions from me, which he must have received ere this . . . among the things now arrived is a splendid specimen of *Befaria* and also seeds of several tropaeolum and fuchsias.

Meanwhile there was still no sign of the Peruvian collection left with the agent in Guayaquil. Lobb wrote again from Panama that he was recovering from an attack of dysentery and was depressed at the thought of returning to Guayaquil. Eventually he forced himself to go back to the port where he found to his horror all his cases rotting in a corner of a warehouse. The agent said that the cases 'had quite escaped his notice' and ants had got in and destroyed almost everything. William saved what he could, repacked the seeds, bulbs and dried specimens and shipped them to Exeter. James sent out a box of glass for making new cases and told Lobb he had to go back to Peru and collect all over again. William, already exhausted, was forced to spend another four months in the interior of Peru. James, who was enthusiastic in describing the colourful and exciting details of William Lobb's travels to Hooker and friends, had little real idea of the appalling trials and conditions his collector was enduring. His determination to receive every last plant collected made him very unsympathetic. In May 1844 William finally arrived home in England after a gruelling three and a half years of travelling and collecting. James, never satisfied if there was one more plant to be found, wrote to Hooker, 'I was disappointed at hearing William Lobb had left Peru, but pleased to hear of his safe arrival in England with many fine plants and seeds in good order. He reached Exeter with his plants on Saturday last and is now gone to his friends.'

Meanwhile the despatch of Thomas Lobb's plants from the other side of the world had also given James Veitch cause for concern. This collection had arrived in London during the freezing winter of 1844. Although the cases of delicate orchids, pitcher plants and hoyas had been well packed, they were delayed through customs and by the time the cases arrived in Exeter many plants were frostbitten and beyond revival. James was beside himself. 'So disappointing to have things brought safely *almost* to your door and then lost for want of care,' he wrote to Hooker while attempting to rescue seeds of a pitcher plant which he tried to 'vegetate in every possible way'. Happily his efforts paid off and the insectivorous *Nepenthes rafflesiana* was the first pitcher plant to be raised in the Exeter glasshouses. At last, in March 1844, the ship *La Belle Alliance* berthed with cases from Singapore containing Thomas's first treasured orchid, *Cypripedium barbatum*, carefully packed in its case. There were also several species of the 'showy' trailers aeschynanthus from Borneo with their clusters of fiery-coloured tubular flowers including the orange-red *Aeschynanthus speciosus*), and *A. purpurescens* which Thomas described as 'growing in woods . . . for the most part epiphytic on old or decaying trees' (see colour-plate section). It was described by Hooker when first exhibited in May 1847 as 'unquestionably the most beautiful species known to us of a genus eminent for the rich colour of its blossoms'. Although a conscientious and thorough botanist, Thomas, like his brother, was a man of few words. It was said that it was difficult to get him to describe a plant but that if he described one as 'very pretty' it was quite sufficient to induce extra care. In Java he discovered the gigantic orchid *Bulbophyllum beccarii* renowned for its rich stink of rotting fish, but it is unlikely that Thomas bothered to warn Veitch's nurserymen as they eagerly unpacked the foul-smelling orchid from its case.

In the late spring of 1844 Thomas finally reached Java from where he sent home a cornucopia of plants and seeds. He also found a number of species of hoya, such as the huge climbing *Hoya cinnamomifolia* which did not reveal its strongly scented wax-white flowers in Exeter for three years. Later, when he crossed to the coast of Burma, Thomas found *Hoya bella* which the *Botanical Magazine* described as 'the most lovely of all hoyas, resembling an amethyst set in silver'. Thomas returned to England at the end of 1847, bringing several sets of herbarium specimens, some of which were sent to Kew, the others being sold at London auction houses for his own profit.

A steadily growing queue of plants was by now being sent to London from Veitch's nursery for Dr Lindley to name and describe, for artists to paint and for Hooker to approve. At one stage James wrote to Hooker that he feared he was overdoing requests to him and he was concerned that his 'repeated applications' might have 'assumed too much the character of an intrusion' (despite the reward of so many fine herbarium specimens) and he begged Hooker to be candid. As the Veitch nursery's new plant collection and its reputation grew, Hooker became increasingly interested in obtaining Veitch plants, both for the botanic gardens at Kew and for his own private garden. James sold large quantities of plants to Sir William Hooker and he regularly sent generous gifts 'for Lady Hooker's garden':

'We have this evening sent to the wharf for the steamer to St George's Wharf, Katherine Dock, London, 100 hybrid rhododendron (between *arboreum* and hardy sorts in variety including *nobleanum*) for the [Kew] Gardens and 50 for yourself.'

William Lobb, having enjoyed an extended period of rest and recuperation at home in Cornwall, was ready to return to Exeter to work on his new introductions in the Veitch glasshouses. James wrote to Sir William Hooker about sending William out again and continued on the lookout for other sources: 'I see by the *Gardener's Chronicle*, [Robert] Fortune has met with some azaleas [in China] and sent home seeds in letters. If you happen to hear of any good things for distribution at Chiswick, will you kindly give me a hint that, as a member, I may make timely application.'

By April 1845 William seemed sufficiently well to be despatched again to South America with instructions to collect hardy and half-hardy trees and shrubs. He revisited the Organ Mountains in Brazil and then moved on to Valparaiso – by sea this time. He collected in the cool cloud forests of the Colombian Andes before going south to the shores of Tierra del Fuego and on to the chain of islands along the south Chilean coast. A description of this journey was published in Paxton and Lindley's *Flower Garden* in 1851: although not by William Lobb, it makes vivid reading.

Rocky precipices stand like perpendicular walls from 200 to 300 feet in height, over which roll the waters from the melting snows, which appear to the eyes like lines of silver . . . In the forest below everything appears calm and tranquil; scarcely the sound of an animal is heard; sometimes a few butterflies and beetles meet the eye, but not a human being is seen. On the sandy tracts near the rivers, the lion or puma is frequently to be met with.

Embothrium coccineum

From this expedition, William sent back seeds of the hardiest and most beautiful of all Antarctic beeches, *Nothofagus obliqua*, and some of our most popular salt-resistent garden shrubs, among them the tall, glossy evergreen *Escallonia macrantha*. Lobb's most memorable introduction must be *Berberis darwinii* (see colour-plate section), first found by Charles Darwin on the island of Chiloe, off the south coast of Chile, and collected by Lobb in 1849. A reporter for the *Gardener's Chronicle* wrote: 'If Messrs. Veitch had done nothing else towards beautifying our gardens, the introduction of this single species would be enough to earn the gratitude of the whole gardening world.' He found the scarlet Chilean Firebush, *Embothrium coccineum*, which was highly praised at Kew – 'Perhaps no tree cultivated in the open air in the British Isles gives so striking and brilliant a display as this does'. He discovered the Chilean Lantern Tree, *Tricuspidaria (Crinodendron) hookerianum*, and the Scarlet Holly *Desfontainia spinosa* with yellow-tipped tubular flowers – in all, a collection of plants that have endured and become popular garden shrubs. William was particularly fascinated by conifers which were becoming increasingly sought after in English gardens. He collected seeds of several South American species including *Fitzroya cupressoides*, from Chile, and *Saxegothaea conspicua*, a yew named after Prince Albert.

William Lobb found many extraordinary plants in South America, but perhaps one of his most beautiful was the climbing lily, *Lapageria rosea* or Chilean Bell flower, now the national flower of Chile (see book jacket). He first saw it climbing high up among the trees, its smooth, slender woody shoots and large dark-green leathery leaves twining around the dense supporting thickets of the Chilean woodlands and he carefully extracted seeds from the long green-yellow berries. For James in his glasshouse in Exeter, coaxing the *Lapageria* into flower, the first sight of the long, pendulous wax-like flowers of a rich crimson, faintly spotted with rose, was enough to make him see that he had a greenhouse winner – still greatly prized today.

MAN-MADE PLANTS

Work in the Veitch glasshouses became increasingly demanding and James spent five critical years persuading Dominy to return to Exeter; he eventually did so in 1846. During these years, James never ceased writing to his other sons scattered around the world, urging them to return to the family business. For the wretched William, who had wanted to become an architect but was forced to train and work in the nursery alongside his brother, all did not 'go well' as his father had hoped, and by 1847 William was dead, aged only twenty-eight. He was buried in Broadclyst churchyard alongside his grandparents, his mother and sister, Anna (her father had once described her as being 'interested in botany'), who had died two years earlier at twenty-two. Anna and William had probably died of tuberculosis. As a family business things looked bleak for James, who it seemed, would now be reduced to only one son in whom he could invest his hopes for the future of the Veitch nursery.

At the beginning of 1848, on his return to England William Lobb was re-united with Thomas who had also just returned from his first expedition to the Far East. Despite seeing so little of each other, the two brothers seemed to have had an affectionate and supportive relationship and spent a happy and productive year working at the Veitch nursery in Exeter alongside James, James Junior and John Dominy. Here, with everyone together, they could begin to appreciate the extent of their achievements: the successful raising and propagation of so many new introductions, including several new orchids and collections of hardy and half-hardy shrubs and conifers from William in South America, and tender, exotic tropical plants from Thomas in Java, Borneo and the Philippines. At last they could begin to enjoy the growing reputation of the nursery, the awards, the medals, and the profits.

James Veitch & Son were learning fast and growing in confidence. But there was still much that botanists and nurserymen did not know or understand. Many species of plant were difficult to propagate; orchids especially did not produce seed for several years, and in the case of the Monkey-puzzle tree, not for twenty years, which made it necessary to keep returning to collect from the wild. Breeding and crossing species meant more was learned about those which seemed particularly suitable for plant breeding. Lobb's new pitcher plants, for example, included one that was small, green and covered with coarse hairs which Veitch hid for the purpose of crossing with more exotic species. He also kept back some rhododendrons and later, some Burma orchids for use as a hybrid parent. Successful, growable hybrids with new forms and colours were starting to attract attention.

Although the word 'hybridisation' was not coined until 1845, experiments had begun in earnest during the 1830s; new varieties were raised to create yet more diversity, as well as hardier forms of garden exotics for the English climate. Flower beds in geometric designs like the old Tudor knots and Jacobean parterres of formal gardens were becoming fashionable again, only now they were planted up with richly coloured massed beds of flowers from South America and South Africa. By the 1840s, the wealth of new creations available ignited a national passion for hybrid roses, begonias, fuchsias, chrysanthemums, dahlias, rhododendrons and many kinds of bedding plants. Nurserymen were able to provide more and more new 'man-made' varieties of popular plants, as they improved their skills in breeding hardier, more colourful and easily produced plants. The nursery trade was booming and it looked as though the Veitch nursery was once again forging ahead of the game.

A new generation of young Veitches was growing up in Exeter. John Gould (named after his mother's family of Gould) was the eldest. His brother Harry, who had inherited his grandfather John's wit, once told a reporter that he was born in 1840, 'the year of the establishment of the penny postage, so that I came cheap!' Young Arthur was born four years later and there were also five sisters, Mary, Anna Harriott, Emma Pauline, Constance and Agnes. The boys walked two miles to school, 'keeping an ear out for the Cathedral bell, which rang five minutes before school started at 7.a.m'. John Gould and Arthur were quite scholarly, but Harry was not a keen pupil. In these happy, carefree days, they rode their ponies out to visit their grandparents at Broadclyst, roamed the countryside around Exeter and helped their kindly but anxious grandfather and zealous and temperamental father as they were 'initiated into the mysteries of the nursery trade'. Some of Harry's earliest memories were of watching the two Jameses sowing seeds sent back by the Lobb brothers in the glasshouses, and whilst they waited for them to grow, he sowed some orange pips and pulled them up from time to time to see how they were doing. The boys spent absorbing hours with the Lobb brothers, listening to tales of their adventures, and John Dominy taught them how to hybridise their own fuchsias.

In June 1848 Sir William Hooker, on a visit to his Devon relatives, made a tour of the Veitch nursery in Exeter. There he admired William's Flame Flower, *Tropaeolum speciosum*, 'framed upon those wire trellises which are now so commonly fixed to garden posts', and he praised Thomas's aeschynanthes and hoyas now flowering in one of the stove-houses. Of the already popular *Hoya bella*, he later commented in the *Botanical Magazine* that 'We had the pleasure of seeing this first gem of the air blossoming in great perfection . . . It is a free bloomer and the flowers last many days in high beauty.' He was full of admiration for the rose-purple *Sonerila stricta* from Java, which had just flowered: 'This, as far as I know, is the first species of the genus that has yet been cultivated in Europe.' Having seen the fruits of the industry in the Veitch glasshouses, the Director of the Royal Botanic Gardens of Kew was clearly impressed.

Another enthusiastic visitor was a Mr Dodman who wrote to the *Gardener's Chronicle* that the nursery quite surpassed his expectations.

> At Mr Veitch's there was a succession of new or rare plants at every other step. Everything was growing in the most vigorous state, but what struck me most was the marvellous specimens of orchidaceous plants; and I think, with reference to the size of the collection, I never witnessed so many fine specimens, so much flower and such good treatment. Mr Veitch leaves his gates open and all walk at free will throughout his grounds and collections, and I understand that the public has given him no reason to repent of his liberality.

THOMAS LOBB'S COLLECTING ADVENTURES IN THE FIELD

For James and son, the horizons must now have seemed limitless. Both Lobb brothers were eager to be off again and the Veitches were equally eager to send them. On Christmas Day 1848, Thomas sailed again for the Far East to search for hothouse plants and shrubs. He was especially ordered to find more varieties of pitcher plants, new rhododendrons and rare orchids.

By the time Thomas Lobb arrived in Calcutta in March 1849, Sir William Hooker's son Joseph was already collecting in north-east India. It was five years since Joseph had returned

Dr Joseph Hooker (1917–1911)

from Captain Ross's scientific expedition to the Antarctic and he had developed into a skilled and experienced botanist, geologist and artist. He was well acquainted with James Veitch's nursery in Exeter and when he heard that one of their collectors was in India, he wrote to his father:

> Tell Veitch by all means to send Lobb to Darj. [eeling], before October if possible, he shall have every opportunity, facility and information I can afford, both as to living and to collecting. May use my collection as much as he pleases in instructing himself on his own . . . it is a chance Lobb may never get again, certainly never so cheaply – You must tell V.[eitch] that I travel as a poor man, and Lobb must not expect great tents and serv'ts.

Despite numerous hardships, Joseph Hooker's distinguished party managed to travel in some luxury with sometimes up to thirty servants, including a personal valet, plus an armed escort in the more dangerous territories. A 'dawk' of six men carried them in litters while the baggage coolies carried tons of equipment. Joseph himself carried a small barometer, a large knife and digger for plants, notebooks, telescope, compass, botanising box, thermometers, sextant, measuring tape, azimuth compass and stand, sketchbooks, several quires of drying papers and strong canvas bags. At one point Joseph wrote condescendingly that 'Lobb passed us with his circus', a scruffy-looking young man with a couple of men and some mules, they were like creatures from different planets. James was never mean in equipping his collectors with

Joseph Hooker's party crossing a river near the Kymore Hills. From his *Himalayan Journals*

what he felt they needed, but Thomas
would have neither needed nor wanted
the trappings of these learned but arrogant 'scientific' gentlemen of class.

Thomas had no intention of joining
up with Hooker and his entourage and
he disappeared to the islands. From
Sarawak he sent the golden-yellow
rhododendron *R. brookeanum*, and more
pitcher plants. He proceeded on to the
Philippines where the *Phalaenopsis*
orchids were top of his list, including *P.
aphrodite*, *P. rosea* and *P. x intermedia*. He
added two attractive hothouse shrubs,
Medinilla speciosa and the even more
striking *M. magnifica*. Slowly making his
way back towards India, he reached lower

The 'Slipper Orchid'
Cypripedium villosum

Burma where he found three unusual rhododendrons from the Moulmain
area, *R. moulmainense, R. malayanum* and, best of all, *R. veitchianum* which is
remarkable for its large, white, crinkle-edged and sweetly scented flowers.
He collected several more orchids, among them *Dendrobium palpebrae* and
Cypripedium villosum (which Veitch later used as a hybrid parent).

A year later Thomas turned up for his meeting with the Hooker expe-
dition, but as Hooker was in Calcutta he saw only a Dr John Thomson.
Thomson found Lobb to be 'a steady, respectable man' and 'very modest
and well-behaved in his deportment', but thought him dreadfully conceited:
'He pooh-poohed Sikkim and has a very poor opinion of Lindley and
Wallich!!!' (Nathaniel Wallich was the Danish collector and Director of the
East India Company botanic garden in Calcutta.) Three months later Lobb
and Hooker finally did meet in a camp in the Khasia Hills. Hooker wrote,
in his *Himalayan Journals*:

> We spent the evening and following morning most pleasantly, but he
> would not stay even a day with us, though in no hurry – it appears
> odd to me – he talks very slightingly of the plants and seeds as usual
> and to judge by what he says he cannot be worth 6d to Veitch &
> Co. His plants he says die en route to Calcutta and that it is almost
> useless sending roots, bulbs or cuttings straight home from this.

James Veitch always instructed his collectors to be secretive about where and what they were collecting and to guard jealously against the encroachments of a rival – even the son of the great Sir William Hooker himself. Thomas's taciturn and evasive responses described by Joseph Hooker and Thomson were probably no more than shyness and an attempt at secrecy. He would soon prove that he was worth over a thousand times more than 6d to Veitch & Co. For Thomas knew the whereabouts of the most sought-after of all orchids, the beautiful Blue Orchid, *Vanda caerulea* (see the colour plate section). First discovered in the Khasia Hills of Assam in 1837 by Dr William Griffiths, a brilliant but wayward botanist, it was later described by Hooker as 'growing in profusion, waving pale blue tassels in the wind, like the flutterings of thousands of azure butterflies' – a vision of the 'rich man's treasure' which one single, cosseted plant in a wealthy collector's greenhouse could never convey. Thomas Lobb had met Dr Griffiths in Singapore on his previous trip and heard from him about the vanda and its exact location.

According to James Veitch, Thomas had already collected 'a man's load' of the orchid near the village of Lernai in the Khasia Hills, a whole month before Hooker's party turned up. Yet according to Joseph Hooker, it was he who told Lobb where he might find it. No wonder Thomas was being so guarded, he had already sent the plants back to Exeter where James was selling cuttings for from £3 to £10 each, making a total of £300. There was wild excitement when Veitch first exhibited *Vanda caerulea* in flower at a Regent Street meeting on 3 December 1850.

In his *Himalayan Journals* published in 1855, Joseph Hooker complained that had he been a 'trader' he could have made large sums by selling his dried specimens for high prices and 'as to the living plants, I quote the load of *Vanda caerulea* . . . which realised £300 at Steven's rooms'.

Hooker had also collected a huge haul of blue orchids but few had survived: 'My want of money to forward my specimens as *those* were forwarded to England, prevented Kew from profiting three-fold from that plant.' Whereas the vanda, which he claimed was 'collected under my sight and directions' for a 'gentleman who sent his gardener with us to be shown the locality', was more successful. The 'gardener' was of course Thomas Lobb. Joseph Hooker estimated that had all Lobb's plants arrived home alive, Veitch would have cleared £1,000. 'An active collector with the facilities I possessed might easily clear from £2,000 to £3,000 in one season by the sale of Khasia orchids.' The use of this anonymous and rather contemptuous description of the Veitch venture was meant to illustrate

Joseph Hooker's long-running argument that his activities as a botanist for Kew, which were surely more important than Veitch's commercial exploits, were not sufficiently well funded by the government. In a letter written to his father, Hooker expressed his frustrations with the inadequate facilities and skills of the gardeners at Kew and complained of the irony that 'plants, especially orchids, sent to Kew were less likely to be successfully cultivated than those sent to a professional nurseryman' – a veiled compliment, at least, to James Veitch and his men. Commercialism had won over science and the gentleman botanist had lost out to the garden boy.

Meanwhile James had decided to send William Lobb to collect 'in a colder climate', partly out of concern for his continuing poor health. For his third trip, begun in 1849, William had sailed to the west coast of North America, with instructions to find conifers from Oregon, Nevada and California, plus hardy shrubs and plants suitable for English gardens. European naturalists had been sending plants from the New World since it was first discovered, but for James Veitch it was an entirely new continent. David Douglas's spectacular collection of conifers, found during his travels for the Horticultural Society, had stimulated such a craze that Douglas wrote to his friend Hooker that 'you will begin to think that I manufacture Pines at my pleasure'. But his collections of live seed were relatively small and, far from flooding the market, Douglas's new introductions only stimulated English gardeners' unquenchable thirst for more. James Veitch quickly saw a potential marketing opportunity and decided to send William Lobb to collect commercial quantities of conifer seeds already made popular by Douglas. Hopefully Lobb might also find other new species that the great collector had missed.

William Lobb arrived in the port of San Francisco at the height of the California Gold Rush. Before he had even disembarked, he saw hundreds of ships in the harbour, abandoned by their crews to join the thousands of hopeful prospectors with 'gold fever'. Like Douglas, William was only interested in horticultural gold and he turned his back on the lawless West and headed south to San Diego. He spent the summer around Monterey and made a fortunate beginning by finding and collecting seeds of the Santa Lucia Fir, *Abies bracteata*, which Hooker later described as 'among the most remarkable of all true pines'. Hooker congratulated Lobb on sending well-prepared specimens of this tree 'with a perfect cone' (it seems that Douglas's ripened cones had fallen to pieces before reaching home). Under James Veitch's orders, William Lobb was the first plant collector to gather viable seed in really large

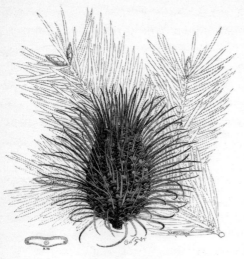

Abies bracteata.

quantities from trees and shrubs that were then still rare in cultivation in England.

Lobb's collecting success in this area was truly remarkable. He sent cones filled with seed of another fir, *Abies venusta*, the Big Cone Pine, *Pinus coulteri*, the Western Red Cedar, *Thuja plicata*, and a number of other conifers that Douglas had originally sent only as herbarium specimens. He also found a small horse-chestnut, the Californian Buckeye, *Aesculus californica*, and the lovely scented *Rhododendron occidentale* which was to become the parent of many even more beautiful Veitch hybrids. By the autumn, William had moved north where he collected sackfuls of seed from the Monterey pine, *Pinus radiata*, the sugar pine, *Pinus lambertiana*, the Western White Pine, *Pinus monticola*, the Knobcone Pine, *Pinus attenuata*, and the world's tallest tree, the coastal or Californian redwood, *Sequoia sempervirens*, first discovered by Archibald Menzies as early as 1794. Later in the year, William continued his searches in the Oregon mountains and California and collected seed from the Noble Fir, *Abies procera*, the Douglas Fir *Pseudotsuga menziesii*, the Giant Fir *Abies grandis*, and the Western Yellow Pine *Pinus ponderosa*. To James Veitch's great joy, he also discovered some new trees – the Western Red Cedar *Thuja plicata*, the Californian Red Fir *Abies magnifica*, the Colorada White Fir *Abies concolor*, the Pacific White Fir *Abies concolor* subsp. *lowiana* and the Californian Juniper *Juniperus californica*.

For gardeners today, William Lobb's collection of hardy shrubs is one of the most significant and rewarding, especially his collection of the glorious blue Californian lilac, *Ceanothus*, including two natural hybrids, *C. x veitchianus* and *C. x lobbianus*. These he found growing in dense brushwood thickets on the dry slopes and ridges of the high Californian chaparral where the winters are short, wet and mild and the long summers are hot and arid. He also collected seeds of deep butter-yellow *Fremontodendron californicum*, a pretty flowering currant, *Ribes lobbii*, and the red *Delphinium cardinale*.

CHAPTER SEVEN

VICTORIAN 'HIGH'

'Where smiling Chelsea spreads the cultur'd lands
Sacred to flora a pavilion stands
Thus, strange to tell! Near London you behold,
The age of fashion, Beauty and of Gold.'
Mr Pratt, *Flowers and Fashion* c1812

BETWEEN 1848 AND 1857 Britain enjoyed a period of almost unprecedented prosperity, confidence and optimism. New lands and new markets were opened up, new sources of raw materials, including gold from California and Australia, were discovered, and new technology was being developed for mass production. The economy was buoyant, profits were high, the professional classes expanded and, for a while at least, working-class employment and wages improved. Britain was at the height of her powers, her Empire extending throughout the world. Prince Albert, as President of the Society of Arts, declared in 1849, 'Now is the time to prepare for a Great Exhibition, an exhibition worthy of the greatness of this country, not merely national in its scope and benefits, but comprehensive of the whole world.'

It was a glorious May in 1851 and visitors flocked to the Great Exhibition held in the specially built Crystal Palace in London. They were awestruck by the spectacle, the novelty and the showmanship: 'the splash of fountains, the luxuriance of tropical foliage, the play of colours from the choicest flowers, carried on into the vistas of the nave by the rich dyes of carpets and stuffs from the costliest looms, enough to fill the eye and mind with a pleasure never to be forgotten.' The new and extraordinary sights at the Crystal Palace were a feast to the eyes of ordinary people who were becoming more aware of an exciting, exotic new world far beyond the shores of England – of beautiful, awesome landscapes, of 'foreign' people, and a vast wealth of unimaginable flora and fauna. The Great Exhibition was planned primarily as an international event to celebrate the latest in manufacturing and commercial raw materials, but, despite its horticultural associations (the building was created by Joseph Paxton, the Duke of Devonshire's ex-gardener and the interior decorated with thousands of ferns, palms and flowers supplied by the largest London nurseries), it did not include horticulture. More than six million people – almost one-fifth of the British population – travelled from every part of the country by railway, steam ship or on newly improved roads to London. Newspapers noted how members of the nobility, gentry, artisan and working classes came together under one roof 'in social harmony'. In his *History of England*, Macaulay wrote that 1851 was 'long to be remembered as a singularly happy year of peace, plenty, good feeling, innocent pleasures and national glory'.

Whilst they were 'up in Town' for the Great Exhibition, people took the opportunity of visiting many of the recently opened museums and galleries as well as visiting the traditional sights of London. The Horticultural Society seized on the prospect of vast numbers of visitors and organised an especially lavish spring show at Chiswick. The *Gardener's Chronicle* observed that 'As usual Messrs Veitch of Exeter stood pre-eminent among the Exhibitions of new or rare plants'. Visitors to Chiswick were amazed by the remarkable spectacle of Veitch's insect-eating plants such as nepenthes from the forests of the Indian Ocean which 'throw abroad their tendrils and suspend their curious bags of green and crimson and white . . .' and sarracenia from the swamps of North America which 'stood erect like living trumpets, or imitated ewers and jugs of green and crimson'. The jury, as they peered at these weird plants, appeared to risk being 'entrapped among the relentless teeth with which the recesses of these cups are guarded'. But they survived the ordeal and awarded James Veitch & Son a Gold Banksian Medal for their magnificent display of sumptuous new plants.

With so many changes taking place in English life it was inevitable that fashions in gardening should change too with an irresistible choice of new trees and plants arriving almost every day from around the empire and even beyond. Many wealthier gardeners had already rejected the once fashionable landscaped pleasure grounds of the eighteenth century. Out went the 'bare and the bald' and in came Italianate terracing and extravagantly colourful flower beds. Huge numbers of new gardeners with smaller gardens were now also free to take what they wanted from a whole range of historic styles and traditions and to choose from a variety of affordable new plants available from nurserymen. Creative combinations of formal and informal styles produced 'pictures' of romance, sentiment, artifice and colourful patterns of such intensity that at first they were found quite shocking. Decorative foliage and architectural plants, evergreens and conifers all became fashionable.

Pineta – plantations of conifers such as those already created by the Veitches at Bicton and Poltimore – started to come into their own and anyone with sufficient land had to have one. Some Victorians developed a passion for themed gardens such as James Bateman's 'China' and 'Egypt' gardens at Biddulph Grange or the popular 'American' gardens filled with hardy flowering shrubs introduced from North America. Special collections of recent discoveries advertised the owner's refined taste and learning as well as the considerable wealth required to own them. For those who wished to be at the cutting edge of horticultural fashion, the prevailing idea was that the garden ought to be considered a work of art rather than an attempt to copy the 'natural' landscape. The overall effect was meant to be a carefully contrived picture, a harmonious combination of artifice and nature. The final composition, however, had to maintain a highly polished look of crisp outlines, neat edges, velvet lawns, perfectly raked paths, with not a mole hill, daisy or fallen leaf to be seen. Nature was transformed into art, but art could never revert to nature. As J. C. Loudon, the great arbiter of garden taste, wrote before he died in 1843, gardens 'are intended to show that they are works of art, and to display the taste and wealth of the owner'.

In her novel *Heartsease*, written in 1854, Charlotte Yonge's newly-wed heroine, Violet, 'held her breath' at the first sight of her wealthy in-laws' 'High Victorian' display garden:

> The grand parterre, laid out in regular-shaped borders, each containing a mass of one kind of flower, flaming escholcias, dazzling verbenas, azure nemophilas, or sober heliotrope, the broad walks, the great pile of building, the innumerable windows, the long ascent of stone steps, their balustrade guarded by sculptured sphinxes . . . reminded her of prints of Versailles.

Wandering further out in the Pleasure Grounds, Violet saw:

> . . . spread out before her a sweep of shaven turf, adorned with sparkling *jets d'eau* of fantastic forms, gorgeous masses of American plants, the flaming of the snowy azalea, the noble rhododendron, in every shade of purple cluster among its evergreen leaves; beds of rare lilies, purely white or brilliant with colour; roses in their perfection of bloom; flowers of forms she had never figured to herself, shaded by wondrous trees;

the exquisite weeping deodora, the delicate mimosa, the scaly Himalayan pines, the feathery gigantic ferns of the southern hemisphere.

This form and scale of garden was extravagantly costly for the owner to create and maintain – but that, of course, was the whole point. It was particularly demanding for the head gardener and required great skill and hard work for his men. The popular horticultural journals extolled the virtues of a seemingly endless choice of new garden ideas and plants. For the nurseryman, who trained the gardeners and supplied the plants, it was an extremely profitable time and the big horticultural nurseries had never been so busy. They watched for the changing trends and sent out new instructions to their collectors tramping the globe in pursuit of novelties. If they were clever, as the Veitches were, they introduced new plants and made them fashionable, created tough, colourful hybrids to serve as summer bedding and rushed out lavishly produced catalogues and advertisements. Fortunately the appeal of the country house remained as great as ever and by the time the building of new country houses and improvements to existing estates had reached its peak, staggering sums were being spent. The nursery establishments were almost overwhelmed by the demand for plant stock and garden layouts.

So many kinds of evergreens and hardy flowering shrubs were needed to brighten the bare beds that nurseries struggled to extend the garden season with new varieties of spring-flowering bulbs and late hybrid dahlias and chrysanthemums for the autumn. James Veitch, John Dominy and his nurserymen also worked overtime crossing and propagating their own stock in order to supply the growing demand for indoor foliage plants, colourful bedding annuals, hardy conifers and flowering shrubs. Increasingly, James found it was necessary to strike a judicious balance between providing rare and valuable exotics for his more discerning patrons and creating popular new species to be available in huge commercial quantities for the general gardener. James would have had to make careful plans and calculations about which plants to order from his own collectors, the Lobbs, who were still labouring in wild, dangerous and unknown parts, shipping back yet more amazing wonders to feed the new fashions in gardens and glasshouses. But for the long, detailed letters and instructions from James which chased the Lobb brothers around the ports of South America and Asia, William and Thomas might have remained unaware of the changes in English garden fashions and of how much their own and other collectors' discoveries were influencing those changes.

This was a period of unprecedented opportunity for nurseries to make huge leaps in the variety, range and size of their stocks. The Veitches were growing and selling ever-larger and more affordable stocks of plants which it was sending out to its expanding clientele on the new railways. The nursery's reputation for quantity and quality as well as novelty was gradually making James Veitch & Son of Exeter one of the most competitive in the country. Yet, when a reporter wrote about the nursery's success in the *Gardener's Chronicle* in the autumn of 1851, he expressed amazement that such a successful enterprise was operating so far from London:

> Near that ancient city [of Exeter] lies a gentle valley occupied by Messrs. Veitch and Son, in which alone will be found more new valuable plants than in any place in Europe, with the single exception of the Royal Botanic Garden at Kew – plants obtained by private enterprise for commercial purposes and not gathered together by the power of mighty Government.

It was a view not shared by Joseph Hooker who believed that the Veitch collectors were better funded than the Kew collectors. Though their collectors' pay was modest, Veitch plant-collecting expeditions were never underfunded as the reporter concurred:

> By means of excellent collectors (two brothers of the name of Lobb) and liberal disbursements, California, Peru, Chile and Patagonia in the west; and the Khasia Hills, the provinces of Tenasserim, Java, Malacca and the ghauts of Malabar in the east have been gleaned, and the result is gathered into hothouses or transferred to the open air in the fertile soils and happy climate of Devonshire . . .

Already on show in the nursery were some of William Lobb's conifers, one of which soon found royal approval – *Saxegothaea conspicua* 'which HRH Prince Albert has permitted to bear one of his names'. There were also many of William Lobb's hardy shrubs, including 'great bushes of Philesia just beginning to produce their crimson tubular flowers' and varieties of *desfontainia*, escallonia, berberis, tropaeolum, the already popular *Embothrium coccineum* and the Quinine tree from Peru 'now flowering for the first time in Europe'. The reporter also greatly admired Thomas Lobb's fine new hoya, an elegant sonerila, quantities of 'Indian' orchids and the giant lily *Cardiocrinum giganteum* from Nepal which was 'hastening to prepare for flowering another year'. Its bulbs were already for sale from 21s. to 63s. according to size. 'In short, turn where you will, the eye meets nothing but what is most fine and rare in this surprising collection of the Messrs. Veitch.'

And there were many more surprises to come, none more so than when William Lobb arrived back in Exeter for Christmas, 1852, a year earlier than expected, with the best present James could hope for. Lobb came home bearing bags of seed of just one remarkable species of tree.

BIG TREE

Whilst in San Francisco packing and sending his conifer collection back to England, Lobb had been invited to a meeting of the newly-founded Californian Academy of Science. There he heard a story of a 'Big Tree' in the mountains. A hunter named Dowd was describing to the enrapt audience how he had been out hunting a large grizzly bear in the foothills of the Sierra Nevada in Calaveras County and tracked it into an area unknown to him. There, to his astonishment, the hunter entered a grove of gigantic trees. He was so amazed by these monsters that he hurried back to camp and insisted that his companions returned with him to confirm that he had not seen them in a drunken vision. They too had craned their necks and stared high above them, marvelling at the height and magnitude of these 'kings of trees'. When he heard the story Lobb knew at once that this was the prize he was dreaming of and hurried back to the Sierran foothills where he too found the now famous Calaveras Grove. Words, never his strong point, failed him and he simply recorded: 'From 80 to 90 trees exist all within circuit of a mile, from 250ft to 320ft in height, 10–20ft in diameter.'

Wasting no time, William Lobb collected all the seed, botanical specimens, vegetative shoots and seedlings that he could carry back to San Francisco and immediately booked himself on to the first ship home. He took a gamble in cutting short his contract, but he knew that, at the risk of angering his employer, he had to get the seeds home before anyone else did. It seemed to have paid off. James was ecstatic and he put aside all other work to concentrate on raising quantities of seedlings.

An editorial in the *Gardener's Chronicle* on Christmas Eve 1853 announced excitedly that Veitch & Son had received branches and cones of a remarkable tree from their collector in California, William Lobb, who described it as 'the monarch of the Californian forest'. Six months later the *Chronicle* reported that Veitch was offering seedlings of the tree at £3. 2. od. each reducing to £1. 1. od. each if twelve pairs were bought. James Bateman was among several enthusiasts who immediately planted an avenue, alternating them with Monkey-puzzle trees.

Unfortunately, Lobb could not claim to be the first to introduce the tree to Britain. He was just beaten to it by a Scot, John Mathew, who only four months earlier had taken some seed back to Scotland. However, as a private gardener, Mathew had distributed only one or two seeds to a few friends.

News was soon out about this mystery tree and James was determined to be the first nurseryman to sell it. He was particularly anxious to have it named and Dr Lindley decided on *Wellingtonia gigantea* to mark the recent death of the Duke of Wellington. But the Americans were not at all happy about this. It was an American tree, they argued, and should be called *Washingtonia* after their own war hero and first President. Elihu Burritt, an American from Connecticut who visited the Exeter nursery and saw some young 'California' pines growing there, complained that British botanists were getting into the habit of giving British names to American trees and plants. He wrote:

> See what they did to the grandest water-lily ever grown on the American continent. They gave it a royal christening in botanical Latin, and called it Victoria Regina!' and they made no mention that it first saw light of life under an American sun . . . there is no telling how far they may carry this propensity . . . next they may transplant and acclimatise our shag-bark Walnut and give it a Latin name, signifying, The Prince of Wales's Own, or they may Anglicise our Sugar Maple and christen it, with its own sweet fluid, Alexandra Melliflua.

While the argument about nomenclature raged on, in California the Calaveras Grove became a tourist attraction. The trees suffered many terrible indignities to please the curious who were attracted to novelty and had no idea about conservation or protection: some were felled to create a large dance floor on one stump, while a bowling alley was created in the trunk of another. The bark of a huge 116-foot tree was stripped and sent to England where it was displayed in the Crystal Palace in its new site at Sydenham. (Happily the Grove is now part of the National Park and its largest and oldest specimen, known as 'General Sherman', is still revered.) Eventually the tree was named *Sequoiadendron giganteum* after the local native Americans and to show its botanical relationship with the coastal or Californian redwood, *Sequoia sempervirens*. But amongst English gardeners it is still popularly known as the 'Wellingtonia'.

THE GREAT LEAP FORWARD

When William, and Thomas, who had finished collecting in India, arrived home in Exeter around the same time, they found the Veitch nursery in a state of excitement and upheaval. Ever since James and son had visited the Great Exhibition and won their accolade at the Horticultural Show, their eyes had been opened to the possibilities of establishing themselves in London; they discussed plans for moving their business to the centre of the commercial world. 'Everyone', the *Gardener's Chronicle* agreed, 'regretted the impossibility of seeing much of so important a collection, so long as it was buried in the heart of Devonshire.' A unique opportunity arose when the large, old-established nursery of Knight & Perry, known as the Exotic Nursery, in the King's Road, Chelsea, was put up for sale. Joseph Knight, with his nephew Thomas Perry, had kept a flourishing business and made a fortune until his retirement in 1852 when he closed the nursery. With

profits pouring into Exeter, James felt he could afford to take over the Chelsea premises. But he decided to continue to cultivate all his plant stock in Exeter where 'more attractive and healthier plants flourished in the fine climate of Devonshire compared with the same things brought under blossom under the murky atmosphere of suburban London'. James Junior would be the Director and take charge of displaying and selling in the magnificent showrooms of the new London branch, which they grandly proposed to call the 'Royal Exotic Nursery', Chelsea. (It is not known whether they obtained royal permission to do so.)

James Junior (1815–1869)

CHELSEA

From the eighteenth century, the King's Road was a private route for the king and his court to proceed from St James and Whitehall to Hampton Court Palace and they made a 'fine sight' as they passed through. But gardeners, farmers, bricklayers and tradesmen were determined to carry their

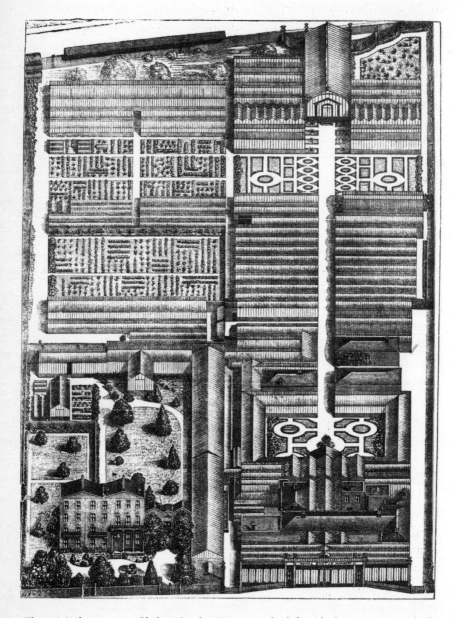

The original nursery at Chelsea. Stanley House on the left with the museum attached.
The rear entrance leads to the Fulham Road and Brompton Cemetery, the front entrance
is on the King's Road. Nothing of this remains and Edith Grove now runs down the
centre of the nursery grounds

goods along it, much to the fury of the Royal Surveyors who erected barriers and tried to charge a toll. An increasing variety of attractions drew people to the area. Royalty, nobility and fashionable society were known to stroll in Cremorne Gardens, successor to the more ambitious Ranelagh Gardens, where they could enjoy concerts, fireworks and galas and ascend in a balloon to look out over the city. Visitors from all over London came to Chelsea for the pleasure gardens, with their rustic arbours and flower walks, the taverns offering skittles and bowling alleys and tea-rooms where they could sample the Chelsea bun. They could purchase the latest plants from nursery gardens which dotted the King's Road and gawp at the curiosities in several museums. There were even a number of tavern-cum-museums with small displays of 'shells, skeletons and curios'.

Chelsea also had important horticultural associations: the eminent botanist Philip Miller and his successors, William Forsyth and William Curtis, held court in the Chelsea Physic Garden and its most famous patron, Sir Hans Sloane, created his extraordinary museum in Chelsea Place (which later formed part of the British Museum). There was also a thriving area of market gardens and horticultural nurseries stretching from the Brompton Road to Fulham and the 'World's End'. Like many outer regions of London, Chelsea and Fulham supplied the city with fruit and vegetables and by 1810 it was reported that half the vegetables sold in Covent Garden were raised here. Over the years, plant nurseries had also moved in and set up their glasshouses, showrooms and shops: among them were Robert Furber, Christopher Gray, Colvill's, Osborne & Co, the Sloane Street Nursery, and many others. By 1830, when the King's Road was opened to the general public, more than twenty-five nurserymen and florists 'exclusively' lined the road with brightly-coloured wooden palings surrounding their show-grounds.

The clean air of Chelsea had also attracted several wealthy families who built themselves large houses and gardens on the King's Road, including the Stanley family, Earls of Derby. At the beginning of the eighteenth century they had replaced an earlier mansion with Stanley House, a 'good, sensible building' which they later rented to the antiquarian William Richard Hamilton. After serving as Lord Elgin's secretary during the Napoleonic Wars, Hamilton accompanied Elgin to Greece and helped bring the Parthenon marbles to London. He added a large hall to Stanley House which he filled with casts of the Parthenon frieze plus a fine collection of statues, pictures, books, minerals and musical intruments.

In 1808, after Hamilton's death, Stanley House and grounds were bought by the nurseryman Joseph Knight who kept the house and laid out horticultural showrooms in the gardens. The area soon became so crowded and popular for purchasing garden plants that the best establishments (including the Veitches later on) kept only their show grounds there and rented growing-grounds elsewhere in Battersea, Slough, Kingston and Sunbury.

When James Veitch bought Knight's establishment, there were several other nurseries nearby; opposite was the Ashburnam Park Nursery, on one side was Mr Dennis, famed for his pelargoniums, on the other was Edward Weeks, builder of horticultural glasshouses. These establishments could by then advertise themselves as being only 'Four miles from London. Omnibuses from the Bank every quarter of an hour'. Chelsea railway station was just around the corner and the small 'cut' or canal up from the Thames at Battersea were ideal for unloading vans and barges with large quantities of nursery stock.

With his customary attention to detail, James spent a considerable period in careful planning and preparation. Every day huge loads of plants were packed into the Veitches' own specially-made railway vans at Exeter and sent up to London. James Junior, his wife Harriott and children, John Gould, Harry, Arthur and their four sisters, set up home in the 'sensible' but nevertheless rather grand Stanley House. The boys never forgot the move from rural Exeter to their new home and the nursery grounds in the city. It was, recalled Harry, the sixteenth of April, 'Grandfather Gould's birthday'. James Junior could walk out of his back door and survey his new nursery which had become rather neglected and, being a practical and energetic man, he at once began to make plans. Like his father, James Junior understood the importance of investment and undertook extensive improvements to the Chelsea premises to make them a grand and fitting theatrical marketplace for selling his nursery stock. Despite its restricted space between the Fulham and the King's Roads, the Chelsea nursery was already well laid out with an extensive range of glasshouses, offices, show house and warehousing with walks and a long 'telescopic vista' ending with a vast bronzed vase with a *jet d'eau*. There was still some good stock, including Knight's collection of banksias, a variety of good conifers and a few plants of the hybrid *Magnolia citriodora*, of which Knight was said to be the sole possessor. Knight also left behind some of the best-trained nurserymen and a well-established list of customers.

All the glasshouses were given a fresh coat of paint and grass borders were laid alongside the central walk where customers could admire the beds of specimen conifers and deodaras, pots of young Monkey-puzzles and standard bays in long rows. Beds of camellias were already flowering freely against a north wall, their blossoms 'very brilliant and perfect'. An old aquarium was used as a temporary house for the pitcher plants with a luxuriance of water-lilies and other interesting aquatics flourishing on the surface of a large slate water tank. One glasshouse was filled with pots of sweet-smelling orange trees from Malta and, while a new orchid house was being built, a small stove-house protected the orchids. There were of course many rare exotics like the lovely *Streptocarpus biflorus*, the free-flowering tree *Statice halfordii* and a handsome twiner, *Hexacentris mysorensis*, 'as much adapted for pot culture as for the rafter of a stove'.

Opposite, in a small greenhouse, were several *Lilium giganteum* which James Senior had discovered were really quite hardy, having stood out in Exeter in seventeen degrees of frost the previous winter. In a long show house near the entrance was a magnificent display of tender azaleas, cinerarias, deutzias and rhododendrons, including the jasmine-flowered rhododendron. Displayed near a fountain in the large, curvilinear conservatory were William Lobb's two rare 'royal' conifers, *Saxegothaea* and *Fitzroya*. The show house at the entrance was entirely remodelled, the flat roof replaced with a triple span of glass supported by trellised uprights with

An aquatic house

wire arches over which tender climbers could grow, including *Magnolia fuscata*, which was trained like a peach tree 'so as to scent the whole of the King's Road from end to end with delicious perfume, like Pine Apple with some Arabian spices'. In the cool greenhouse were rows of low-growing, flowering plants such as 'showy' small rhododendrons and Chinese primulas which, patrons were assured, could be grown in either the garden or the conservatory. All the paths were relaid with flagstones and several new walls were erected to hide the offices and packing sheds from the customers' view.

James Junior installed the most up-to-date heating system using hot-water pipes instead of the old flues. He experimented with improvements to the ventilation in the glasshouses and adopted Moore's patent ventilators which consisted of long panes of glass about six inches wide arranged like Venetian blinds and moved outwards or inwards by means of a lever acted on by a string. When the new orchid house was eventually completed it was filled with the famous Veitch collection. In the newly-built propagating house customers would be able to view pots of seedlings of William Lobb's most exciting new 'Big Tree', *Sequoiadendron giganteum*, and try to imagine them growing into 'the enormous Californian tree which is now everywhere occupying so much attention'.

There was a cool, dank fernery for Thomas Lobb's ferns. Shade was provided by laying 'tiffany', a gauze muslin, over the roof. The sides were made of irregular masses of citrified brick held together with Roman cement with crevices in which luxuriant mosses and small ferns thrived. A mound of mossy rockwork was surrounded by a winding white gravel walk; rising from its centre was the marvellous royal fern, *Osmunda regalis*. A little waterfall trickled over the rocks into a basin with floating Cape pondweed. Across the King's Road, on a large piece of waste ground, James Junior created a new ornamental garden in which customers could stroll and admire the plants in a more natural setting. 'Exmouth' magnolias graced the walls and there was a walk through the middle with chain borders on either side 'formed into beds by means of narrow pathways made of Derbyshire spar'.

At last, in early spring of 1853, James Junior was ready to open the doors of the Royal Exotic Nursery. He published an advertisement 'respectfully' informing the nobility, clergy and gentry, and the public generally that the new Veitch horticultural nursery was open for business and that its Director had ambitious plans to exhibit at Chelsea many of the 'beautiful and rare

plants of recent introduction to this country . . . for which the establishment at Exeter has been so distinguished'.

SECRET HISTORY IN THE GLASSHOUSE

Although James Senior, increasingly affected by heart trouble and ill-health,
remained in Devon, there was no doubt as to who was still in charge. All
the plant stock continued to be raised in Exeter and sent up to London;
James decided which plants were the most attractive, the best quality and
when they were ready for sale. All plant introductions from collectors had
to be delivered to Exeter where James could receive and evaluate them
and give new seeds and plants his special skills and attention. His highly
trained nurserymen and hybridists under the brilliant John Dominy would
continue to work in Exeter, propagating and raising the newest, best and
most marketable stock. Indeed Dominy was distinguishing himself as 'Messrs.
Veitch's indefatigable and very intelligent foreman' with his 'skills and assid-
uous perseverance' as a specialist hybridiser. He had already created several
successful crosses with fuchsias and with some of Thomas Lobb's rhododendrons and pitcher plants. Secretly, unknown to anyone but James,
Dominy was also working on the horticultural holy grail, the creation of
a hybrid orchid.

Orchids were notoriously difficult to raise from seed, and so it was necessary to keep going back to the wild to replace stocks. Some years earlier
the Rev. William Herbert, Dean of Manchester, had published a paper on
hybridising plants, especially orchids, but had failed to produce an orchid
hybrid himself. However, he wrote, 'An intelligent gardener may do much
for science by attempts of this kind, if he keeps accurate notes of what he
attempts, and does not jump to immature conclusions.' John Dominy was
just this sort of man and, with help and advice from his friend, Dr John
Harris, an Exeter surgeon, plus enthusiastic support from his employer,
Dominy quietly started making history in the glasshouse. He began by
cross-pollinating cattleyas and then making a cross of *Calanthe furcata* and
C. masuca. But it would be some years before results of Dominy's patient
and persistent work would become public news.

The new London nursery was already proving to be a wild success and
James, who had dreamed of finding exotic plants in foreign lands, had now
fulfilled another dream – of creating a profitable, reputable and fast-
expanding business. Yet, just as he had never travelled, he did not seem to
have any desire to expand with his success. What fired James were not the

trappings of wealth and fame but a private and spiritual dedication to the pursuit of knowledge and the profit that could be gained from it. He was a workaholic, an autocrat, passionate about his plants and his business, but nevertheless content to remain modestly in Exeter and to drive the business from there. James Junior, however, was motivated by quite different ambitions. He wanted to create a reputation for himself in the centre of the horticultural world. James Senior might have felt some misgivings as to whether his clever but volatile son could cope with the cut and thrust of the competitive nursery business in London. There were showrooms and glasshouses where plants must always look their best and most appealing, a class and range of hugely demanding clientele requiring both patience and courtesy; there were offices keeping accounts and sending out bills, catalogues to compile and print, and a large horticultural and administrative staff to train and oversee. It was quite different to business life in the provinces and with James Junior's short temper there were inevitably problems ahead.

There is little doubt that James Junior had great affection and respect for his father but he must also have felt frustrated by the restrictions placed upon him. Many people spoke of his untiring zeal and energy, his keen perception, his clear-headed business habits, his horticultural skills and his great personal influence. As time passed, however, they also observed James's quick temper and 'an impatience of opposition'. Many friends, colleagues and employees experienced the wrong end of his violent outbursts, especially if he was crossed in any way. He liked to inaugurate new schemes and ideas and vigorously and single-mindedly drove them through committees. It was this very determination and refusal to brook opposition that later brought James Junior the respect that he yearned for.

What Veitch plant collectors William and Thomas Lobb made of the sudden transformation of a provincial nursery to this grand and extravagant London shop displaying their hard-won discoveries and introductions is not recorded. For a year they had worked on their collections in Exeter and watched as expensive improvements and alterations at Chelsea continued. But by the middle of 1854 it was decided that both brothers were to be sent out again to collect fresh seed and plant stock. James was keen to obtain some plants from Japan, whose flora was still relatively unknown in England, and had negotiated the purchase of some conifers from a contact in the Dutch East India Company. In August, Thomas was sent to Java to collect and ship the order home. He then set off to North Borneo to explore Mount Kinabalu on whose slopes he hoped to find some giant pitcher plants including, at James's request, *Nepenthes rajah* which was said to reach a circumference of nearly nineteen inches. However, there was so much civil unrest in the region that Thomas was unable to climb the mountain but instead fortuitously discovered *Nepenthes veitchii*. It does not seem to have been a particularly fruitful trip and Thomas cut it short and returned home where he made himself useful in the Exeter nursery unpacking his cases, potting the plants and sorting dried specimens for Kew.

William, despite persistent ill-health and pleas from his family in Cornwall to stay and rest, insisted that he was fit enough to travel again. In a letter to Sir William Hooker, James remarked on 'a sort of restlessness about him' which was also noticed by his family: 'He seems taken with a sort of monomania, which it is difficult to describe and which he could not explain himself, a sort of excitability and want of confidence.' Unknown to his family and employer, William was almost certainly exhibiting symptoms of syphilis, probably contracted in the ports of South America where, not surprisingly, he would have sought occasional companionship and solace from his lonely travels. Putting aside his concerns, James sent William back to California for another three-year contract. Perhaps William dreamed of another 'Big Tree' but he found nothing more and sent only repeat collections of conifer seeds. James wrote to Sir William Hooker in January 1857, 'We hear Lobb has been ill, his writing appears shaky and I am inclined to think it probable he will soon return.'

William Lobb did not return home, but James's youngest son, Robert, finally did. James had never given up hope that his surviving sons, John, Thomas and Robert, would one day return to take up their positions in the family firm. At some point Robert had left his job in Turkey and joined his brother Thomas to farm in the South African Cape district of Somerset East. There Robert specialised in growing fruit, especially the Cape apples for which the region was famous. He had corresponded regularly with his father and step-mother and no doubt heard all about the great successes at home, of the growing Exeter nursery and the already profitable new London premises. His father was struggling on his own in Exeter in failing health and Robert probably realised that, if he was to come home, now would be the best time. With his French-born, South African wife, Sarah, and their four young sons, Robert moved into James Junior's old house in Exeter. Although an expert in apple growing, Robert knew little about horticulture. But he soon settled down to learn and help his father, who wrote that he was 'now getting on very well with so much assistance'.

What James had not anticipated was the return of his son Thomas whom Robert had fallen out with and had been happy to leave behind in South Africa. Thomas had become a wastrel and a drunk. When he arrived back in Exeter, he made himself more unpopular by opening a rival seed business which staggered on for nearly a year before going bankrupt. A friend of the family wrote that 'The Veitches have been and are in much sorrow on account of the reckless conduct of their worthless son, Tom. He seems wholly given up to drunkenness.' John, the eldest son, who had gone to sea as a medic, was by now a doctor living with his family in England.

William Lobb remained in California after his contract expired in 1858. He had expressed his wish to withdraw his services at the end of the contract but James informed him that he still had obligations to fulfil. Lobb started sending a few things to private collectors and to the Low nursery in Clapton who were very happy to receive the seeds of a new fir, *Abies concolor* subsp. *lowiana* and the rare *Pinus torreyana*. He also caused great embarrassment to the Veitches by sending herbarium specimens and live plants direct to Kew. In his only known surviving letter, dated 4 February 1858, William Lobb informed Sir William Hooker that he had shipped five cases of seeds, specimens and plants all marked and numbered: 'Should this reach you before the arrival of the steamer at Southampton due March 15, it would be advisable that some person should see the Cases opened at the Custom House and the contents carefully handled . . . I am sir, your obdn't servant. W. Lobb.'

'Your letter from WL could not have astonished you more than it has me,' James wrote to Hooker. For many months, neither William's family nor James received any further news from William and they had all become alarmed. 'We thought he had given up collecting plants, for Californian gold,' James wrote unkindly. 'His conduct towards us seems inexplicable and I am tempted to make strong comments.' There followed some rather tight-lipped correspondence between Veitch and Kew which resulted in James Junior being despatched with a cheque for £250 to buy five cases of Lobb's last collection and thus prevent them falling into the hands of competitors. In one careworn letter to Hooker, James complained of 'so much to try and perplex me this past year'. Tired and suffering from rheumatism and gout which made it painful for him to write, he tried to take comfort in his faith and quoted a hymn to Sir William for the New Year:

Still has my life new mercies seen
abounding every year.
Behold the days that yet remain
I trust them to Thy care.

Feeling able to entrust the nursery to his son Robert, with help from head nurseryman John Dominy and Thomas Lobb, who was then working in Exeter, James and Rebecca took a well-earned holiday. Typically, James first took a rail van loaded with orchids to an exhibition in Manchester before going on to tour Wales for three weeks.

Dominy was meanwhile still absorbed in his own challenge – the 'slowest and most patience-taxing of all operations connected with the gardener's art' – creating a hybrid orchid. He eventually managed to obtain seed from a cross between *Calanthe furcata*, a species from the Philippines, and *Calanthe masuca*, a Himalayan species bought from the Rollison nursery. On 28 October 1856, the seedlings flowered. A plant was shown to Dr Lindley who wrote that a botanist '. . . would have considered it either as a purple-flowered *C. furcata*, or as a fork-spurred, small-flowered *C. masuca*. Had hybrids been suspected to occur among Orchids the plant would have been pronounced a cross. And such it was.'

The hybrid was an immediate sensation in horticultural circles and Lindley named it *Calanthe x dominii* to honour 'the first man who succeeded in this operation'. Orchid hybridisation could finally be seen as a real possibility.

James Veitch did not stand idly by basking in his nurseryman's achievement. Lindley had noted that Dominy had succeeded in raising such plants from seed 'as a matter of horticultural business' rather than for science and James wasted no time in promoting and mass-producing *C. x dominii* for sale. The botanists, however, were initially less enthusiastic in welcoming the new plant, being suspicious of hybrids which they called 'mules'. Dr Lindley, realising the nomenclatural implications now facing taxonomic botanists, exclaimed to Dominy, 'You will drive the botanists mad.' And he was right, though it was a different kind of madness that was to infect many more than just a few botanists.

Dominy's success sparked off another family row, this time with James Junior, who had always regarded himself as the family expert on orchids. This, after all, was the kind of glory that he longed for himself and for his nursery in Chelsea. On his many travels to exhibitions, James encountered wealthy and

Professor H. G. Reichenbach
(1823–1889)

distinguished men who, like him, were passionate about orchids. He was gradually building up an orchid network, an important reputation and a substantial collection of his own. When the great nursery of Loddiges closed, their huge collection of orchids was put up for auction and James Junior was one of the first at the door of the auction house to buy some of the rarest and best plants. He also bought many of the finest orchids from James Bateman's valuable collection. The great plantsman, now getting old, introduced James Junior to his collector, George Ure-Skinner, a Scottish businessman who had spent many years trading in Central America, and the two became close friends.

Meanwhile John Dominy had produced more hybrid seedlings, this time of cattleya orchids, and in August 1859, five flowering plants were displayed at a meeting of the Horticultural Society. This new hybrid was named *Cattleya x hybrida*. In November plants of another cross, *Cattleya x dominiana* (*C. x dominyii*) from *C. labiata* and *C. intermedia*, produced their first flowers. There were two types, *alba*, with pale sepals and petals and *lutea*, with a large yellow disc on the lip. It was described as a 'very grand hybrid' (see colour-plate section). Professor Reichenbach of Hamburg, who ranked with Dr Lindley as the greatest authority on orchids at the time, became a regular visitor to the Chelsea orchid houses. In October he wrote in the *Gardener's Chronicle*:

> I may here remark that a son of the proprietor [either John Gould or Harry, sons of James Junior, who were both by then training in horticulture], who kindly showed me over the nursery, informed me that a great deal of success that attended their orchid growing arose from a careful consideration of the climate and habits of the plants in their native countries, and assimilating as much as possible that state here, instead of jumbling them up together as is often done to the utter ruin and destruction of many valuable plants.

This kind of praise may have led James Junior to feel, not unreasonably, that the skills of John Dominy would be better used in London. But his father would have none of it. Dominy would remain in Exeter where he had produced even more hybrids of exotics, such as the still-popular winter-flowering orchid hybrid, *Calanthe x veitchii, Cattleya exoniensis*, some beautiful cypripedium hybrids, and new hybrids of pitcher plants, such as *Nepenthes x dominiana*, plus several fuchsia hybrids. A compromise was reached when James Junior employed John Seden, a young gardener from

John Seden (1840–1921)

Essex who showed great promise and ability in the Chelsea orchid houses. Seden was sent to Exeter to train under John Dominy and learn from him the secrets of hybridisation. Dominy continued his experiments, becoming renowned as the authority in the field of orchid hybridisation. For fifteen years Veitch's was the only nursery where orchid hybrids were produced. The nursery remained extremely secretive about its activities and it gave them a huge lead in the highly competitive world of orchid collecting.

SOCIETY BUSINESS

As the Chelsea business flourished, James Junior proved that he was not only an able businessman but also a very knowledgeable and skilled horticulturist; he was becoming an eminent and respected figure in the world of horticulture. In 1865 he was elected to the council of the Horticultural Society, at a time when the Society's finances were still in a poor state, when the membership was increasing, but funds were not. Desperate measures had had to be taken in earlier years to reduce outgoings which were well in excess of income. Their expensive and luxurious publication, *Transactions of the Horticultural Society*, was discontinued but plant-collecting expeditions went on, with Robert Fortune in China and Theodore Hartweg in South America. Adding to the Society's increasing debts was the recent costly construction of a conservatory in the Society's garden at Chiswick. There were also the expensive exhibitions and shows which were very popular but never financial successes. The Society started a disastrous policy of selling off its assets. The precious herbarium and many stove plants, including specimens contributed by Society collectors and nurseries such as the Veitches', were sold. The auction of orchids, tree ferns, palms and greenhouse plants included the finest specimen ever seen of *Phalaenopsis amabilis* which Robert Fortune had sent home from the Philippines. A huge *Laelia superbiens* carrying 220 pseudo bulbs, which was still attached to the wood on which it had been found in Guatamala, was sold for £36.15s. This 'appalling act', which realised a total of only £1,044, did little to solve the Society's mounting debts. There was even a proposal to terminate the tenancy of the Chiswick garden which was rejected: 'A horticultural Society without a garden would be like a crew of sailors without a ship,' wrote one correspondent. James Junior was so horrified at the idea of giving up the Society's garden that he donated all the prize money won by the Veitch nursery for one year to help with its upkeep.

In 1858 Dr John Lindley was elected Secretary to the Society and Prince Albert succeeded the Duke of Devonshire as President. Yet the situation continued to deteriorate and members of the Council despaired. By December, James Junior, who was never shy of forcefully expressing his opinion, even if it was unpopular, proposed a resolution that the present Society be wound up and a new one formed with a 'Charter . . . better adapted to the interests of Horticulture'.

Although James Junior was a highly respected figure, his resolution was fiercely fought by others determined to save the Society, including Dr Lindley, who had given thirty-six years' devoted service. The idea was abandoned and the beleaguered council continued to shore up its debts by selling off the Society's assets, including its Regent Street headquarters and, worst of all, the magnificent library with 1,500 original drawings, for a mere £1,112. James Junior, whose loyalty to the ideals and principles of the Horticultural Society was never in question, turned his energies to fresh ideas of his own that would have considerable significance for the Society's future.

The Society had set up a number of committees such as Finance, Garden and Exhibitions, but curiously none to deal with the plants themselves. In 1858 James Junior proposed the creation of a Fruit and Vegetable Committee to monitor and encourage cultivation, experimentation and quality of every type of fruit and vegetable. It was to become the first of a series of standing committees (the Floral Committee followed a year later) which now play such an important part in the Society's work. James Junior's involvement with the Fruit and Vegetable Committee encouraged him to take a greater interest in the nursery's own stocks of specimen fruit trees and he began a programme of experimenting with raising vegetables. But the nursery had been expanding so fast that this meant yet more land would be required.

Twenty minutes' walk from the Chelsea nursery down a narrow lane near Parson's Green in Fulham lay the old orchards and market gardens of Mr Fitch who had recently died. James Junior immediately bought up the land, felled the fine old apple and pear trees and laid out an entirely new nursery with a range of vegetable trial beds such as early peas, lettuce and asparagus and regular rows of young fruit trees between gravel pathways neatly edged with box. The Fulham nursery, under the 'able management' of Mr Reid, supplied trained trees of every description including the then fashionable 'cordons' – cordon oblique, horizontal, vertical, dwarf, one-armed or two-armed – 'whatever one might desire' as well as orchard-house trees grown in pots. A correspondent for the *Journal of Horticulture* described the Veitch policy of only raising one-year fruit trees for trans-planting in the autumn when 'they are so nice and sturdy, so strong yet not gross, and so beautifully budded, that, to use a common expression, one could do anything with them'.

The new Royal President had meanwhile proved both a blessing and a curse for the Horticultural Society. Many members of the Royal family enthusiastically signed up as Fellows and Queen Victoria herself made generous contributions. The Prince Consort arranged for the Royal Commissioners to lease to the Society twenty-two-and-a-half acres of land in South Kensington (now the site of the Natural History Museum), for a new garden more conveniently placed than the one at Chiswick. Creating a new garden was very expensive – £50,000 – but with royal support and generous contributions from Fellows the sum was somehow raised. The Prince presided over plans and designs for the new gardens with the same energy and enthusiasm that he had brought to the Great Exhibition a decade earlier. In May 1861 the Horticultural Society was granted a Royal Charter and a month later the gardens were formally opened by Prince Albert, attended by the Prime Minister, Lord Palmerston, along with Mr Gladstone and Mr Disraeli. During the ceremony the Prince planted a *Sequoiadendron giganteum*, watched proudly no doubt by the entire Veitch family. Did anyone spare a thought for William Lobb languishing in his final years in California?

This Royal event sealed the Society's recovery and membership rock-eted, with nearly a third of the new Fellows being women. In September a dahlia show was held in the new Kensington garden and the Veitch Royal Exotic Nursery showed some 'sumptuous specimens'. But the most admired exhibit was a superb pot-grown specimen of William Lobb's *Lapageria rosea*, owned by the Dowager Duchess of Northumberland, which clambered over a huge trellis, smothered with countless flowers. The Victorian passion for pursuing their entertainment in pleasure gardens and at exhibitions was becoming a tempting source of revenue for the Society. The need for funds and the Prince's passion for things 'artistic' was pulling the Society in a different direction to its original aims of promoting horticultural science, research and education. In his speech opening the new garden, Prince Albert had referred to the valuable attempt to re-unite the science and art of gardening to the sister arts of Architecture, Sculpture and Painting. To this end, fountains, bronze statues and *objets d'art* were bought by the Royal Horticultural Society's new Fine Art Committee and musical promenades and 'tea parties' were organised by its Music Committee.

In December 1861 the Prince Consort died of typhoid fever. Before withdrawing into deep mourning, Queen Victoria announced her intention to keep the Kensington garden under her personal patronage and protection in memory of her beloved Albert. But a large number of Fellows and members of the Council, especially James Junior, had become alarmed by the drift away from horticulture and by the huge costs of the 'arts' and entertainment attractions at Kensington. Experimental work continued in the reduced trial gardens at Chiswick, where talks and lectures were still held, but they were not so well attended as the more popular attractions at the Kensington garden. In the following year a Fellow wrote to the *Gardener's Chronicle* reminding members that the Society was formed 'for the purpose of the Improvement of Horticulture in all its branches, ornamental as well as useful' and he queried how this was reconciled with the 'feats of Mumbo Jumbo, tight rope dancers, blazing burgees, Brigands and all the other vulgar absurdities which have so intensely disgusted of late that public which has really at heart the improvement of Horticulture'. James Junior's own uncompromising nature and capacity for loudly expressed indignation reached boiling point and in November 1863 he resigned from the Council.

Despite his impatience with matters of administration and finance, James Junior thrived in committees and meetings where he was an imposing and irritable presence. When any kind of horticultural or botanical question was debated, he would be in the thick of it. He held regular social evenings at Stanley House which went on into the small hours as learned men sat smoking, talking and drinking around the dining table, while occasionally small processions sortied into the night with a glass of port and a glowing cigar to explore the nursery glasshouses in search of a leaf or bud of some specimen to prove a point or simply to admire and discuss a new or particularly interesting plant. Harry and John Gould, when they were still teenagers, remembered these evenings with some amusement: '. . . we used to get tired of hearing the numerous conversations about the Society and when those discussions began we used to imitate the turning of the handle of a barrel-organ.'

Stanley House became a Mecca for men of science and horticulture from several countries and many new schemes were discussed or concocted in the parlour.

NEW COLLECTORS

The premises of the Royal Exotic Nursery at Chelsea were extremely restricted and could never be more than a showcase and shop for the Veitch stock. After the successful purchase of the small Fulham fruit gardens, James Junior decided it was necessary to find larger grounds in the suburbs where plant stock could be cultivated. Thirty-five acres of land were leased from the estate of the Dukes of Cambridge at Coombe Wood on Kingston Hill, just a few miles beyond Putney Bridge, and at the south end of the King's Road known as 'World's End'. The Coombe Wood nursery was to become as famous as the show nursery at Chelsea. The successful raising and marketing of a great variety of trees and shrubs was partly due to its unique position and soil with varying aspects of slopes and hollows, different soil types and temperatures. It was also free from London smog. The grounds were dug over, prepared and planted with rows of young trees and shrubs, then a long avenue of Monkey-puzzle trees and fine specimens of *Sequoiadendron giganteum* as well as William Lobb's conifers to advertise the exciting and unique collection of Veitch evergreens.

Increasing numbers of Veitch men, trained in the nursery grounds at Exeter and Coombe Wood and the glasshouses at Chelsea, were now going out to important posts around the world. But those who stayed, such as the Lobb brothers, John Dominy and John Seden, found opportunities to show their skills in the Veitch nurseries as nurserymen or as collectors. One such was Richard Pearce from Plymouth, a cheerful, good-looking and intelligent young man who had worked at the Pontey nursery before entering service with Veitch where he had trained under Thomas Lobb in 1858. Pearce

Richard Pearce (c1836–1868)

soon caught the collecting bug from Lobb, who showed him how to dry specimens and pack plants. Pearce persuaded James to replace the errant William with himself and early in 1859 he was packed off to South America where he made two fruitful expeditions to Chile, Peru and Bolivia. His orders were to look for hardy trees and shrubs, stove and greenhouse plants and orchids, and to collect more seeds of William Lobb's introductions, including the Monkey-puzzle tree and *Lapageria rosea*. Pearce also found the much rarer and stunning looking *L. alba*. Victorians were becoming keen on unusually grained and coloured South American wood for furniture and panelling and Pearce was particularly instructed to find seeds of the tree from which it was believed the famous Alerze timber was produced. It was through his diligent research that the tree, *Fitzroya patagonica*, was identified.

Unlike the Lobbs, Pearce wrote lively descriptions of his travels. While exploring the Cordilleras, he described the contrast between the gentle, undulating meadows and placid lakes with the surrounding mountains and their 'foaming cataracts, deep gorges and frightful precipices, over which tumble numerous dark, picturesque waterfalls reaching the bottom in a cloud of spray'. Nor did he find the vegetation any less beautiful or interesting:

At an elevation of 4,000 ft, the vegetation exhibits a totally different character from that of the coast. Here one finds Antarctic beeches (*Fagus antarctica* and *F. betuloides*) which constitute with *Fitzroya patagonica* the large forest trees. The *Embothrium coccineum, Desfontainia spinosa, Philesia buxifolia*, three species of berberis, pernettya and gaultheria are the most abundant of the flowering shrubs, whilst the numerous pretty little rock-plants meet one at every step with their various forms and colours.

In Chile, Pearce collected seeds of one of his most glorious finds, *Eucryphia glutinosa*. One of the few trees that can be found flowering in midsummer in English gardens with its huge, pure white blossoms and deep golden stamens, it quickly became a popular specimen tree in many gardens. Pearce

found the bright green Chilean
or Plum-fruited yew, *Prumnopitys
elegans*, and another small tree,
Azara microphylla, bearing tiny
polished evergreen leaves and
small vanilla-scented, fluffy yellow
flowers. Down on the plains near
Valdivia, he found an unusual
berberis with globose yellow
flowers, and in the forests, the
coral plant *Berberidopsis corallina*
with flowers similar to those of
the berberis. At the year's end
Pearce sailed home with six large
cases of plants and huge quanti-

Eucryphia glutinosa

ties of seeds. James Veitch was extremely pleased with his new collector,
who had shown great skill as well as 'energy and daring'.

Whilst in Chile, Pearce found a pretty purple daisy, *Perezia viscosa*, a
golden flax, *Linum chamissonis*, and the striking orange daisy-flowered
'climbing Gazania', *Mutisia decurrens*. He collected the tufted yellow *Mimulus
cupreus* which became the parent of many hybrids and a new creeping
ourisia, *O. pearcei* with crimson, blood-red-streaked tubular flowers. In the
spring of 1862 Pearce travelled north to Peru and Bolivia in search of stove
and greenhouse plants, and especially handsome foliage plants. He found
Calathea veitchiana, the handsome *Maranta veitchii* and *Dieffenbachia pearcei*,
all of which became very popular.

Meanwhile Thomas Lobb had set out on his last expedition to the Far East
to collect more orchids and new ferns for the fernery house at Chelsea. It
proved a valuable trip, producing many good ferns, including new species
of davallia. From North Borneo came the magnificent *Alocasia lowii* var.
veitchii which James Junior exhibited at Ghent where it received the highest
award for new foliage plants. Lobb also hoped to collect the extraordinary
giant *Nepenthes rajah* which Hugh Low had first found in 1851 after heavily
bribing the local people to help him locate it. Thomas Lobb also tried to
climb the mountain where the pitcher plant was thought to be, but having
no gifts to offer, he was turned back by the hostile natives and *N. rajah*
grew on undisturbed for more than twenty-five years until another Veitch

collector reached it. From Burma came an unusual variegated fern and a new rhododendron, *Rhododendron lobbii*, with bright scarlet, tubular flowers. At some time on his travels Thomas badly injured his leg and in May 1859 he was forced to return home. He was on duty at the Veitch stand at the summer Horticultural Society show where he and his plants drew large crowds but as he was a shy man of few words, he allowed the plants to speak for themselves. His leg was painful and had not healed properly and so as soon as the show stands were packed away, Thomas went home to Cornwall to live with his sister, Jane Mitchell, and her family.

The house standing in the Coombe Wood grounds was used as a country retreat by James Junior and Harriott. Their children were now nearly grown up. The eldest, John Gould, had studied botany at University College and was an extremely bright and personable young man, fluent in French and German, cheerful, charming and very handsome. Harry was sent at the age of fourteen to Germany to learn the language and then went on to train in the famous horticultural nursery of Vilmorin-Andrieux in Paris. Arthur, who was still at school, seemed headed for the business side of things. John Gould's interests were clearly more in botany than commercial horticulture and he particularly admired Joseph – now Sir Joseph – Hooker and longed to emulate his travels and plant-collecting achievements. James Junior, who saw the perfect opportunity to send his own 'Chelsea' collector, willingly acquiesced to John Gould's entreaties to be allowed to travel. In 1860, after much deliberation and careful planning, it was arranged that he would travel to the almost unknown Japan.

Before he left, John Gould visited his grandparents in Exeter to say goodbye. Both were unwell, particularly James, whose health had deteriorated badly, confining him to his house. Nevertheless, he still kept involved, writing endless letters, and recommending his trained gardeners – 'one to go to India to make new plantations'.

CHAPTER EIGHT

A VEITCH IN JAPAN

Nature seems to have united in Japan the beautiful with the astonishing . . . so fond are they of flowers, that all their females are known by names taken from the most beautiful of them.
Samuel Curtis, *Monograph on the Genus Camellia*, 1819

JAPAN HAS ALWAYS been a country of mystery and paradox, both beautiful and violent. In 1693, Japan had closed its borders, permitting only the Chinese and Dutch some restricted trade. It was a German physician, Englebert Kaempfer, employed by the Dutch East India Company in the 1690s at their trading post on the tiny island of Deshima, who first discovered Japan's horticultural treasure house. It was compulsory to make an annual 'Embassy' or pilgrimage with lavish gifts to the Royal Court in Yeddo (Tokyo) and the long and heavily guarded journey offered an opportunity to botanise along the way although actual collecting was forbidden. Kaempfer carried on his horse a very large 'Javan box' which he took great risks in secretly filling with plants, flowers and the seeds of trees such as ornamental maples.

Eighty-five years later a Swede, Carl Peter Thunberg, was similarly employed and found conditions not much better. He was reduced to searching for seeds of wild flowers in the hay sent in to feed the horses. What both men noticed was that the ordinary Japanese people (unlike the feudal princes or *daimyos*, who swore to massacre all foreigners) were curious but friendly, loved their rich landscape of trees and flowers and were keen gardeners. They also learned that Japan already had a large number of thriving horticultural nurseries. After smuggling home as many of the scarcest and most interesting specimens as they could, both men returned to their own countries and published their *Flora Japonica*, which included the first descriptions of many species of shrubs and plants then unknown in Europe – aucuba, skimmia, hydrangea, chimonanthus, bamboos and gingko, and numerous new varieties of lilies, magnolias, prunus, azaleas, camellia and tree peonies. It was an astonishing revelation to gardeners in Europe.

In 1826 another German, Dr Philipp Franz von Siebold, took up the position with the Dutch East India Company and found restrictions still in force. A skilled eye surgeon, 'arrogant, power-loving and unscrupulous', Siebold's main interests were in politics and ethnology – and he may have been a spy. He was also a keen plant collector and used his visits to patients as a pretext for botanising as well as acquiring information about Japanese customs, economics and politics. Siebold was caught in possession of forbidden maps and expelled from the country but took with him a large consignment of plants which he had prepared for shipping in the Dutch-owned gardens at Deshima. In Holland he got himself a favoured position in the Dutch East India Company and used it to bring more Japanese plants back to Holland where he set up his own nursery business, Siebold & Co., selling to gardeners clamouring for exclusive new 'oriental' plants.

News of these new plants spread like wildfire around Europe and nurseries vied with each other to obtain as much of this scarce flora as they could. European demands for trade with Japan increased until the Japanese government realised their policy of isolation was untenable. In 1854, a treaty was signed, opening two ports for trade. Always alert to every opportunity, James Veitch had immediately arranged to buy some Japanese plants which Thomas Lobb shipped home. Later, further ports and consulates were estab-

lished, though travel inland remained restricted. The opening of Japan had begun and nurseries rushed to send in their plant collectors. With their usual entrepreneurial flair, the Veitch nurseries sent in the first collector on 20 July 1860, the twenty-one-year-old 'brilliant young botanist' John Gould Veitch.

In April of that year, Dr Lindley echoed Sir Joseph Hooker's disquiet about the failure of English scientific establishments to act quickly, when he wrote of John Gould in the *Gardener's Chronicle*:

John Gould (1839–1870)

As soon as he ascertained Japan was open he eagerly sought the means of proceeding thither – under the protection of powerful persons in this country . . . It will be seen that he will soon have skimmed the cream of the flora and those who follow him will have little novelty to gather. Thus we shall again see the value of private enterprise in English hands, and how far more efficient it proves than missions entrusted to mere Government agents.

John Gould's journey got off to a bad start when his ship the *Malabar* was wrecked off Ceylon and he lost all his equipment. He found another passage with a P&O ship and finally arrived in Nagasaki via Hong Kong, Canton and Shanghai. He wrote home requesting a new set of instruments, but he had some difficulty in getting new glass cases made: 'they think me mad to try and send plants to England in this manner.' His letters to his parents were full of youthful humour, confidence and enthusiasm for Japan, its scenery and its people. Nagasaki had the 'finest scenery I have ever met with, surrounded by mountains covered to the top with vegetation'. Everything was so fresh to the eye and so exciting.

Japanese officialdom, however, was unpleasant and government officers routinely spied on each other, making it impossible to deal with them. Restrictions were still in force and a ten-mile limit was set on trips out of town. But the people were obliging and helpful and John Gould made great efforts to learn the language, which he claimed was quite easy to pick up. He thought Japanese women were friendly, contented and not at all shy. They were quite open about looking at him and admiring his clothes but they did not like European whiskers, particularly John Gould's bushy, long black 'wheepers', and they begged him to cut them off and 'be like Japanese men'. The ladies spent many hours having their glossy, jet-black hair professionally dressed in many different ways including the latest 'tea-pot fashion'.

As was the practice for the handful of foreigners who had already arrived, John Gould obtained safe lodgings in a Buddhist temple where he was pleased to find three other Englishmen who all turned out to be 'Devonshire men'. He had a small room, about ten feet by six, with a Chinese servant to cook for him. One of his new friends, Mr Rice, 'brother to the musician at Exeter', proved to be especially helpful in caring for John Gould's plants whenever he was away. John Gould persuaded the monks to let him use part of the large temple garden where he prepared the ground to keep his plant collection. He built a bamboo shed covered with oiled paper to protect them from the summer sun and from wind and rain in the colder months.

As it was mid-summer and no ripe seeds could be collected, John Gould decided to collect some living plants and to find and note the localities where interesting trees were growing in order to return to them later for their seeds. Travel outside the ten-mile limit was impossible but he seemed confident that he could find plenty of good things despite the restrictions imposed on his collecting activities. He rambled 'without fear' over the hills within the permitted neighbourhood carrying his baskets and cases, collecting plants of the more common species such as camellias, viburnum, *Aralia sieboldi* and some bamboos and hardy ferns.

He was becoming quite accustomed to the customs of the people. The locals were friendly and would call out cheerful greetings to him. The children pestered him for English buttons which were very popular, while the adults invited him into their homes to drink their refreshing and delicious tea. They showed him their wood houses with floors of bamboo matting and strange pillows and were happy to let him look around their gardens, pleased to give him any plant that took his fancy. John Gould found an endless variety of plants in the towns as 'the Japanese are great lovers of flowers and shrubs and I find quantities of plants grown by them in their gardens which I never see growing wild, nor can I ascertain where they are to be had in a wild state'. He potted up about fifty plants and put them in the safety of the temple garden where, he wrote with a hint of homesickness, 'I almost fancy myself at Chelsea while I am watering them' and he tried to reassure his mother that he was 'as comfortable as I possibly can be away from home'. The priests were particularly kind and took a great interest in his plant collecting. 'Scarcely a day passing without their bringing me some novelty in their eyes. I always received their presents and thank them very much although I generally throw them away afterwards.'

John Gould was eager to move on to the region of Yeddo (Tokyo) where he believed the vegetation would be much more varied and interesting and he was keen to find specimens of the scarcer conifers there. He got a berth on a 'man of war' steaming up the Inland Sea to Yokohama. His only regret at leaving Nagasaki was not having received any letters from home.

Sir Rutherford Alcock, the British Consul-General, sent John Gould an invitation to join him on the first permitted European expedition to the summit of Mount Fusi Yama (Fuji) the 'sacred Mountain' where thousands of Japanese pilgrims travelled every year 'for deliverance from sickness and misfortune' (though women were allowed only once in every sixty years).

Araucaria araucana. The Monkey-puzzle or Chilean Pine. Many of the oldest specimens still alive in England today can be traced to William Lobb's seed collection of 1844.

Hamamelis mollis. The Chinese Witch-Hazel. One of our most popular winter flowering shrubs. Found in China by Charles Maries but 'lost' in the Veitch nursery for twenty years.

Aeschynanthus speciosus. One of several aeschynanthus introduced by Thomas Lobb on his travels; he found *A.speciosus* in 1846 in the mountains of Java growing on the trunks of forest trees.

Berberis darwinii. Introduced in 1849 by William Lobb from Chiloe, an island off the south coast of Chile. It remains the best known of all the berberis species.

Lilium auratum. The Golden-rayed Lily. One of the plants of which the Veitch nursery was most proud. This 'aristocrat of lilies' was sent from Japan by John Gould Veitch in 1862.

Vanda caerulea. The Blue Orchid. This 'fabulous' orchid, introduced by Thomas Lobb from India in 1850, was the cause of considerable ill-feeling between the Hooker and Veitch families.

Rhododendron vernicosum. Wilson collected over forty species of rhododendrons during his travels in China which, he wrote . . . 'should be a most welcome addition to English gardens.'

Cerasus pseudo-cerasus var. 'James H. Veitch'. James Herbert's order of flowering cherry trees from nurseries in Japan started a popular trend in English gardens which still endures.

Primula obconica. Collected by Charles Maries during his unhappy expedition to the Yangtze Gorges in China in 1878. One of many primulas also collected by Ernest Wilson and William Purdom.

Cattleya x dominana (C. x dominiyii). John Dominy's third historic hybrid orchid raised in Exeter in 1850. Described in *Hortus Veitchii* as one of the 'grandest' of all hybrid cattleyas.

Davidia involucrata. The Handkerchief or Dove Tree. This spectacular and unusual tree is one of Ernest Wilson's most famous introductions for the Veitch nursery from China in 1900.

Begonia pearcei. Found by William Pearce in La Paz, Peru in 1865. The second of his famous begonias which became the wild ancestors of many modern hybrid tuberous begonias.

Cantua buxifolia (C. dependens). The 'Magic Tree'. This beautiful evergreen half-hardy shrub was sent from Peru by William Lobb and flowered for the first time in Exeter in May 1848.

1. ARALIA VEITCHII.   3. ADIANTUM PERUVIANUM.
2. PANDANUS VEITCHII.   4. BEGONIA SEDENII
            5. TODEA WILKESIANA

Pollett, Horticultural Printer.   Bridgewater Gardens Barkham

Two colourful selections of Veitch plants offered for sale in their catalogue of the 1890s including several varieties of exotic-looking foliage plants.

1. CROTON VEITCHII.   4. RHODODENDRON LOBBI.   7. DRACÆNA MOOREI.   10. ORTHOSIPHON STAMINENS.
2. CROTON CORNUTUM.   5. DRACÆNA CHELSONI.   8. BEGONIA SEDENI.   11. DAVALLIA MOOREI.
3. CROTON UNDULATUM.   6. DRACÆNA ALBICANS.   9. ARALIA OSYANA.   12. ADIANTUM RUBELLUM.
                              13. BLANDFORDIA AUREA.

H.M. POLLETT. LONDON.

Viburnum fragrans (V. farreri). Still much loved for its fragrant winter flowers, it was found by William Purdom in 1911 growing in a temple garden in Minchow, China.

Sir William Hooker had written to Alcock to say that British botanists were very anxious to learn about the flora of Japan, particularly the mountainous region of 'Fusiyama . . . of which absolutely nothing is known'. As only official foreigners could travel, Alcock appointed John Gould 'Botanist to her Britannic Majesty's Legation at Jeddo' and with this honorary status John Gould wrote jovially, 'I at once grew six inches taller.'

The expedition had grown to a 'cortège of a hundred persons', included eight Europeans from the Legation travelling on ponies accompanied by armed guards, twenty Japanese officials and their attendants, including umbrella and spear bearers, and the ubiquitous 'ometsky' or spy. Alcock had hoped for something a little more informal and intimate; instead everywhere they went the local people turned out along the road 'to behold the foreigners'. But the journey proceeded uneventfully and John Gould was amazed by the immense variety and dense mass of luxuriant trees, including stately avenues of pines and the huge and majestic Cedar of Japan, *Cryptomeria japonica*, which he believed was the most magnificent tree in Japan, growing alongside all the principal roads. Across the hillsides and along the river banks grew luxuriant foliage, forests of conifers and broadwoods covered in rich autumnal tints mingled with wild hydrangea, smothered in huge clusters of white and lilac flowers, and tall, graceful bamboo. Although they were not allowed to stray far from the prescribed route, John Gould still managed to return from his brief forays laden with ferns, bamboo and seedling trees, including *Thujopsis dolabrata*, one of the protected 'five trees of Kiso' which Thunberg had enthusiastically described many years earlier and which John Gould alone would have recognised, since the only known European specimen grew in his father's nursery. (It had been part of James Veitch's Japanese purchases six years earlier and was growing well.)

When John Gould excitedly showed *Thujopsis dolabrata* to Alcock, who knew little about botany, the Consul-General expressed some disappointment but tactfully suggested that perhaps Thunberg's admiration had been so great that disappointment was inevitable. He did, however, concede that it was 'a noble tree of the pine species, with unique silver lining . . . but scarcely calculated to throw any but a botanist . . . or the first to discover it, into ecstasies!'

Along the way, John Gould collected ripe cones and seeds from conifers growing in gardens near the 'flea-ridden' resthouses and temples which proved a rich source of plants, including the venerable-looking Temple juniper, *Juniperus rigida*. He never failed to express his admiration of Japanese horticultural skill, particularly in one monastery garden where he saw conifers, aucuba, maples, azaleas and an interesting new species of magnolia set among 'waterfalls all blended together with exquisite taste and without formal appearance'. Every house, it seemed, had a garden, however small, like a miniature imitation of a wilderness, with dwarfed trees, rockwork, a mini-lake and lawn. Plants were brought from many parts of the country and high prices were often paid for rare specimens.

Climbing the sacred mountain was not too arduous although it rained heavily and the ponies had to wear straw shoes to prevent them slipping. At one temple they were welcomed by priests in their saffron robes where 'great preparations had been made' and they enjoyed a hot saline bath and cold douche which 'soon refreshed us'. When they finally reached the summit, the party indulged in typical Victorian-British insensitivity by hoisting the Union Jack on a make-shift pole, firing a twenty-one gun salute with their revolvers, drinking to the health of Her Most Gracious Majesty and shouting 'God Save the Queen'. They then descended in a 'thick Scotch mist'.

John Gould and Rutherford Alcock ascending Mount Fuji. From Alcock's *Capital of the Tycoons*

During his trip to Mount Fuji, John Gould discovered a new variety of the Japanese cedar, *Cryptomeria japonica* var. *elegans* as well as four new pines, including the red-barked pine, *Pinus densiflora*, which he found growing in huge plantations on granite and volcanic debris high on the slopes of Mount Fuji. Its resin was used to heal wounds and sores and cure lung disorders. He also took seeds of the Japanese larch, *Larix kaempferi*, which has become one of Britain's favourite larches, and another tree valued for its beautiful wood, the Japanese elm. He sent home cones of the Sawara cypress and the huge Hinoki cypress, *Chamaecyparis obtusa* which the Japanese consecrated to the Goddess of the Sun for its valuable wood, used in building temples and making highly polished bowls and fans using slips of the wood held together by fine, silken thread. His most interesting discovery was the rare pyramidal 'Parasol Fir' or Umbrella pine, *Sciadopitys verticillata*. A remarkable tree, des-

Sciadopitys verticillata

cribed as one of the finest conifers in all Asia, it derives its name from having leaves in dense whorls like the struts of an umbrella and is the only species yet discovered.

John Gould was taking quite a risk in collecting and sending out of the country seed of so many trees that were highly valued for their timber and rigorously protected. Of one in particular, a silver fir which Dr Lindley named *Abies veitchii*, John Gould could send only an herbarium specimen. (Live cones were eventually returned by another Veitch collector, Charles Maries, in 1878.) Obliged to travel with an escort, it was tantalising to ride past trees and shrubs loaded with seeds and not be able to stop and gather them. Instead Gould sent out native collectors with drawings to illustrate what he required.

John Gould began making a collection of different kinds of timber trees which would be the 'first of the kind made in Japan' and, most significantly, he wrote that in his opinion most trees grown in Japan 'would flourish in European gardens and would prove of sufficient hardiness to withstand the most severe of our winters where they will flourish as luxuriantly as they do in Japan'. John Gould's collection was quite the largest and most valuable received by any British nursery at the time. No fewer than seventeen new conifers arrived at the Veitch nursery including, apart from those already mentioned, the Japanese Fir, *Abies firma*, Alcock's Spruce, *Picea bicolor* (previously known as *P. alcockiana*), the Tiger-tail spruce, *P. polita*, and the Hondo Spruce, *P. jesoensis*, the Japanese Black and White Pines, *P. thunbergii* and *P. parviflora, Juniperus chinensis* 'Aurea', and the cedars, *Chamaecyparis obtusa* and *C. pisifera* 'Squarrosa'.

Magnolia stellata

But some of John Gould's most valued garden contributions were two of today's favourite magnolias, *M. liliflora* 'Nigra' and the lovely star-shaped *M. stellata*, plus a number of beautiful Japanese maples such as the attractive and popular *Acer palmatum*. He introduced the Boston or Japanese ivy, first named *Ampelopsis veitchii*, and now known as *Parthenocissus tricuspidata*, which can be seen covering houses and walls all over Britain and North America where it is particularly popular. He sent home some lovely primulas such as *P. amoena, P. cortusoides* and *P. japonica*. But perhaps his most exciting find was the great Golden-ray lily, *Lilium auratum*, which caused a sensation when it was first exhibited at South Kensington in July 1862 where, according to Dr Lindley, 'some ten thousand eyes beheld it', the ladies gasped and men took off their hats (see colour-plate section).

After a short trip north, John Gould returned to Tokyo and stayed at the British Legation. When he heard that Japanese fruit and vegetables were considered to be insipid and flavourless, he happily set about laying out a vegetable garden 'on English principles' in the Legation grounds and planted vegetable seeds sent out from Veitch's Exeter nursery. Meanwhile, in his official role as 'Legation Botanist' he was asked to pack up cases of plants for Kew and for Queen Victoria's gardens at Osborne on the Isle of Wight. Sir William Hooker wrote that he was particularly interested in 'some curious dwarfed things' found in the packages sent to Osborne. One was a tiny *Thujopsis dolabrata* and also a podocarpus, 'the whole tree not a foot and a half high, quite covered with innumerable little crooked branches'. These dwarf trees or bonsai soon became quite a novelty, much sought after and very expensive. John Gould found it 'quite astonishing to see that amount of industry and perseverance which the Japanese must have devoted to the production of these ancient, miniature firs and pines'.

The British Legation in Tokyo was filling up with foreigners eager to benefit from the partial opening of Japan. A Prussian expedition arrived with a German collector and John Gould's knowledge of German was put

to good use. His energy and youthful sense of fun made him particularly welcome in the semi-confinement of the Legation. He helped create a comic newspaper, the *Illustrated Fuji Yama Gazette*, in which everyone was caricatured, especially John Gould: 'I am represented with a specimen case on my shoulders with trees, etc. growing from all parts of it.'

One particularly eminent guest who arrived in November was Robert Fortune, one of the greatest in the long line of successful Scottish plant collectors. Fortune had already made three celebrated expeditions to China for the Horticultural Society. Now middle-aged, he had been in Japan for about a month collecting for the nursery of John Standish of Bagshot in Surrey, a close rival of the Veitches in collecting and selling new plants from the Far East. Fortune had been visiting the elderly Siebold who had been allowed to return to Japan and was living in his house near Nagasaki where he kept a small nursery. Fortune, like John Gould, was adept at using his charm and good manners to get around travel restrictions to visit numerous nurseries and private gardens. Both collectors found baskets of plants brought to the Legation by gardeners who had heard of their activities: 'it was seldom that I did not find something amongst them of an ornamental or useful character that was new to our English gardens,' wrote Fortune.

John Gould, who had been in Japan rather longer than Fortune, was busy preparing and packing his collection for his return home. When Fortune put his own collection on board the SS *England* bound for Shanghai, he found John Gould's plants already installed. He wrote that by the time the ship left port

the whole poop was lined with glass cases crammed full of the natural productions of Japan. Never before had such an interesting and valu- able collection of plants occupied the deck of any vessel, and most

devoutly did we hope that our beloved plants might be favoured with
fair winds and smooth seas, and with as little salt water as possible –
a mixture to which they are not at all partial, and which sadly disagrees
with their constitutions.

Fortune's collections arrived home in such good condition that Standish
was able to exhibit some of the plants at the Horticultural Society a few
days later, looking 'as if they had been luxuriating in the pure air of Bagshot
all their lives'. Among the conifers some confusion arose as to which were
Fortune and which Veitch discoveries, especially John Gould's *Sciadopitys verticillata* and *Thujopsis dolobrata* which *The Times* attributed to Robert Fortune.
With characteristic fury James Junior wrote a letter making it clear that these
trees and many other new conifers had been introduced by his son for the
Veitch nursery, the first seeds having arrived in England in September of the
previous year, 'nearly a month before Mr Fortune reached Japan'. While
collectors in the field were often happy to co-operate and keep good relations, the horticultural nurseries for whom they worked were not.

John Gould did not return home with his plants as expected. His father
had written to tell him that, because Thomas Lobb had injured his leg and
been forced to return home early, he was to go on to the Philippines for
a further six months where he would collect phalaenopsis, the native orchids
of the islands which were then extremely rare in European glasshouses. He
arrived in Manila before the rainy season and almost immediately experienced a violent earthquake, 'an extraordinary phenomenon, which made
the river heave and boil like a simmering cauldron and the riverbed rose
up'. He found the dense vegetation totally different from anything he had
met with before. The heat was terrible, the 'natives' friendly but lazy and
his lack of Spanish a drawback. But, he wrote, his searches in the islands
for orchids gave him the unique experience of a real jungle 'which one
requires to see in order properly to appreciate it'. More importantly, he
learned some valuable lessons about the habits and cultivation of orchids
by seeing them grow in the wild. He wrote to Dr Joseph Hooker:

I felt convinced in my own mind that our greatest mistake in England
is that we confine the roots too much and keep them in a random
state. I never met with a good specimen in any other position than
where the water (rain or otherwise) will immediately run off.

Phalaenopsis particularly will not bear their roots being covered and sodden.

He was also surprised to find many orchids had adapted to higher altitudes than had been thought possible and he collected some fine specimens, among them *Phalaenopsis amabalis*. He was thrilled to discover a new orchid, *Cypripedium philippinense*, growing on rocks by the seashore on the island of Guimares. Despite one shipment of Philippine plants being lost, John Gould successfully shipped home a large and important collection of orchids as well as many attractive foliage plants which he found flourishing in the tropical climate. Included among them was a particularly fine species of alocasia, *A. zebrina*, its huge green arrow-shaped leaves on long stalks, beautifully marbled and mottled with dark green on a yellowish-green ground.

When John Gould returned to Japan in time for the seed season in 1861, he found a very different state of affairs. The British Legation in Tokyo had been attacked by one of the many feudal princes who continued to hold a fanatical hatred of all foreigners. Two Englishmen had been severely injured. John Gould described the violent scene with walls still smeared with blood, furniture and bedding hacked, books cut through with sabres and house screens and mosquito nets slashed to shreds. The situation was still so dangerous that 500 Japanese soldiers were guarding the compound. John Gould found Richard Oldham, a young and inexperienced collector sent out by Kew, frightened and keen to go home, but busy preparing dried specimens. The elderly Siebold was also taking temporary shelter there: 'he appears to be annoyed at so many Englishmen coming here collecting.'
  John Gould seemed impervious to danger and continued buying plants from outlying nurseries, accompanied by mounted and armed guards. He wrote of his admiration for Japanese nurseries: 'I was more impressed than ever with the enormous extent of ground devoted to the culture of plants . . . the Japanese must be great amateur gardeners, and large sums must be spent annually to support such numerous establishments.' He gazed at hundreds of pots of gorgeously coloured and shaped chrysanthemums which he felt sure 'would not disgrace even a London exhibition' and he noted that the Japanese preferred evergreens, conifers and plants with variegated foliage that could be enjoyed all year rather than flowering plants. He was impressed by the order and cleanliness in the nurseries and the arrangement of different species of plants classed by themselves, 'so that one can see at a glance the

extent of the whole collection'. Unlike English nurserymen, who seemed bent on cut-throat rivalry and secrecy, John Gould observed that the proprietors of the different nurseries in Japan seemed to get on well. They did, however, appear to have one thing in common: 'they are invariably unanimous, viz., to get as much out of the *Tōjen* (foreigner) as they can!'

In the autumn of 1861 John Gould stayed in Yokohama where he packed up his final collection of plants and seeds, including some new conifers and bamboos. So much had changed during his six-month absence from the port where a large European settlement had risen, no doubt, to the consternation of the Japanese authorities. Sir Rutherford Alcock was there waiting for his battered residence in Tokyo to be rebuilt. Everyone, wrote John Gould, feared more violence: 'The Japanese do not, or will not understand that foreign nations are equal to themselves and must be treated as such. The Minister's tasks here are not easy, and no one envies Mr Alcock's position. We have two men-of-war here now.'

With relief but also regret, John Gould set sail from Japan one bright November evening. He took his last sight of Mount Fuji, its glittering cone of snow towering in the distance far above the surrounding ranges of hills, glowing, as the sun set behind it, in its solitary grandeur.

After his return to England John Gould began to suffer from increasing bouts of ill-health. Whether he knew that he had tuberculosis is not known, but he threw himself into work with his characteristic enthusiasm. His family, especially his younger brother Harry who was training in the nursery, was thrilled to see him safely home and their father made them both partners in the firm. John Gould spent long hours in the grounds at Coombe Wood, sorting and cultivating plants and seeds from his Japanese and Philippine collections. At Chelsea, an entire glasshouse was filled with the Japanese golden-ray lily, *Lilium auratum*, that was causing such a stir: 'If ever a flower merited the name of glorious it is this, which stands far above all other Lilies . . . its perfume of Orange blossoms sufficient to fill a large room, but so delicate as to respect the weakest nerves.' Reporters fell over themselves in their efforts to describe this extraordinary new flower adequately:

> Imagine upon the end of a purple stem no thicker than a ramrod, and not above 2 feet high, a saucer-shaped flower at least 10 inches in diameter, composed of six spreading somewhat crisp parts rolled back at their points, and having an ivory white skin thinly strewn

with purple points of studs and oval or roundish prominent purple stains. To this add in the middle of each of the six parts a broad stripe of light, satiny yellow losing itself gradually in the ivory skin. Place the flower in a situation where side light is cut off, and no direct light can reach it except from above, when the stripes acquire the appearance of gentle streamlets of living Australian gold . . .

Although the lily was grown and displayed in a glasshouse, John Gould felt sure that it would prove hardy in England since it grew in regions of Japan experiencing as much as sixteen degrees of frost and he supervised the Veitch nurserymen in experimenting with its hardiness. For the Veitch Royal Exotic Nursery, *Lilium auratum* was already proving to be 'living gold'.

Another glasshouse in the Chelsea showrooms was filled with a display of richly coloured and textured foliage plants collected by Thomas Lobb and John Gould, including their extraordinary collections of alocasias from Borneo and the Philippines and a *Cyanophyllum magnificum* showing off its huge ribbed purple undersides and beautiful velvety gloss on the upper surfaces. The plants were shaded from the harmful rays of the sun by the spreading canopy of an *Allamanda schottii* trained along the roof. Yet another house kept pots of green-leaved, berry-bearing and variegated kinds of aucuba which were quite new to English gardens; 'when better known they cannot fail to occupy a front rank among hardy shrubs'.

While many young conifers were still protected under glass at John Gould's insistence, the majority were being successfully cultivated outdoors in the near perfect conditions at Coombe Wood. In less than a year, this young man had introduced to the British Isles a selection of the most remarkable, beautiful and – as he had correctly predicted – hardy conifers. No nursery played a more important role in the introduction of conifers to English gardens than James Veitch & Son through their collectors William Lobb and John Gould Veitch.

Veitch's wasted no time in advertising their new hardy Japanese conifers as soon as they were in a saleable state and in sufficient quantity: 'The Royal Exotic Nurseries, Exeter and Chelsea [offer plants] . . . potted singly, and although necessarily at present small, are sufficiently established to travel with perfect safety.'

The advertisement also promised that a number of other fine things were being raised, foremost amongst them the Umbrella pine, fast becoming as sought after as William Lobb's 'Wellingtonia'. At Coombe Wood customers could also buy a selection of some of the most popular and now commonly grown hardy shrubs and plants brought home by John Gould. Despite his young age, he was already a celebrated collector, nurseryman and botanist of considerable distinction whose knowledge and advice was regularly sought. When Sir Rutherford Alcock returned to England and wrote about his three years' residence in Japan in his book, *The Capital of the Tycoons*, John Gould provided an appendix of trees and flora unique to Japan. He was invited to sit on the committee of the Botanical Congress formed before the opening of the International Horticultural Exhibition and for the first meeting a number of papers were read to which John Gould contributed. Despite the strong relationship forged by James senior and Sir William Hooker, Dr Joseph Hooker, who had succeeded his late father as Director of the Royal Botanic Garden at Kew, continued to resent the success of 'commercial ventures' against what he perceived as inadequate budgets and lower standards of government-funded botanical activities. There is an extraordinary and abject letter written by John Gould after his return from Japan dated 29 December 1866 in reply to a letter written on Christmas Eve by Dr Hooker in which he appears to have accused John Gould of failing to provide Kew with dried specimens from his expedition (which he was under no obligation to do.) John Gould wrote; 'I was much grieved to receive your letter . . . and can only assure you that you *wrong us* altogether, for our desire is, and always has been to assist Botany and Horticulture in any way in our power.' John Gould promised to send a few specimens made in Australia, but, he explained, many were burned in the ship (appropriately named *Fiery Star*) on the way home. 'As regards Japanese specimens,' he wrote, 'I have very few as most of my time was occupied with living plants and the reason that I saw *two* men collecting for you in Japan [one of whom was Richard Oldham] and I felt sure that you would receive far more than I could give you.' He pointed out that Dr Hooker already had a large herbarium of Japanese plants, 'and I felt ashamed to send the few I had.' He begged Hooker to forgive him. 'I trust you will accept this explanation and believe we are all very desirous to aid you in any way in our power, the more so as all our family always met with such kindness at your father's and your hands.'

In January 1863 James was making plans in Exeter to send Richard Pearce out again on another three-year contract to Peru. Several of Pearce's handsome foliage plants such as *Dieffenbachia pearcei* and *Calathea veitchiana*, collected in Ecuador on an earlier expedition, had proved so successful in the Chelsea showrooms that another South American venture was thought worthwhile. Pearce based himself in the Indian town of Cuzco from where he collected maidenhair ferns and new exotics such as sanchezias and a scarlet-orange aphelandra, *Aphelandra nitens*. Back in Exeter events took a terrible turn when on 7 May 1863, James's wife Rebecca died. For over thirty years Rebecca had selflessly cared for her dead sister's children and loyally supported her husband in his endeavours. He cannot have been an easy man to live with but she had shown patience, tolerance and a great love for him. A week later, James went into his beautiful garden at Graslawn, filled with so many memories and unique Veitch plants, to pick an armful of lilies to place on Rebecca's grave. Overcome with grief and distress, he collapsed with a heart attack and died.

James Junior wrote to Sir William Hooker on black-bordered paper that 'All of us mourn the loss of one of the best of men and the very best of parents'. Whether or not, by the standards of his age, he had been a good parent, James Veitch was one of the very best of nurserymen – a skilled and patient horticulturist, a pioneer of plant collecting and plant hybridisation, and a brilliant, entrepreneurial businessman. Without James Veitch there might never have been a story to tell.

The funerals of James and Rebecca were to be the last, sad family gatherings in Devon. Crowded into the small corner of Broadclyst churchyard where the Veitch graves lie, stood James Junior and Robert, with their families, along with many other members of the Veitch, Gould, Tosswill and Acland families as well as old friends, patrons, customers and nursery employees, including John Dominy and John Seden who carried James's coffin to the internment.

A year later almost to the day, forgotten and alone in San Francisco, William Lobb died of 'paralysis', or most probably, syphilis. William was arguably one of the finest but least-known of collectors who gave gardeners some of the most remarkable trees and loveliest plants ever grown. When he was buried in a public plot in Lone Mountain cemetery, there were no mourners. His headstone was moved in 1927 to South Ridge Lawn and later, in 1940, to a crypt at Cypress Lawn Cemetery by the California Academy of Sciences.

SOUTH SEA ADVENTURES

Like many plant collectors, John Gould could not stay still for long. This 'intelligent and adventurous traveller' was so infected by the 'spirit of enterprise and the desire for further important discoveries' that he longed to undertake another expedition. In the summer of 1864, a year after the deaths of his grandparents, John Gould sailed for Australia and the South Sea Islands, leaving Plymouth Sound for Sydney in the ship *La Hogue* along with many 'old Australian colonists returning home'. He was kept busy tending a collection of plants in Wardian cases destined for various friends and botanists in Australia. Early in November they berthed in Sydney where John Gould was disappointed to see the brown, burnt-up appearance of the surrounding country. When he visited the botanic gardens and nurseries, however, he was amazed to find plants which would be classed in Britain as stove, greenhouse, bedding and hardy all growing together in outdoor beds under the 'propitious climate'. Although impressed with one or two gardens which had fine collections from all over the world, John Gould was surprised at their limited number. It was, he supposed, because most people stayed in the colonies only long enough to 'realise a fortune' and then hurried home to enjoy it.

John Gould was invited to go on a cruise on HMS *Salamander* to explore the east coast of Australia where he found a rich collection of ferns, palms, and a few 'tree-perching orchids [dendrobiums]'. On Cape York they stayed at a newly-founded settlement where two men had been killed by the natives. Now well accustomed to danger, John Gould went out collecting accompanied by several aborigines who brought him plants and seeds in exchange for tobacco. He found some interesting new palms, and three species of Screw-pine as well as some foliage plants and ferns. He explored the numerous islands along the Great Barrier Reef, admiring the rich sea and wildlife, but saw few plants to excite him. He visited other regions of Australia, some of which were botanically exciting and some disappointing, and he complained that everywhere were 'the same brown dingy Gum-trees'.

The following June, John Gould joined a four-month Royal Navy excursion to the Polynesian and Melanesian Islands where, he believed, he would be the first person to collect living plants for introduction to Europe. The prospect of 'lighting for the first time upon some fine plant previously unknown to English gardens' was exciting and he prepared eight Wardian cases, took hatchets, knives, fish-hooks, red cloth, and much else 'to barter with the natives'.

He set sail with four other naturalists on the flagship 23-gun frigate HMS *Curaçao* where he was made an honorary member of the mess and became quite a favourite among the ward-room officers: it was, he wrote, 'a most agreeable, jovial party'.

After a visit to the hospitable but eccentric 'far-famed' Pitcairn Islanders on Norfolk Island who were making themselves at home in the old convict settlement, John Gould got down to some serious botanising and found a tree fern, numerous dwarf ferns and a relative of the Monkey-puzzle tree, the Norfolk Island pine (*Araucaria heterophylla*) which is now so popular in Mediterranean countries: 'The whole effect was so abundantly green in comparison to the dingy brown bush of Australia.' Before the *Curaçao* left Norfolk Island, a ball was held on board ship at which many of the young ladies 'were dressed in strict accordance with the latest fashions, even including crinolines'. They sailed on, calling in on a number of Polynesian and Samoan islands where they were greeted like tourists, bartering with native outriggers, entertained with feasting and war dances. They were treated to a 'genuine Polynesian dinner' consisting of a pig, yams and taro cooked in an oven of heated stones, washed down with plenty of kava, the native beverage. On one Samoan island John Gould found a rare new palm which was named after him, *Veitchia johannis*, a beautiful fan palm, *Pritchardia pacifica*, and some species of pandanaea, including *Pandanus veitchii*. The orchids were not, he thought, showy enough to be worthwhile but he did collect a rich supply of mosses and ferns, varieties of stately arums and some foliage plants such as a vast alocasia.

They sailed on to the Tongan Islands which, by contrast, were flat, civilised and full of missionaries. The islanders grew in their well-kept gardens a great variety of fruit and vegetables, delicate Chinese hibiscus, sweet-smelling gardenias and the attractively coloured foliage plant, *Croton variegatum*. Here, wrote John Gould, the main occupation seemed to be beating the bark of the Paper mulberry to make the native cloth.

Quite different to these peaceful scenes were the mountainous Islands of Fiji where Wesleyan missionaries were still attempting to stamp out the 'savage and barbarous vice of cannibalism'. Here John found the flora rich and varied and he collected some of the best species of palms, ferns and foliage plants.

On the Islands of the New Hebrides the native peoples were still active cannibals, and killing female babies and the old was a common practice. It was considered far too risky to venture out botanising, despite being able to see several new plants from the safety of the ship, including an unusual red-foliaged musa or banana tree. As in Japan, John Gould was frustrated by the sight of a land teeming with interesting vegetation, a rich botanical field which he was unable to visit because of the dangers. However, on one island he was allowed ashore to collect for a few hours, whilst a native chief was held on board ship as guarantee of his safety.

The Solomon Islands, 'the most interesting and peculiar group of islands', were rich in ornamental-foliaged plants while hoyas and other climbers overran the forests so vigorously that they had to hack their way through and wade in rivers and marshes up to their armpits. Here too John Gould was vexed by the sight of so many promising places which he was not able to explore properly because the 'natives were not friendly'. In his travel journal, published in the *Gardener's Chronicle*, John Gould wrote that when the South Sea Islands had been 'civilized' there would be a rich botanical harvest for some future traveller. At the end of this journey John Gould brought home a unique collection of foliage plants, some of which are still popular as house-plants, new ferns and palms and a few interesting orchids. His adventures and botanical studies had probably been more exciting than the commercial results of his collecting.

Compared to the Lobb brothers and other collectors who had struggled alone through appalling conditions and dangers to find plants in the wild, young John Gould's adventures were rather different. He was well educated, had extensive botanical training and very good connections. His youthful charm, good manners, knowledge of languages and intelligence gave him the advantage. He certainly had to suffer some discomfort and considerable danger. While some of his collections came from the wild, because of the restrictions in Japan and difficulties in Australia, many plants were bought from gardens or nurseries. Nevertheless, he made several important contributions to horticulture and botany and western gardens are the richer for many fine Japanese conifers, some beautiful acers such as *Acer palmatum*, the lovely *Magnolia stellata* and the magnificent golden-ray lily, *Lilium auratum*.

CHAPTER NINE

FAMILY AFFAIRS

'A tribute to botanical explorers is, we must say, well earned.
Of all the deadly occupations this is surely the most fatal.'
Gardener's Chronicle, 1858

FTER THE DEATH of his father, James Junior had hoped to set about arranging things in the way he wanted. But even in death his father seemed to thwart him. James had left the house, Graslawn, the 'Pleasure Gardens' and a large income to Rebecca. But because she had predeceased him, it was two years before his will received probate in 1865. Robert was given the right to purchase the nursery business in Exeter, its grounds, stock and considerable lands and properties at a fair price and on easy terms, but if he was not interested, it was to be offered to James Junior. The proceeds from the sale were to be split three ways between Robert, James Junior and John. Tightly controlled funds were left in trust to James's fourth surviving son, the 'worthless' Tom and his wife and child. James Junior inherited the portrait of his grandfather and his father's most prized possession, the silver salver won for his dahlias. After all the sales and legalities had been dealt with, James's estate was valued at £23,000, a huge sum in those days.

No mention is made in James's will of the Royal Exotic Nursery in Chelsea. It would appear that, after ten years, James Junior was the sole owner. Two years before James Senior's death, father and son had made an agreement regarding plants 'jointly introduced', and when matters were finally settled, James Junior hurried down to Exeter where he packed up and removed all the best nursery stock. He took John Dominy and John Seden back with him to Chelsea where he installed Dominy in the orchid house and put Seden in charge of the fern collection. Soon after, John Heal, another promising nurseryman whom James Senior had sent to Coombe Wood to learn to hybridise Malayan rhododendrons, was transferred to Chelsea where he was told to concentrate on hybridising begonias. At last James Junior had a first-class team of nurserymen at Chelsea,

John Heal (?–1925)

just as he had wanted. He seems to have taken no further interest in the Exeter nursery and severed all business ties, though possibly not family ones. However, his children kept their Devon connections close in their affections for the rest of their lives.

Harry Veitch, who had followed his brother's adventures in Japan, Australia and the South Seas with great enthusiasm, never showed any desire to travel. After his training in Germany and France he had settled down to 'learn the business' and while John Gould was away, had started at the bottom, working as an 'office-boy' in the nursery and taking the letters to the post. This entailed a brisk run to the post office at Sloane Square over a mile away. Packages had to be carried even further, to the railway station at Paddington which required paying a toll of sixpence if he took a short cut through the Brompton Gate. Like his brother, Harry was a lighthearted and cheerful character, but he was also an untiring and dedicated worker.

One employee, William Camp, who spent many years working for the Chelsea nursery, recalled his month's trial period as a clerk:

Veitch's were tremendously busy, and long before my month was up I was severely tested. The hours were nine a.m. to seven p.m., but there were so many invoices to get out that Mr Harry Veitch, who was then in the office, said, on one occasion, he would go back after dinner to finish them. He came back at eight, we worked until ten, and I do not think we made one mistake.

Camp's relations with James Junior were rather different: 'Everybody in the nursery stood in awe of James Veitch. He could never bear to be interrupted, and was very angry if disturbed.'

Camp worked at the Chelsea nursery for two years until his previous employer, Thomas Rivers, who ran a nursery in Hertfordshire, persuaded him to return to him as chief clerk. On hearing of his departure, James Junior shouted, 'What a fool you are . . . just got your foot on the ladder and going back to bury yourself down there.' Harry, a much more approachable character, gradually took over supervision of the business side of the nursery while his father visited important patrons and customers, attended exhibitions in England and on the Continent and sat on several committees and juries. Five years later, when Camp returned to work at Veitch's, he found the atmosphere had improved considerably.

Soon after John Gould had returned from plant collecting in Japan, James Junior admitted him and Harry to partnership of the Royal Exotic Nursery. Young Arthur, who was not horticulturally minded, went to work in the offices of Rothschilds Bank. The horticultural event of 1866 was the International Horticultural Exhibition and Botanical Congress held at Kensington in May and James Junior and John Gould and Harry served on several planning committees. Afterwards, members of the committee of the Botanical Congress were invited to a 'magnificent *déjeuner*' in the grand hall at Stanley House in Chelsea. Present were the leading botanists and nurserymen of England, France, Germany, Belgium, Italy and Holland, among them Professor Lecoq, Dr Reichenbach, and Messrs Vilmorin, Linden and Van den Hecke. Toasts were drunk and speeches made with the foreign gentlemen politely expressing their admiration at the 'pre-eminence of British horticulture'. In response, John Gould, who had already shown considerable skills in diplomacy and public relations, made complimentary remarks in perfect French about the visiting dignitaries. After a bibulous lunch and a tour of the nursery to admire the collection, including some new novelties brought back by John Gould from his travels in Japan and the South Seas, the visitors were given their *carte-de-visite* as a souvenir. For Harry the exhibition was a defining moment in his career and the start of a lifetime of committee work concerning, most particularly, orchids.

SCIENTISTS AND ORCHIDS

When John Dominy took his place in the Chelsea nursery, the orchid houses were already bursting with one of the finest collections in the country and his pioneering orchid hybrids were creating huge excitement. His first laelia hybrid flowered at Chelsea in May and was named *Laelia* x *pilcheriana* after Mr Pilcher, head gardener to one of Veitch's most important patrons, the orchid enthusiast Sigismund Rucker. When it was finally exhibited four years later Professor Reichenbach, the great German orchidist, wrote: 'This is a very glorious product of the Veitchian Nursery, obtained by the efforts of Mr Dominy, who would appear to be quite as skilful in the fertilisation of orchids as the insects themselves . . . We would most earnestly exhort Messrs. Veitch never to put an end to their glorious experiments of crossing orchids.'

But there were still people who did not approve of hybridisation, including James Bateman. In a lecture given at the RHS in 1864 Bateman said that the day was rapidly approaching when there would be no new plant species left to collect and 'our Lindleys and Reichenbachs, our Benthams and Hookers will find their occupation gone'. It was religion, not conservation concerns, which lay at the root of Bateman's and several other botanists' objection to hybrids. They regarded it as tampering with the work of God. Bateman was possibly the anonymous correspondent who wrote of Veitch's orchids: '. . . among which, however, I must not be supposed to include some of the hybrid triumphs of Mr Dominy's misplaced ingenuity, *Cattleya dominii* and so forth. Hybridise everything else if you will, but spare, oh spare the orchids!

James Junior's abiding passion was always for orchids and his friendships and patrons reflected this obsession. Species were still pouring in from a wide source of suppliers – the Brussels collector and nurseryman, Jean Jules Linden, Colonel Benson in India, the Rev. William Ellis, a missionary in Madagascar, and the veteran Scottish orchid collector, George Ure-Skinner, one of James Junior's greatest friends. After buying the entire Bateman/Ure-Skinner collection, James regularly purchased new specimens of cattleyas, odontoglossums and laelias from Central and South America, especially Guatemala, where Ure-Skinner lived and ran his business. At Chelsea, James

Laeliocattleya dominiana langleyensis. One of Dominy's earliest orchid hybrids

created a special hothouse to display Ure-Skinner's orchids and the collector could always be found there during his regular trips to England, happily admiring his discoveries and Dominy's genius in raising them. The whole Veitch establishment fascinated Ure-Skinner and the Veitch family were especially close to his heart, as he was to theirs.

As James Junior's reputation grew, an extraordinary mix of scientists and orchid enthusiasts passed through the doors of his nursery – great names such as Professor Reichenbach, Sir Joseph Hooker, Dr Lindley, Professor Huxley and Charles Darwin. In 1864 Darwin rocked the foundations of natural history by publishing his work *On the Origin of Species*. It aroused considerable suspicion and hostility among scientists, yet many did begin to support his views. One of Darwin's major interests was the mystery of reproduction in the orchid family which he studied assiduously. Whilst preparing his treatise *The Various Contrivances by Which Orchids are Fertilised by Insects*, Darwin's friend Joseph Hooker recommended he visit the Veitch nursery. James Junior proudly showed Darwin the rarest and most unusual specimens in the orchid collection and presented him with a number of plants, including the first specimen Darwin had seen of *Catasetum saccatum*, a genus which had a particularly interesting reproductive system. Darwin made several visits to the nursery where he cross-examined Dominy. The two men spent long hours discussing the problems of orchid reproduction, one having developed his remarkable skills empirically, the other through scientific observation and study, both without the benefit of genetic knowledge. James often sent plants of special interest to Darwin's house; among them was *Cycnoches ventricosum* from Central America about which Darwin wrote: 'Mr Veitch was so kind as to send me on two occasions several flowers and flowerbuds of this extraordinary plant.'

Darwin was also fascinated by the movement of plants and spent many hours at Chelsea examining the twiners and climbers such as the passion flower and tropaeolum from South America. He studied the huge nepenthes or pitcher plants which needed considerable support: 'I observed in Mr Veitch's hothouse that the stalk often takes a turn when not in contact with any object' and he concluded 'it would appear that the chief use of the coiling, at least while the plant is young, is to support the pitcher with its load of secreted fluid.'

James Junior thoroughly enjoyed rubbing shoulders with the greatest scientific minds of the day. He also devoted considerable time to the wealthiest orchidists who kept exceptional collections in their homes – Baron

Schröder at The Dell in Egham, Leopold de Rothschild at Gunnersbury, Joseph Chamberlain from Birmingham and Sigismund Rucker of West Hill, Wandsworth. These men owned vast glasshouses and made considerable demands on James's time and expertise. Other nurseries looked on the Royal Exotic Nursery with ill-concealed jealousy, for James now possessed many of the rarest and most priceless specimens to be found in the country and, what is more, with the nursery's closely guarded secret methods, he was exclusively creating orchids of his own.

Despite the huge numbers and varieties of orchids arriving in the west, surprisingly little was known about how to cultivate them. Orchid growers failed to understand the difference in cultural needs between different kinds of orchids such as terrestrial and epiphytic species (which were then thought to be parasitic). It was generally assumed that orchids only came from tropical jungles and so all were grown in heated stove-houses in a humid and steamy atmosphere, without ventilation. This made conditions unpleasant and uncomfortable for both the orchids and the gardeners who had to look after them. Regardless of type or origin, orchids were planted in mixtures of rotted wood and leaves and their pots were plunged in beds of tanners' bark or sawdust. In this environment hundreds of thousands of orchids died. Sir Joseph Hooker was heard to remark that England had become the 'grave of tropical orchids'. For an orchid to have reached England at all was a miracle; to survive English cultivation was a double miracle.

Joseph Hooker and James Veitch Senior had in earlier years both experimented with wicker baskets and moss to allow the air to circulate and later John Gould had implored growers to go easy on the watering. At the Chiswick Horticultural Garden, Dr John Lindley started a systematic study of how, and under what circumstances, different orchids grew in their native habitats. He reported that:

Some grow on trees, some on stones, many on the ground itself. Some bask in the hottest sun, others luxuriate in the open places of deep forests, or ride aloft on the branches of trees. There are highland races that can only exist on the sides of mountains where clouds are always condensing, or that even struggle onwards towards the limits of alpine vegetation . . . it is not enough to tie them to a block of wood or to pot them among peat of leaves or potsherds, or to keep the air about them always damp, as some imagine.

Slowly a better knowledge of orchid cultivation was developing. Sigismund Rucker had accidentally discovered the growing habits of *Stanhopea* when his gardener dropped some pots which smashed and revealed flower scapes desperately trying to get out. New arrivals from higher altitudes which perished under hot treatment were tried with cooler growing conditions; Joseph Paxton was one of the first orchidists to abandon stoves and adopt the new ideas. He opened his greenhouse to air and sunlight, giving his plants cool, buoyant conditions, and they began to thrive. It was a turning point in orchid culture and beautiful, cool-growing orchids such as odontoglossums, became attractive and attainable propositions.

As for James Junior at Chelsea, 'No other establishment', wrote the *Gardener's Chronicle*, 'has made greater efforts to obtain a continuous supply of new orchids from all parts of the world and none has been at greater pains to make their hard-earned treasures thoroughly at home.' When John Gould conducted a reporter around the nursery, he explained that a great deal of their success was due to careful consideration and re-creation of the climate and habits of the plants in their native countries 'instead of jumbling them up together as is often done, to the utter ruin and destruction of many valuable plants'.

English horticultural science and orchid study came to an abrupt halt in 1865 with the deaths of three of their biggest advocates, Dr John Lindley, Sir William Hooker and Sir Joseph Paxton. The German orchidologist, Professor Heinrich Reichenbach, succeeded Lindley as the 'Orchid King' and specimens from all over the world were now to be sent to Hamburg for identification. Although Reichenbach regularly visited England and wrote weekly reports for the *Gardener's Chronicle*, orchid enthusiasts and nurserymen disliked having to send their specimens to Germany. Reichenbach recorded and kept everything he received in his herbarium until it eventually rivalled Lindley's collection at Kew. Orchid collecting suffered further setbacks in the following years with the deaths of the Devon naturalist and orchidist, Hugh Cuming, who had spent a lifetime roaming the western oceans for unusual orchids, and Josef Ritter von Rawicz Warszewicz, the Polish-born orchid collector, who had shipped numerous valuable orchids from Central and South America to botanical gardens in Poland and Germany. The death of George Ure Skinner in 1867 was a particularly great blow to James Junior who lost an important friend. Although gravely ill with yellow fever, Ure Skinner had written his last letter to James Junior from Panama, full of high spirits and plant gossip:

'I went to Paraiso on Friday afternoon, and slept there. The scarlet passion flower was in great beauty – but no seed. I have two slips in earth to root and bring back with me. I travelled over on a hand-car much of the way, and found another passion-flower, very pretty and sending forth a scent such as can be equalled to a thousand violets! I have sent home a box with orders that it may be sent up to you at once. You will find an Ionopsis which may be good, Pleurathalis, and some very curious Epinendra. Some seeds and a branch of the purple-and-white passion flower: do you know this? It is brilliant: but no scent. . . . I sail from Panama on the 10th instant, and shall be in Guatamala on the 18th.'

But on 9 January Ure Skinner was dead, struck down with yellow fever. The ship that carried the letter to Chelsea also carried the news of the orchidist's death. James Junior was left shocked and depressed. 'There was,' James Bateman lamented, a 'temporary gap in the supply of south American orchids.'

James Junior seemed to have forgotten that his late father's collector, Richard Pearce, was still travelling in South America. Pearce's discoveries had already drawn him to the attention of a number of botanists. Some particularly fine dried specimens of his collection of maidenhair ferns, sent to Kew for naming, had so impressed the keeper, Mr Baker, that he wrote, 'Mr Pearce appears to have had a singularly keen eye for discovering meritorious novelties.' In Peru he found the striking orange-scarlet flowered orchid, *Masdevallia veitchiana* (which became Harry's favourite orchid). In the region around La Paz, the capital of Bolivia, he had collected several varieties of hippeastrum, such as *Hippeastrum pardinum*, described in the *Botanical Magazine* as 'a truly magnificent plant', while another was so admired by King Leopold of the Belgians when he saw it exhibited at the South Kensington Royal Horticultural Show in June 1869 that he gave permission for the plant to be named *Hippeastrum leopoldii*. Pearce's most important introductions, however, were the tuberous begonias which were to become the parents of the modern pot-plants and summer bedding so favoured today. The first species of tuberous begonia, *Begonia boliviensis*, was found by Pearce in the Bolivian Andes in 1865. In Peru he found *Begonia veitchii* with immense

vermilion flowers, and high in the
mountains, the *B. davisii* and *B. rosaeflora*
and the only yellow flowering species,
Begonia pearcei (see colour-plate section).
The Veitch nursery hid these begonias
away while one of their top hybridists,
John Seden, worked on them to create
several crosses. It would be several years
before the first hybrid begonias were put
on sale.

When he heard of James Veitch's
death, Pearce had written to James Junior
reminding him of the signed agreement
with his father which allowed Pearce
to collect herbarium specimens for
himself. James Junior replied that, in his

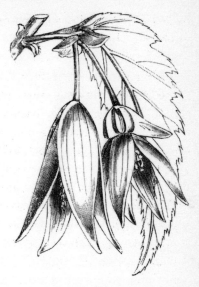

Begonia boliviensis

view, Pearce had permission to collect for scientific purposes and not for
sale but that he 'would agree to anything that my father agreed to'. Richard
Pearce overstayed his contract by nearly two years and finally reported back
to the Veitch Nursery in 1868 with plenty of good seeds for Veitch. He also
sold a beautiful collection of butterflies and some of his fine herbarium
specimens. By their usual arrangement with Veitch, Sir Joseph Hooker (who
had succeeded his father as Director of Kew) requested some of Pearce's
herbarium specimens. James Junior replied: 'I have sent off a large parcel of
Botanical specimens which I have made Mr Pearce select out of all our
specimens, being one of each of which we have a duplicate. We have many
others of which there are no duplicates, and which we should be glad to
have named from our specimens if this could be arranged.' James then seemed
to imply that he had no further plans for his late father's collector as he
wrote: 'Mr Pearce, having nothing in particular to do whilst he is waiting
for some appointment, would like to be able to come some time to your
Herbarium if you could oblige us in this matter.'

Two days later, Pearce delivered another parcel of eighty dried specimens to Kew. It was the opportunity he had been hoping for when he
could, without Veitch's knowledge, offer his own 'private' collection of 1,500
specimens. Sir Joseph was very keen to buy Pearce's particularly fine collection but told him that he had first to get Veitch's permission.

James Junior was furious with Pearce's deviousness and dishonesty. 'I had no idea,' he wrote to Hooker, 'that he had these by him which he has offered to you. He has stayed six months at my expense, yet he has never told me he had such a lot of specimens.' James Junior reminded Hooker that his father had always sold the Lobb brothers' herbarium specimens for them through Hewards of Kensington and, after deducting his expenses, paid them the profits. Reminiscent of a similar row his father had had with William Lobb, James wrote, 'I think he has some time been using us.' At this point Pearce produced his contract with James Senior plus the letter from James Junior agreeing to whatever his father had signed to. There was nothing that Veitch could do about it.

Richard Pearce did not work for the Veitch nursery again. Instead he walked round to Wiliam Bull's nursery next door where he was immediately signed up to travel again in South America. Only a few months later in Panama, Pearce contracted yellow fever and died. Twenty years on, the anonymous author of an article in *The Tuberous Begonia* wrote that 'Though a man of small stature, Richard Pearce had a lion's heart and his early death was a great loss to British horticulture'.

While Pearce was outstaying his contract, James Junior decided to send another collector to the potentially lucrative collecting fields of Brazil and Columbia. Early in 1866, in a joint deal with William Wilson Saunders, the new Secretary of the Royal Horticultural Society, the Veitch nursery sent David Bowman, a Scots foreman in the Society's Chiswick Garden, to Rio de Janeiro. From Brazil, Bowman sent back several interesting stove-plants such as *Dieffenbachia bowmanii* and *Paullinia thalictrifolia*, a pretty greenhouse climber with beautiful fern-like foliage. He found two interesting orchids, *Odontoglossum crispum* 'Alexandrae', and *Cyanophyllum bowmanii* which was awarded a first-class certificate by the RHS's Floral Committee. Unfortunately, just as he was about to sail for home, Bowman was robbed of much of his collection and James insisted he prolong his stay and recollect. He bravely carried on despite an attack of dysentery which 'ultimately brought him to an early grave' in Bogota in 1868.

In his relentless search for more orchids, James Junior shipped another equally inexperienced man out to Java. Henry Hutton was the son of a former head gardener to Lord Houghton and was said to have been 'an ardent student and promising explorer'. But after a year in Java, where he was unable to cope with the extreme climate, Hutton's health broke down and, like Bowman, 'he fell a victim to his enthusiasm' – if not his own, then certainly his employer's. Before he died Hutton did manage to send home a new species of cymbidium, *C. huttoni, Saccolabium huttoni, Dendrobium huttoni* and an aerides which he found on the Island of Timor. He also rediscovered and successfully introduced the very rare tawny-yellow *Vanda insignis*. It flowered in Chelsea for the first time in 1868 but remained very rare in British collections until it was re-introduced by a later Veitch collector.

The supply of enthusiastic young men seemed inexhaustible so long as there were new and exciting orchids and stove-plants to be found and James wasted no time in sending out another, even less successful collector. Carl Kramer, a German, was also a gardener's son whose employer in Hamburg had a fine orchid collection. In 1867 Kramer went to Japan in order to supplement John Gould's collection, but the mission was a failure. Surprisingly, Kramer was immediately sent out again, this time to Costa Rica and Guatemala to look for orchids. According to *Hortus Veitchii*, the Veitch 'history' privately published in 1906, Kramer 'proved entirely unsuitable for the work he had undertaken, and apparently had not that adaptability and resource essential to successful exploration'. His only recorded find was a species of odontoglossum, *O. krameri*, allied to *O. citrosmum* which he found in Costa Rica. A second German, Gottlieb Zahn, was initially more successful. James Junior sent Zahn to Central America between 1869 and 1870 from where he sent several consignments of plants, mainly orchids and a number of ferns. Zahn was supposed to be searching for the rare *Odontoglossum warscewiezii*, first discovered in 1849 by Warscewicz and subsequently lost, but he failed to locate it. Poor Zahn was drowned in a river in Costa Rica. His name is associated with the beautiful bromeliaceous plant *Tillandsia zahnii* with its crimson-striped leaves and scarlet bracts.

Why was James Junior less successful in his collectors than his father? Possibly it was his propensity to rush headlong into things, perhaps it was because he failed to ensure proper training and preparation; he was more demanding for quick returns and thus less rigorous in controlling his expeditions. None of the individuals or nurseries were noted for their concern for the

Tillandsia zahnii

welfare of their collectors. Everyone knew it was a gamble, a risky business. Perhaps James was unable to appreciate the difference between hardened, wily old collectors like his friend Ure Skinner, who lived and breathed
orchids and the countries they inhabited, and the innocent enthusiasm of
young nurserymen.

In April 1867 John Gould took a correspondent from the *Gardener's Chronicle*
round Coombe Wood, its extensive grounds now forming 'a valuable adjunct
to the great plant emporium at Chelsea'. Trees planted in the grounds were
growing to maturity, including the fine avenue of Monkey-puzzles. John
Gould's own particular interest was in plants that could be shown to be
hardy in English gardens, and Coombe Wood was now filled with some
lovely specimens that were proving him right. There was the Patagonian
holly, *Desfontainia spinosa*, which after three winters was flowering profusely,
William Lobb's *Escallonia macrantha* from Chile and the elegant Australian
shrub *Grevillea rosmarinifolia*, now out of the greenhouse and growing happily
through the English winters. There were healthy specimens of the shrubby
Cotoneaster simonsii from India and a number of small trees such as the black
walnut, *Juglans nigra*, a variegated plane tree 'with large yellow and green
blotches like the plumage of a parrot' and a strange golden chestnut from
California, *Castanopsis chrysophylla*, its 'cupules having an outer coating of
bristles like the quills of a porcupine'. Large stocks of numerous varieties
of John Gould's Japanese conifers were now growing vigorously; junipers,
firs, cypresses and cedars such as the Japanese Red Cedar, *Thujopsis dolabrata*,
which 'was revelling away now that it is of some standing and Mr John
Veitch assures us that it is quite hardy and that he found great trees of it
growing in the north of Japan at a high altitude where snow lies nearly
five months of the year'. The visitor admired the Japanese Red Pine, *Pinus
densiflora*, 'which Mr Veitch called the "Scotch Fir" of Japan which is here
in quantity' and the fabled Hinoki Cypresses which were also doing well,
attaining the same height of a tree in Japan and keeping their golden colour
all the year round.

TWO WEDDINGS AND TWO FUNERALS

During the summer of 1867 there were two family weddings. Harry married
Louisa Johnston and lived close to the Chelsea nursery in Redcliffe Gardens.
John Gould married Jane Hodge and settled into the house in the grounds

Harry Veitch (1840–1924)

at Coombe Wood where their sons, James Herbert and John Gould Junior, were born.

Harry was occupied with setting up the firm's display for the Paris International Exhibition where his father was acting as a juror. John Heal, one of their trio of head nurserymen, accompanied them and their efforts were well rewarded. The young garden designer, William Robinson, writing as correspondent for *The Times*, wrote that Messrs Veitch had won 'First for new kinds and for the best fifty species'.

John Gould, weakened by the stress and strains of his years of travelling, was now in the deadly grip of tuberculosis. He and Jane spent the winter in the Mediterranean where his health improved slightly.

James Junior was also experiencing ill-health, possibly suffering from the same heart condition which had killed his father. But any advice that he should take it easy and cut down on his work load was anathema to a man who 'was the epitome of energy, often working until two o'clock in the morning while regularly prepared for the day's work at six o'clock'. James Junior was aware that he had a weak heart and that his condition was likely to shorten his life. Unknown to his family, he visited the Brompton Cemetery which lay across the road from the rear entrance to the Royal Exotic Nursery and chose a site for a family grave. He also knew that his eldest son was not likely to survive for long.

On 9 September 1869 Thomas Lobb, who had remained in Cornwall and out of touch with the Veitch business for some ten years, took a train to London and in the evening, visited Stanley House. He had been summoned by James Junior who, knowing that his son would never collect again and having failed so miserably with others, was desperate for an experienced and successful orchid collector. Despite his ill-health, James Junior had ambitious plans for a new expedition and he was planning to persuade Thomas Lobb to collect for Veitch's again. But, as usual, James Junior's efforts at persuasion gave way to his overbearing manner. In the parlour, where so many lively meetings had been held late into the night, there was a heated argument and Thomas limped away into the night. Before dawn, James Junior suffered a fatal heart attack. He was fifty-four years old.

One can only guess at what had passed between the two men. Was Thomas angry at the way he had been treated after providing the Veitch family with so many valuable and profitable new plants? There is no record of a pension nor payment for his injured leg which had left him unable to work again. Summoned to London after so many years of silence, he might have been filled with bitterness to have been cast off, unrewarded and forgotten, whilst his plants became household names and made his ex-employers a fortune. Perhaps too he had nursed a great resentment at the way his brother William had been virtually abandoned and left to die in San Francisco. Despite the compliments and public credit which James Senior occasionally made sure they got, the Lobb brothers would have had every reason to feel exploited and forgotten. James Junior's obituary described his 'concientiousness and straightforwardness, a disgust to all semblance even, of meanness or underhandedness, and a warmth of friendly feeling that can be adequately gauged only by those who knew him'. Yet he does not seem to have found such feeling for those who worked for him in the nursery or for the men who faced great dangers and even died in the field while collecting for him.

The most curious thing about the many fulsome articles written during James Junior's life and in his obituaries is the long list of plants which he is credited with introducing through his many collectors. His father is never mentioned and the famous discoveries and introductions made by the Lobbs and Pearce are all ascribed to James Junior. Almost every book that mentions the Veitch family confuses its members, especially all the Jameses. But this cannot be the explanation for the strange 'air-brushing' of James Veitch Senior from the records, denying him the credit for some of the greatest achievements in the story of the Veitch nursery, indeed the pioneering foundation of its most successful principles.

James Junior may have been abrasive, even a bit of a bully and impatient with those who did not share his view, but he was an untiring advocate of selfless service to the highest of horticultural ideals. His stern belief that horticulture, though a hobby for amateurs, was a serious business for nurserymen and should not include the pursuit of unrelated matters, however superficially entertaining, did not endear him to general gardeners. He had lived his life at the centre of everything horticultural and botanical, and he counted some of its greatest names amongst his friends and colleagues. He had been an active member of the Council of the RHS although it was noted in his obituary in the *Gardener's Chronicle* that he 'had not entirely succeeded in bringing the majority of the Council round to his way of thinking'. Although they had not always seen eye to eye with him, members of the Council met to discuss the most suitable means of raising a memorial to the late James Veitch. With the indefatigable James Bateman as chairman, the sum of £809 18s. 4d. was raised by fellow nurserymen and members of the Society. After much discussion it was agreed to establish the Veitch Memorial Medal which has ever since been awarded annually to those who have helped in the advancement and improvement of the science and practice of horticulture.

A year later tragedy again struck the Veitch family. On 13 August 1870, John Gould suffered a relapse, his lungs haemorrhaged and he died. He was only thirty-one and left a widow and two young sons. The family grave in Brompton Cemetery was re-opened and once again a procession walked slowly down the tree-lined path. The coffin was carried by members of staff, including John Dominy and John Heal who had already borne the coffins of both James Senior and James Junior to their last resting places. John Gould's obituary in the *Gardener's Chronicle* was fulsome in its recognition:

So we part sorrowing from one of the most gifted and promising of our younger commercial horticulturalists . . . one who, if his life had been spared and his health had permitted, would have worthily filled a prominent position in the world of horticulture; one, moreover, whose memory will continue to be cherished by those who had the pleasure to know him intimately as that of a straightforward, single-hearted, earnest and sincere friend.

It was a terrible loss to botany and horticulture, a waste too of one of the most charming, intelligent, warm-hearted and witty members of the Veitch dynasty. The Veitch Memorial now would always be associated with the memory of both father and son: 'So long as British horticulture lasts, so long will the names of these earnest labourers in its cause, call up feelings of respect and regret.'

CHAPTER TEN

THE GREAT DECADE
(1870–1880)

'The plant-collector's job is to uncover the hidden beauties
of the world, so that others may share his joy . . .'
F. Kingdom-Ward,
From China to HKamti-long, 1924

A FTER THE DEATH of James Junior, relations between the two Veitch
nursery businesses in Exeter and London became more cordial with
increasing co-operation. Robert Tosswill Veitch had done well since
leaving his apple farm in South Africa. Now settling into middle age and
living the life of a prosperous provincial nurseryman, he was a large, solid,
bearded figure whose powerful appearance and manner reminded one more
of Africa than Devon. Robert had worked hard to readjust to English ways
and his South African wife, Sarah, an accomplished flower arranger, had won
a number of prizes for her 'drawing-
room arrangements'.

After his father's death, and despite
James Junior's removal of Dominy
and the best stock to London, Robert
had successfully built up his own
business. At first he specialised in fruit
stock and became a respected expert
in pomology, especially the many
varieties of Devon cider apples, so
important to the thriving West
Country industry. In Robert Hogg's
famous *Fruit Manual*, the list of the
best of these apples came from details
supplied by 'Mr R. T. Veitch nurseryman, Exeter'. Robert kept up the

Robert Veitch (1823–1885)

Veitch contracts with big Devon estates, planting newly-introduced trees and shrubs, and updating the gardens at Bicton, Poltimore and Killerton.

In the years since the Veitch family had left Budlake Farm at Killerton, the Aclands had prospered but also suffered their own misfortunes. After Lady Lydia's death in 1865, Sir Tom found great solace in the gardens. James, and later Robert, had continued to visit, bringing new plants and trees grown from seed brought back by the Lobbs for Sir Tom's gardener to 'try out' in the rich soil and balmy climate. Some of the first sequoia seedlings were now growing tall and Sir Tom loved to inspect them after Sunday morning service in the Chapel and 'look over' several species of new Veitch flowering shrubs being 'cared for' at Killerton. His slow progress around his estate, discussing the gardens with Robert, was now Sir Tom's greatest pleasure. A traditionalist to the end, he continued to admire the old 'landscape' style, disliking the fussiness and order of the new Victorian garden. Once summoned before a magistrate for neglecting to have hedges trimmed and trees lopped in parts of the Killerton estate, he justified his inaction on the grounds that this was the intended 'picturesque effect' as it was first planned, nearly a hundred years ago, by the 7th baronet and his steward John Veitch. The 'Great' Sir Tom died in his eighty-eighth year in 1871 after his usual drive around the gardens. His death 'left a gap in the Devon landscape as if a great tree had fallen'. But the Acland–Veitch relationship lived on for many more years with both the Exeter and Chelsea nurseries continuing to send seeds and plants to Killerton.

Robert's growing reputation for design work gained him a contract for an ambitious project which would propel the Veitch name in an entirely new direction. In 1866 Richard Thornton West, a millionaire East Indian merchant, bought a house on the outskirts of Exeter which he pulled down and replaced with a classic Victorian Italianate house. He contracted Robert Veitch to create new gardens and a pinetum. Thornton West is reported to have spent over £80,000 on the house itself and a further £70,000 on laying out and planting the new estate – a fabulous sum even for today. After five years' work, Streatham Hall, as it was called, was completed. (It is now the grounds of Exeter University.) The gardens covered very steep slopes, 'so that of necessity, the architect and gardener have worked hand in hand, creating a series of terraces in the Italian style, with many noble flights of steps at contrasting angles' and plenty of classical statuary. A description of the gardens thirty years later gives a picture of a grandiose scheme around the house and a large conservatory and palm house filled with palms, ferns, foliage plants and numerous varieties of exotics. The pleasure grounds led through mature woodlands of conifers, hollies, flowering trees and specimen rhododendrons, to a lake covered in huge lilies.

Robert was fortunate to be able to buy stock from the huge range of rare trees at the Veitch nurseries in Chelsea. Many of those he planted were raised from seeds brought back by William Lobb from North and South America and by John Gould from Japan. Robert created imaginative and liberal plantations around the terraces with some of the finest trees set in solitary splendour on the lawns. Along the drive he planted an avenue of twenty-four paired specimens of John Gould's *Chamaecyparis nootkatensis* and opposite the south front of the house, half a dozen *Thujopsis dolabrata*. Grouped here and there were variegated weeping hollies, particularly popular at the time. On the lawns surrounding the terracing, Robert planted Lobb's cypresses from Oregon and north-west California, several kinds of junipers, the slow-growing mountain hemlock and the Santa Lucia fir. Nearby he planted Chinese junipers and Tiger-tail spruce and specimens of John Gould's famous Hinoki cypress and Japanese cedar, while on the lawns by the house were set two beautiful golden yews.

As well as tree-planting and the laying out of formal parterres and flower beds, Robert created a large rockery at Streatham Hall. For this, he employed F. W. Meyer, a German rockwork expert. Meyer had studied at the Royal Horticultural College in Silesia and was probably a friend of Robert's son, Peter, who had been doing horticulture training in the region. Veitch and Meyer joined forces and began to advertise their new speciality of rock and water gardens using natural stone. (In 1865 James Pulham had invented an artificial stone but Pulhamite rockeries never proved as popular as natural stone.) By the late 1870s, Robert Veitch & Son with F. W. Meyer were one of the two leading companies specialising in the design of rock and water gardens and Meyer published a popular book on the subject.

Their work also kicked off new fashions in conservatory planting with a rapidly growing demand for new rockery plants such as hardy ferns, small conifers and alpines in which the Exeter nursery wisely started to specialise. The growing craze for exotic displays of plants depicting a 'natural' setting in conservatories and glasshouses called for a backdrop of tropical jungle or 'picturesque scenery'. Gardeners used arrangements of rock and water in which orchids, ferns, mosses and foliage plants could luxuriate. At one

Devon and Exeter horticultural show, the Veitch display was done in an extraordinarily 'novel and artistic manner'. Creating a *trompe-l'oeil*, the plants were set against an imaginative scene of rockwork with a little 'pond' of silvered glass which appeared to run back among caves formed by the rocks until lost to sight. Ferns, reeds and pitcher plants graced the sides of the 'pond' with alpines, such as anemones and edelweiss, covering the rocks. Tall tree ferns made a canopy for orchids and the whole display was backed with huge specimens of *Eucalyptus globulus*.

Outside in the garden, fairy caves, grottos and romantic ruins became all the rage. They appealed to the Victorian spirit of romance and adventure and provided the thrill of a wild Alpine rockface with cascading mountain streams. Imitative 'sublime' scenery became a popular theme in British gardening during the last third of the century and enormous projects were undertaken using extraordinary scale-model construction and tumbling water effects, among them the Khyber Pass in East Park, Hull, the Matterhorn at Friar Park, Henley-on-Thames and Mount Fuji in the Japanese garden at Fanhams Hall, Ware. But not everyone liked them: the garden designer Reginald Blomfield wrote that it was absurd to suppose that a love of wild nature could be shown by trying to reproduce it on a small scale in a garden – 'Any one who loves natural scenery will want the real thing; he will hardly be content to sit in his rockery and suppose himself to be among the mountains.' However, for some who had not travelled it was the next best thing and, for the true gardener, the rockery offered an ideal environment in which to grow and display their special collection of rare alpine plants.

One of Veitch and Meyer's most complex rockery creations was at Bystock, near Exmouth. Here they transformed five acres of field and clay-pit into a magical world of 'waterfalls, ornamental lakes, precipices and masses of rugged rocks, pierced with caverns, chasms and flowery valleys'. The huge rockery, extending horizontally for 200 yards above the pit, was filled with alpines, ferns and dwarf azaleas, while a variety of handsome creepers cascaded over the precipice below. The extensive collection of alpines included many varieties of saxifrages, primulas, harebells, phlox and veronicas, with bright blue trumpets of *Gentiana acaulis*, a small pink and white pea, *Coronilla varia*, from the Mediterranean and a blue daisy, *Catananche caerulea*. Rough steps led to the entrance of a large cave which was shaded by an ancient oak and rustic seats were strategically placed so that the whole effect could be admired in comfort.

TWO VEITCH NURSERIES

In 1870, Robert's son, Peter, returned from training abroad to work in Chelsea, assisting his cousin Harry who was faced with the enormous task of running the Royal Exotic Nursery without either his father or the brother whom he had loved and admired. Harry knew that a new generation of Veitches was necessary to give the business a sound future; Arthur, his youngest brother, was working for the Rothschild family (some of whom were regular patrons and close friends) and they readily allowed Arthur to return to Chelsea to help Harry and Peter with the office work.

Peter Veitch (1850–1929)

The London nursery had grown in size and reputation in its seventeen years. Yet, as everyone in the nursery trade knew, without a strong director, it could equally quickly collapse. Many wondered how Harry, still only thirty years old and now its sole director, would cope with the challenge.

Friends also worried as to whether he would be able to shoulder his responsibilities as head of a family which now consisted of his widowed mother, four unmarried sisters and a widowed sister-in-law with her two boys. But Harry had four great strengths: his deep religious convic-tion, the calm, confident support of

Arthur Veitch (1844–1880)

his wife Louisa, his own pleasant but tough personality and robust good health. He was stockily built, with broad shoulders and a long, bushy beard which in later life became his hallmark. His strong physique was coupled with a 'cheerful and breezy humour', and his charm, wit and pungent comments recalled his great-great-grandfather John and his brother John Gould. He was from quite a different mould than his father and grand-father, the two Jameses.

Under Harry's management, the character of the Chelsea nursery also changed from the rather lofty and intense air of science and specialist plantsmen to a broader-based business. Harry was just as skilled, knowledge-able and passionate about horticulture as his forebears but he could see that gardening was increasingly a popular activity for all classes. When he took control of the Royal Exotic Nursery, the firm was pre-eminent in the field of orchid hybridisation and housed one of the finest collections of cultivated orchids from around the world. Much of this collection had been created through judicious purchases as well as remarkable finds. One of Harry's first concerns was whether the nursery should continue its pioneering plant collecting and compete in the still highly elitist yet expanding mania for orchids.

ORCHIDOMANIA

Shortly after noon the doors of Steven's Auction Rooms – the leading venue for plant sales – were opened to admit a crowd of strangely assorted men and one or two women. Ranged round the walls of the rooms were rough tables covered with various lots of bulbs and bundles of dry-looking sticks of every shape and size, 'withered or green, dull or shining' or 'a mass of roots dry as last year's bracken'. There were no bright blossoms with brilliant or subtle markings, nothing to suggest that buried in this strange array of plant matter lay some of the most beautiful and exotic flowers in the world. The men strolled along the tables, lifting a root and scrutinizing it with a 'practised eye that measures its vital strength in a second'. The talk was of orchids and everyone knew each other. It was like a family party, but like families, not always friendly. On the whole, a cheerful familiarity ruled and disputes were usually referred to as 'misunderstand-ings'. These were men of breeding, wealth or professional standing. A duke compared notes with a clergyman, a banker made enquiries from a nursery-man standing by his display of pots of flowering plants, discreet whispers were made between buyers and auction attendants. There might be Baron Schröder who had the finest orchid collection in the country, Baron Leopold de Rothschild or his gardener, Sir Trevor Lawrence, son of the celebrated gardener Mrs Lawrence of Ealing Park, a representative of His Grace the Duke of Marlborough, Mr Buchanan of Scotch whisky fame, Joseph

Chamberlain, MP and passionate orchidist, Sir George Holford of Westonbirt and the regular and curious figure of the Reverend Kineside of Tunbridge Wells, 'always dressed to the nines, smoking a fine Havana cigar and looking more like a city magnate than a clergyman'.

On some days the air was electric with excitement and anticipation when news of the arrival of a new collection of orchids spread through the 'bush telegraph' of orchid houses. Then the London auction rooms became so crowded that the cigar smoke hung in a thick cloud, almost obscuring the assembled company of orchidists, nurserymen and traders. All were eager to buy the specimens in the hope that, if they flowered, something would appear of outstanding merit, either a new natural hybrid or a new type of species. A few of the 'lost' or 'disappeared' orchids, such as the fabled *Cattleya labiata*, carried a mysterious cachet and extremely high price tags.

The deaths of Lindley, Paxton, Hooker and Ure Skinner five years earlier had done little to quench the ardour of orchid growers and collectors; indeed they had brought a change in the wind of orchid collecting – or hunting, as it was now sometimes called. Science was giving ground to commerce and younger upstarts were arriving on the scene to challenge the position and authority and seize the crown from the orchid kings, Veitch, Rollison, Charlesworth and Low. Just ten years after Thomas Lobb had made his first voyage to India in search of tropical orchids, the *Gardener's Chronicle* published details of a sale at Steven's Auction Rooms. It covered over 600 lots, from South America, India and Asia, sent in by collectors such as Josef Warszewicz and Jean Linden. Prices ranged from ten shillings to nine pounds a plant. At each succeeding sale the prices rose until single plants could sell for over 100 guineas. One journalist wrote: 'I hear almost every day of some new person starting up, and further, I find that the collectors in the upper classes are also increasing.'

Over the next twenty-five years orchids poured into London in ever-increasing quantities, prices continued to rise, especially for rare or new plants, until it was not uncommon for several hundred guineas to be paid for a rare or 'lost' plant. Orchid fever held wealthy Europeans and Americans in its grip and profits for nurseries were staggering. As long as the power of imperial Britain seemed unassailable and the capacity of its territories to supply luxuries and decorative pleasures infinite, orchids remained the jewels of empire. They became synonymous with the Victorian image of power, wealth, romance and exoticism and nurserymen vied to produce the most magnificent flower arrangements. Indeed, bouquets for Queen Victoria's

Golden Jubilee were composed of every variety of orchid 'produced within Her Majesty's dominions'. The orchid had become an object of status in Victorian society and gambling on plants was once again in vogue.

Despite being one of the leading orchid suppliers, Veitch's no longer had collectors in the field. But if Harry had not already made up his mind by this time, the decision was soon made for him. One day early in 1870, Harry's secretary brought him a letter bearing a Chilean stamp. It came from a young man named J. Henry Chesterton who was employed as a valet to a gentleman travelling through South America. Chesterton wrote that he had a passion for orchids and had gathered a fine collection but needed advice as to how best to bring it safely home. Harry quickly replied and arranged for Chesterton to meet one of his shipping agents in South America who would show him the correct methods for packing his plants. Nothing more was heard from the 'valet' until many months later when he arrived unannounced at the gates of the nursery. Harry and John Heal hurried down to meet the stranger who was anxious to show them his collection, so carefully packed and well looked after that it had arrived in perfect condition. Harry immediately offered to buy all of Chesterton's plants.

After many long conversations and a period of time spent studying and working in the Veitch orchid houses, Chesterton was offered a contract to return to South America, this time not as a valet but as a Veitch plant collector in search of orchids. There was one goal in particular, the much-talked-of and long-desired scarlet *Miltonia vexillaria*, often seen by collectors, but never successfully introduced, which Chesterton did eventually find in the northern Cordillera Occidental, in Columbia. His first successful expedition rocketed the Veitch nursery out of a period of collecting inactivity and encouraged Harry to set out on another forty years of plant collecting.

Harry wisely started by using experienced men already in the field. It was thirty-odd years since James Veitch had first sent William Lobb to South America and travel conditions had improved immensely. There were new roads as well as colonial outposts offering facilities which made a plant collector's life considerably easier and less dangerous. But some hardened veterans remained who had survived far tougher days. One was a German, Gustave Wallis, who was deaf and did not learn to speak until he was six. Left penniless in Southern Brazil by a horticultural company which went bankrupt, Wallis joined others working for the Belgian nurseryman, Jean Linden (an early pioneer of orchid collecting and an old friend of the Veitches). Wallis crossed the entire continent, starting at the

A group of masdevallias orchids including several found by Veitch collectors

mouth of the Amazon River and traversing the total length to its source, penetrating the wildest, unexplored areas of jungle. He was a tough and experienced man who knew his orchids and his territory. Yet, for some reason, when Harry Veitch decided to hire Wallis, instead of allowing him to continue searching in the rich orchid regions of South America, he sent him to find fresh species of phalaenopsis in the Philippines. Not surprisingly, the venture was an expensive failure and Wallis had to be recalled. Realising his mistake, Harry sent Wallis back to Colombia, a country that he already knew, where he settled down to several profitable years collecting many valuable orchids as well as some fine tropical plants. Another experienced collector, A. R. Endres, who was already in Costa Rica, was described in *Hortus Veitchii* as 'a half-caste'. He was recommended to Harry by the veteran orchidist James Bateman. Endres was employed to carry on the work of James Junior's ill-fated collector, Gottlieb Zahn, who was drowned in Costa Rica. In particular Endres was to search for two rare orchids, *Cattleya warscewiczii* and *Cattleya dowiana* as well as new anthuriums, a fashionable species of exotic greenhouse perennial with long-lasting red or greenish-white spathes.

Harry adopted a policy of instructing his men to collect a limited number of any one species, and to pack them with expert care so that he could be as certain as possible of propagating and marketing them for the highest possible prices. He knew that the greatest threat to orchids was their journey home and, as Dr Livingstone had recommended so many years earlier, Harry began a practice of sending someone out to meet his collector and escort the plants home to ensure that they were well protected from the worst hazards of a long sea journey. Seyfarth, a young German gardener, was sent out to Manila to bring home Wallis's thin collection from the Philippines. Similarly, George Downton, a prize-winning student gardener from the RHS garden at Chiswick, was sent first to Central America, where he made a good collection of orchids, then on to join Endres in Costa Rica, pack up their joint collections and escort them home. For some reason the Veitch nursery did not regard Endres as a success, despite his delivering to them surviving specimens of the longed-for *Odontoglossum warscewiczii* which was renamed *Miltonia endresii* in Endres' honour. He also found the rare *Anthurium scherzerianum* which was small with colourful flowers, making it more manageable than the giant *A. veitchii* and still a very popular pot-plant.

Whatever Endres' shortcomings, Harry was satisfied with George Downton

who was sent on a second trip to
Chile. He was instructed to collect
fresh supplies of seed of William
Lobb's *Embothrium coccineum, Tropaeolum azureum* and *T. tricolor*. Downton
also visited the then little-known Juan
Fernandez Islands where he discovered some rich new treasure in
the form of several half-hardy
shrubs, some fine ferns including a
tree fern, *Dicksonia berteroana*, and
various species of berberis.

While Harry's new collectors
were to come and go, with varying
degrees of success and failure, there
was always great excitement in the
New Plant Department at Chelsea.

Dicksonia berteroana

Several plants of the scarlet *Miltonia
vexillaria*, which Chesterton had successfully located and sent back, had flowered for the first time. Professor Reichenbach praised Chesterton for introducing the miltonia, which became much sought after by Veitch's
ever-increasing number of wealthy orchid growers. He had also delivered
several fine *Odontoglossum crispum*, one named *O. chestertonii* by the Professor,
and some fine masdevallias including the beautiful *M. coccinea* var. *harryana*,
which Chesterton had found growing abundantly high up on the Sierra
Nevada de Chita. This extraordinary orchid changes its colour according to
the altitude at which it grows, from light yellow at the highest altitudes
through to reds and oranges to crimson at its lower limits. Sir Trevor Lawrence,
Leopold de Rothschild and Baron Schröder made sure they were first on
the list for this new natural hybrid named after their favourite nurseryman,
Harry Veitch.

By 1873 George Downton had ended his contract and gone to work on
an English coffee plantation in Central America. Endres too had ceased to
work for Veitch, whilst Wallis and the indomitable Chesterton were still
busy in South America. Harry meanwhile had been watching some of his
own nurserymen in the hope of finding those qualities that were essential
for a successful plant collector. One possibility was Walter Davis from
Hampshire, who had trained under Dominy in the New Plant Department

and having proved himself, was elevated to foreman of the nepenthes and fine foliage plants' collections. Harry decided that Davis was the perfect candidate and in August 1873 he was shipped off to South America with the special object of collecting a good quantity of *Masdevallia veitchiana* which Richard Pearce had first introduced but which was still very scarce and highly valued. Over the next three years Walter Davis crossed the Cordilleras of the Andes in Peru and Bolivia no less than twenty times at elevations of up to 17,000 feet and, like Wallis, he traversed the vast continent from one side to the other, along the whole length of the Amazon valley. He found *M. veitchiana* growing in the crevices and hollows of rocks very high up 'where vapour is constantly rising from the streams and valleys below' and gathered a large and valuable collection of new orchids, in particular the bright orange-yellow *Masdevallia davisii*, named by Reichenbach in his honour. He also added one new tuberous begonia, *Begonia davisii*, to Pearce's collection which the Veitch nursery were still using for their best-selling begonia hybrids. When Davis finally returned from his adventures, he happily settled back to work in the Veitch propagating departments.

Harry's cousin Peter, meanwhile, who had been helping him run the nursery at Chelsea, was given responsibility for transport and supervision of exhibits at continental shows; he took a large consignment of delicate stove plants and nepenthes to the 1873 International Exhibition at Florence. Since he clearly enjoyed travelling, Harry decided to send Peter on a training and plant-collecting trip to Australia and New Zealand. Peter seemed intent on following in the path of his late cousin John Gould, for on his arrival he immediately set off on a cruise to the Fiji and South Sea Islands. But he experienced a number of disasters, losing his Fiji collection in a gale and being shipwrecked on his way to New Guinea.

Harry now turned his attention to the possibilities of finding rare African orchids. At that time travel in most parts of Africa was difficult and dangerous owing to the hostility of the people, particularly the traders who were suspicious of foreigners and prevented them from penetrating into the interior. In 1876, Guillermo Kalbreyer, another German, set sail from Liverpool on the long voyage to the west coast of Africa. Kalbreyer, who was both courageous and determined, reached as far as the Cameroon Mountains but heat and disease took their toll and within a year he had returned to England. He brought home five species of mussaenda, the new *Gardenia kalbreyeri*, plus two new orchids, *Brachycorythis kalbreyeri*, a terrestrial species named for

him by Reichenbach, and *Pachystoma thomsoniana*, an epiphyte named at
Kalbreyer's request, in honour of the Rev. George Thomson who for many
years was an 'earnest missionary in that unhealthy region'. After recovering
from his African adventures, Kalbreyer was sent off to the more 'delightful
highlands and mountain slopes' of Colombia where he did much better.
Kalbreyer travelled into the eastern Cordillera where he found quantities
of *Odontoglossum pescatorei* and *O. triumphans*. Unfortunately he was held up
by exceptionally low river tides on his way back to the coast and the delay
meant that by the time he reached England, more than half his collection
was lost.

Kalbreyer, however, continued to prove himself a valuable orchid collector
and made three expeditions into Colombia where he found several new
species as well as introducing living specimens of others that were known
but still rare in England. He later found the giant *Anthurium veitchii* with
leaves over six feet in length and collected seeds of more than a hundred
species of palms. Apart from his many valuable orchids, including several
species of the curious, large-flowered masdevallias, Kalbreyer collected over
360 dried ferns of which eighteen were new to science. He was a particularly concientious collector and always wrote lengthy reports on the habitats of his collections which were invaluable to nurserymen in the Veitch
New Plant glasshouses. He was praised for his 'judicious packing and careful
superintendence of the transport' of quantities of the scarce *Odontoglossum
blandum* which, in 1879, all arrived in very good condition. After his final
expedition in 1880 Kalbreyer returned to Bogota in Colombia where he
set up his own business as a nurseryman and exporter of orchids – always
sending his best finds to Harry Veitch.

THE ORCHID WARS

During the early 1870s Veitch, Low and Linden continued to be the main
traders employing 'orchid hunters' in South America and Asia. But around
1876, a new and aggressive young upstart appeared on the scene, Henry
Frederick Conrad Sander, the most energetic of the new commercial orchid
specialists. Born in Bremen, he worked in various German and British nurseries until he married the daughter of a wealthy printer and could afford to
start his own nursery in St Albans, Hertfordshire. He met Benedict Roezl,
one of the most prolific German collectors, who had lost his right arm and
used an iron hook to bring down orchids from the trees. Roezl, who boasted
he had sought orchids in more lands than he could count on his fingers

Anthurium veitchii

(presumably when he had both hands) agreed to send Sander a substantial number of the orchids that he found. Professor Reichenbach, a fellow German, became a close friend and ally of Sander whose collectors were usually of German extraction. Rather as James Senior had used Sir William Hooker, Sander used the Professor as an intelligence agent, pumping him for information about movements of other firms. Sander was passionate, single-minded and ruthless in his love and pursuit of orchids and his success was astonishing. Numerous orchids found by his men were named after him and within ten years he had been appointed 'Royal Orchid Grower'. In one year alone, Sander had twenty 'orchid hunters' combing the jungles and mountain ranges of Asia and South America. He drove them hard and would not countenance failure.

Sander quickly learned all the underhand dealings employed in orchid hunting after one of Hugh Low's men had attempted to trick one of Sander's collectors out of his secrets. 'You must be a snake, not a fox,' Sander told his man. More and more stories filtered back to London of 'hunters'

who spent days tracking their competitors and trying to throw rivals off
the scent and of spies planted among the native bearers. The more experienced hunters, especially the self-employed like Roezl, moved swiftly and
silently, never disclosing their movements to anyone, even fellow employees.
A few even disappeared and 'went native'. All kinds of tricks were used to
hamper the progress of rival collectors and to hold up their consignment
of delicate plants. The nastiest practice was to urinate on the packed dried
plants waiting for shipment, causing them to 'bolt' during the voyage and
arrive in useless condition.

Nurserymen and dealers in London fought as hard as their collectors,
especially Sander with the wily old Low. Hugh Low was a shrewd and
cunning nurseryman, but Sander had the fire of youth and relished the battles
in the field, at auctions and in the nursery. At home the race to flower first
was intense and secrecy in the orchid houses was vital – no wonder the
Veitch glasshouses had no door handles! Sander wrote copious and fierce
letters to his men: 'Keep your gob shut, 1,000 plants would be worth £10,000
if they arrive and are genuine. A fortune, but silence!' Careless talk meant
that the journals would get hold of the news 'and their buyers will tell Veitch's
travellers' – hardly the voice of Victorian gentlemen. Veitch, though an old-
established and more respectable outfit, was not averse to taking advantage
of any slip in information and of obtaining new plants wherever and however
it could. Sander, though, understood one crucial thing: 'He who cultivates
them best will sell them best' and here Harry Veitch and his nurserymen still
held the leading position. When Sander introduced a new cattleya, it was the
Veitch nursery who, within the year, first sold flowering plants of it.

However, there were occasions when Harry and his team failed to beat
Sander at his own game. In 1878, a customer had asked the Veitch nursery
to send someone to inspect a lovely but apparently unknown orchid which
had recently flowered in her glasshouse. This was not an unusual occurrence
since orchid plants were arriving in all sorts of ways; sometimes unidentified ones turned up mixed in with others. A nurseryman duly arrived and
identified the lady's orchid as a fine specimen of *Cypripedium spicerianum* and
on the spot offered her a cheque for seventy guineas. Back in the Veitch
Orchid House, the plant was divided and sold for far more than its own
weight in gold. Having profitably sold all the plants, the nurseryman went
back to the lady to enquire if she knew where it had originated so that
more plants could be collected. Probably feeling rather cheated by Veitch's
dealings, the lady firmly refused to help beyond saying that it had appeared

unexpectedly amongst a bundle of *Cypripedium insigne* which she had been sent. This orchid was to be found in a vast region within the Himalayas and even as far east as Assam, yet when news got out every nursery raced to put collectors on the trail of this now highly sought-after orchid.

Only Sander had the nous to return to the lady in Wimbledon and charm her into revealing, over tea and cakes, the address of her brother who often sent her plants from his tea plantation near the border of Bhutan. One of Sander's numerous orchid hunters was immediately despatched to visit the brother and, by using some very devious tactics and embarking on a terrible journey, facing fever, man-eating tigers, hostile natives and impenetrable jungle, he tracked down *Cypripedium spicerianum*. There at last was the plant he had suffered and searched for growing at the summit of a vast rock wall in great sprays. He built a bamboo ladder, climbed up and cut them down and, to be sure of his exclusive find, took every single one. Some months later, Sander offered 40,000 plants of *C. spicerianum* at Steven's Auction Rooms. Sander had succeeded where Veitch and other nurseries had failed: it never occurred to them that the key to the mystery lay in Wimbledon.

Harry was not to be ruffled. His establishment had many years of respectability, science and experience behind it and still held the lead in orchid hybridisation. Sander could have his coups, but the Royal Exotic Nursery at Chelsea and its suburban satellites was still the largest and most prestigious in the country. For more than twenty years the Veitch nursery had been the only place where orchid hybrids (a total of twenty-five in all) were available. Competitive hybridising started around 1874, but Veitch continued to be at the cutting edge until Rollisons and later Sander joined in. Reichenbach sarcastically remarked that 'All Orchidic England is now engaged in the procreation of mules'.

But hybrid orchids were not to everyone's taste and the search for new, wild orchids continued unabated. Whether Harry relished his part in the orchid wars is not known, but it is unlikely that he lost much sleep over them. On the whole his men kept their hands clean and behaved with dignity and professionalism. A few, however, were lost to the opposition. After ten years of profitable collecting for Veitch, Chesterton, with his reputation for finding rare plants, was seduced into joining Sander's expanding team and was put to work searching for the ultimate 'lost orchid', *Cattleya labiata* var. *vera*. It was a free-flowering orchid of particular splendour (first found in 1818 for William Cattley) but its known habitats had been destroyed by de-forestation. As its rarity increased, so its value rocketed. Sander had developed so fierce an obsession that he did not let up in his search until he tracked down fresh supplies of the orchid in the virgin forests high up in the mountainous state of Pernambuco. By then Chesterton had died at Puerto Berrio and his obituary of 30 January 1883 read: 'Poor Chesterton's reckless spirit rendered him very efficient as a plant collector.' The irony in these words tells us much about the extent to which the obsession and madness for orchids drove these men.

Orchids were fast falling victim to their own success and the vast quantities of orchids that were being taken from their wild habitats was beginning to cause concern. In May 1878 the King's Road nursery of William Bull boasted the arrival of 'two of the largest consignments that have ever been made' – estimated at two million. Commercial collectors were being sent out in their droves and whole areas of orchid habitats were plundered. In one particular search for *Odontoglossum crispum* in Colombia, 10,000 were collected with 4,000 trees felled in order to strip them of their epiphytes. As one area was cleared, collectors moved on, hacking down more trees and depleting the natural wealth. Orchid hunters never sent back less than thousands of plants and many thousands more were discarded as being too small or scraggy. The Director of the Zurich Botanic Garden wrote that 'Not satisfied with taking 300 or 500 specimens of a fine orchid, they must scour the whole country and leave nothing for many miles around – the

environs of Quito and Cuenca have been perfectly plundered and no collector henceforth will find any odontoglossums there'. But orchid hunters were not just collecting for themselves; they were stripping out the habitat in order to prevent their competitors from finding anything. The region where Chesterton had rediscovered *Miltonia vexillaria* was later said to have been cleared as if by forest fires. Gardening journals published passionate outcries against the desecration. 'Collectors in all quarters are ransacking the forests to send home plants,' a concerned resident wrote from the British colony of Penang. 'Our jungles are nearly stripped of all the orchidaceous plants.' It was nothing less than 'wanton robbery'.

Professor Reichenbach wrote fierce articles about the waste of orchids that were so badly packed that most arrived 'in a putrid mass'. He spared no one in his attacks and described one collector in South America who 'has done his best to destroy the orchids in the district of Ocana by sending thousands of dead masdevallias and putrid odontoglossums'. He had nothing good to say about Sander's Roezl and only Veitch's collector Kalbreyer and Linden's Wagener were singled out for praise. Reichenbach described collectors as being 'like wandering locusts . . . only intent on accumulating masses and sending them in a careless manner'.

But Reichenbach's criticisms fell on deaf ears. The public had never seen an orchid growing in the wild, nor been in a jungle. They had little interest in the idea of conservation and believed that Nature's bounty was infinite and that the domain of the orchid was limitless. Indeed, it was argued, if wild game hunters were free to go out and shoot countless numbers of wild animals, why shouldn't plant hunters similarly take all they wanted? After all, these exotic and delicate plants would be far better off in the safety and comfort of a glasshouse than unseen and unappreciated in their primitive state deep in the jungle or hanging precariously off a mountainside.

But many of the orchid grounds were drying up. With the exception of Kalberyer's continuing good work, Harry decided to turn his back on South America, believing correctly that most of its orchids had been discovered and taken. Although orchids were always an important part of his life and his nursery, Harry was first and foremost a horticulturalist and commercial nurseryman. He knew better than to gamble his business entirely on the sale of one genus of plant. Victorian gardeners wanted variety and were curious about all kinds of fresh ideas and new plants arriving from previously unknown parts of the world. Harry's confidence in his ability to train and pick good men from his own nursery was, on the whole, paying off.

There had however, been one disastrous and expensive expedition to South Africa by Christopher Mudd, the son of a former curator of the Cambridge Botanic Gardens. Although great things had been expected of him, he was not Veitch trained and Mudd showed no aptitude for collecting and 'entirely lacked the explorer's instinct'. Harry nevertheless, felt that he was ready to embark on the most intense period of plant collecting thus far, using his own trained men. His ambitions were fixed on Japan and China.

FORAYS INTO CHINA AND JAPAN

China, like Japan, had at last been compelled to open some treaty-ports and allow foreigners, including missionaries, freedom to travel inland. Amongst these missionaries were keen botanists whose letters home suggested a rich undiscovered flora far inland up the headwaters of the great rivers if only collectors could penetrate the difficult terrain. For some time Harry had been in correspondence with Jesuit missionaries in the central and eastern districts of China where, since the Peking Treaty of 1860, their presence had been tolerated. With the lifting of restrictions, Harry grasped the possibilities of exploring the vast Chinese hinterland for new plants. All he needed was the right man for the job.

Charles Maries was a grammar-school boy from Stratford-on-Avon who had acquired a love of botany from his headmaster, Professor Henslow. Maries joined Veitch at Chelsea where he proved to be an industrious and steady workman who caught Harry's approving eye. Harry decided to send Maries to China to concentrate his search along the valley of the Yangtze for plants that would be hardy in England. He would also be sent to Japan to collect conifer seeds, including more of those found earlier by John Gould Veitch.

Maries sailed for China early in 1877 full of excitement and enthusiasm. His first ambition was to find a lovely 'lilac' which he had heard grew in a garden in the Chinese coastal city of Ning-Po – Robert Fortune's old territory. Although he successfully

Charles Maries (1851–1902)

traced the garden, Maries could not find the plant. Imagine his astonishment and delight when in Shanghai buying tickets for his trip to Japan he
saw a man carrying a bunch of lilac-like flowers. The man took Maries to
a local nursery-garden and showed him a shrub covered in flowers: it was
not a lilac, but *Daphne genkwa*.

While the west was falling in love with Chinese plants, there was no
love lost between the Chinese people and the western travellers moving
in to convert and exploit them. Maries found the Chinese understandably
aggressive and resentful and he was glad to move on. After obtaining plants
from the relative safety and comfort of the British compound in Shanghai
where life revolved around tennis and polo matches, Maries happily sailed
to Japan. He much preferred the company of the Japanese who seemed
more friendly and polite and appreciated Maries's skills as a shot and as a
talented musician. They were delighted when he learned to play the Japanese
'shamsin' a kind of banjo, and readily joined in their musical celebrations.

Japan had changed dramatically since John Gould's visit seventeen years
earlier. An industrial exhibition was open to visitors in the palace of the
Mikado at Kyoto where formerly it would have meant death to enter. But
many of the great gardens of the Shogun and Daimyos were abandoned
and derelict, although in one Maries managed to acquire the 'curious and
ornamental' square bamboo, *Chimonobambusa quadrangularis* (a native of
China but also cultivated in Japan). Although Maries wrote that he thought
gardening in Japan was dying out, he found many of the nurseries so
admired by Veitch and Fortune still flourishing. They had created a lucrative export trade in lily bulbs and were sending many of the now popular
and established Japanese plants direct to Europe in Wardian cases.

With civil war raging through the south, Maries travelled northwards
500 miles overland, finding several plants including a new white-flowered
azalea. He reached the northernmost port of Aomori from where he planned
to take a steamer to the northern islands. Whilst waiting for his boat, Maries
saw a conifer in a garden which was new to him and he learned that it
grew in quantity on Mount Hakkoda which towered over the little port.
He climbed as high as he could and there found the trees tantalisingly close
and loaded with cones, but an impassable barrier of bamboo scrub prevented
him from reaching them. Undaunted, the following morning Maries made
an ascent on horseback from the north side and was rewarded with a sackful
of seeds of a new species, later deservedly named *Abies mariesii*. He also
collected seed of *A. veitchii* which John Gould had discovered on Mount

Fuji. When Maries returned triumphantly to his lodging he found that the mostly timber-built town had suffered a terrible fire and been reduced to charred ruins. Fortunately his baggage and plant collection had been saved and he took the steamer across the straits to Hakodate.

Maries was the first plant collector to explore the forests of the remote northern island of Hokkaido. There he discovered the Hornbeam Maple, *Acer carpinifolium*, and the Nikko maple, *Acer nikoense* (*A. maximowiczianum*), a species with large trifoliate leaves that in autumn turn brilliant shades of red and purple. He collected various hydrangeas, viburnums, the fragrant *Styrax obassia* and the magical Katsura tree, *Cercidiphyllum japonicum*. He spent many weeks exploring around Sapporo where he found a new variety of the Chinese Bellflower, *Platycodon grandiflorus* var. *mariesii*, which have large, deep purplish-blue flowers. Maries stayed in Japan until the autumn, happily exploring the mountains and making extensive entomological and botanical collections. Well satisfied, he loaded his treasures on to a Japanese ship bound for Hakodate carrying a cargo of dried seaweed. But the ship was old and started leaking, causing the seaweed to swell until it burst the hull. Some boxes of seeds were rescued and put on to another boat which capsized and sank. The wretched Maries, like scores of collectors before him, was forced to turn back and start again.

TWO YOUNG MEN IN BURMA

The news of Maries's lost collection in Japan reached Chelsea around the same time as Harry received a letter from his nephew Peter Veitch who had

Platycodon grandiflorus var. *mariesii*

been travelling in Australasia and the South Sea Islands for nearly two years. He too had recently lost his collection in a shipwreck off the north coast of Australia while on a voyage to New Guinea. Peter wrote that he was intending to go home and help his father in the Exeter nurseries. But Harry had other ideas and, after studying the map of the world that hung in his office, he seemed to think – as armchair travellers so often do – that far-flung parts of the world are near each other. He wrote to Peter asking him to sail immediately to Borneo via Sumatra and the British settlements of Penang and Singapore. There he was to meet Harry's new man Frederick Burbidge.

Burbidge was a highly intelligent and literate young man who had excelled in both practical and scientific training at the RHS Chiswick gardens and later at Kew. He had also worked for five years for William Robinson's paper *The Garden* as well as writing three horticultural books of his own. Burbidge was ready for an adventure and in 1877 Harry packed him off to Borneo with orders to find orchids, pitcher plants and ferns, all highly popular with nursery customers for growing in their conservatories and indoor *terraria*. Peter's instructions were to join Burbidge in the northern tip of Borneo where they were to climb Mount Kinabalu, the Sugar Loaf Mountain. On its upper slopes they would locate and collect seeds of the fabled giant pitcher plant, *Nepenthes rajah*, which, years before, Thomas Lobb had been prevented from reaching.

After nearly three months at sea, Peter staggered into the

Frederick William Burbidge (1847–1905)

British port of Labuan to find Burbidge staying in some comfort. The two young men were similar in age and temperament and seem to have hit it off at once. Burbidge was more botanically gifted than Peter, but both shared a love of nature and adventure and they became firm friends over the long and arduous journeys ahead.

The terrain around Kinabalu, still one of the most dangerous in the world, posed serious challenges. But as the collectors struggled high up into the mountains, they were rewarded by the sight of several pitcher plants, including one they described as a 'tall-growing species bearing beautiful white pitchers, elegantly ewer-shaped, diaphanous like "egg-shell" porcelain and most daintily blotched with reddish crimson'. As they continued climbing, all around them these extraordinary and delicate giants clambered high into the trees, reaching up to forty or fifty feet. Everywhere they looked they saw nepenthes sprawled in 'luxuriant health and beauty', the long, red-pitchered *Nepenthes edwardsiana*, the epiphytal-like *N. lowii* and, at the highest point, *N. villosa*, a beautiful plant with rounded pitchers of the softest pink colour with a crimson-frilled orifice. 'All thoughts of fatigue and discomfort vanished as we gazed at these living wonders of the Bornean Andes!' wrote Burbidge.

'Here on this cloud-girt mountainside were vegetable treasures which Imperial Kew had longed for in vain.' There were also several beautiful phalaenopsis, rich, silky-green mosses, fabulous varieties of tree ferns and palms and giant insectivorous plants, their pitchers bloated with half-digested insects. It was a once-in-a-lifetime experience.

Burbidge and Veitch spent three days on the mountain enduring daily torrents of rain and cold early morning mists. One night they became separated from their bearers. Lost, drenched and cold, the two men sat down under a tree with no food except a couple of wet biscuits and a flask of brandy which they shared, finding them '. . . sweeter than

Phalaenopsis in the wild. From Burbidge's
Gardens of the Sun

the choicest viands would have tasted had we been in dress clothes and in comfortable quarters'. Peter searched his bag and found a couple of cigars and a box of matches. 'Sitting in the smoking room of a comfortable club, or in the billiard-room at home, one may smile on such a discovery; but, situated as we were, cold and wet, a cigar added much to our comfort.' The two young explorers spent a memorable night alone in the jungle cheerfully chatting and smoking.

They made several other journeys along the Bornean coast exploring inland rivers by boat and on buffalo, and by steamboat to the nearby islands of Sulu where they joined in a royal pig hunt and collected several beautiful new orchids, new ferns and rare mosses. Burbidge found a bulbophyllum which he proposed naming *B. peterianum* after his 'travelling companion' Peter Veitch. Indeed, the names Veitch and Burbidge were given to several new species found on this extraordinarily productive expedition, including a new palm, *Pinanga veitchii*, and even a new genus, *Burbidgea nitida*. After a year of exploring and collecting, Peter and Frederick returned home in triumph with their huge collections, providing the Chelsea nurseries with many years of productive work with their introductions. Burbidge's appreciation and knowledge of South-east Asian flora and fauna is richly described in *The Gardens of the Sun* which he wrote on his return home. His botanical enthusiasms were always tempered with a good understanding of the horticultural purpose of his travels. Although he was successful in introducing living plants and seeds of many extraordinary species, a large number have proved too large or too difficult to grow and few find homes in English greenhouses or gardens today. (Burbidge was appointed Curator of the Botanical Gardens at Trinity College, Dublin where he remained until his premature death in 1905.)

Veitch and Burbidge. From *Gardens of the Sun*

CHAPTER ELEVEN

THE GOLDEN AGE

*'The Horticulturalist, when he steps into his Department,
aspires to the top of his art.'*
Abercrombie's Practical Gardener, 1834

O N HIS RETURN to England in 1878, Peter Veitch decided to join his father in Exeter as partner in the newly named firm of Robert Veitch & Son of Exeter. It was a great disappointment to Harry, particularly as less than two years later his younger brother Arthur died of typhoid, leaving another widow and six children for the Veitch firm to provide for. And it was the loss of one more young Veitch from the London family business.

But Harry was blessed with a loyal, skilled and hard-working team of nurserymen: William Court and George Tivey, both brilliant hybridisers, especially of nepenthes, and the 'three Johns', John Dominy, John Heal and John Seden. Seden had created numerous hybrid orchids since his first, *Cypripedium x sedenii*, and several hybrids of cattleyas, phalaenopsis, including masdevallias, calanthes, and many other plants, such as *Escallonia x langleyensis* and *Hemerocallis x luteola*. John Heal had made his name crossing various forms of hippeastrum (amaryllis), streptocarpus and the 'gorgeous-flowered' phyllocacti. Earlier, by crossing Thomas Lobb's Javan and Malaysian introductions, Heal had been very successful with hybrid greenhouse rhododendrons such as *R. balsaminoeflorum*, remarkable for their large, compact trusses of rich and varied-coloured flowers.

It had been many years since Dr Lindley had told John Dominy he would drive botanists mad. Now Professor Reichenbach suggested they might instead go crazy with excitement. In 1878 the long-awaited flowering occurred of a handsome intergeneric hybrid between *Cattleya dowiana* (named after a helpful packet captain on the South American run) and *Laelia purpurata*. It was Dominy's last hybrid and 'a fitting climax to his labours'. Professor Reichenbach named it *Laelia x dominiana* and described all the staff of the 'Veitchian nursery' gathered in the main showroom in

Rhododendron balsaminoeflorum

great excitement about the new seedling: 'There are thousands and thousands of seedlings at the Royal Exotic Nursery . . . but the seedling was understood by a kind of universal suffrage to be Mr Dominy's . . . There were three beautiful buds and one expanded on Sunday, August 11th, just at 12 o'clock to the ecstasy of those present.' When the two other plants flowered they were sent, like so many other famous Veitch hybrids, into the exclusive and expensive collections of Baron Schröder and the Hon. Joseph Chamberlain, MP.

After thirty-five years' service with the Veitch family and having achieved so many triumphs, John Dominy, the pioneer in the hybridisation of orchids, fuchsias and nepenthes, was heading for retirement in 1881. Honours were heaped on him: the RHS awarded him a Gold Flora Medal, the twenty-first volume of *The Garden* was dedicated to him, and an enthusiastic subscription headed by the wealthiest and greatest orchidists raised 200 guineas and a gold watch in acknowledgement of the services Dominy had given to horticulture generally and to orchids in particular. (Dominy retired to his home in Exeter where he died in 1891.) Having cracked the secrets of orchid hybridisation, Dominy passed them to John Seden who went on to create *Masdevallia x chelsoni* and *Sophrocattleya x batemaniana*, named for James Bateman, the veteran orchidist who, despite his initial disapproval of the practice of orchid hybridisation, remained a loyal supporter and friend of the Veitch family.

John Heal took over Sedens's work hybridising South American tuberous begonias from plants which Richard Pearce had first introduced. The goal now was to create begonias with the largest flowers and to produce the first white forms. By 1878 Veitch had exhibited their large-flowered, orange-scarlet 'Emperor' and were advertising their first white begonia, 'Queen of the White', selling at half a guinea a plant. Harry bought a new begonia, found on the island of Socotra, *Begonia socotrana*, which he got Heal to cross with one of the firm's Central American plants, *B. incarnata*, in order to produce the first winter-flowering begonia. The result was 'Autumn Rose' which was not thought quite perfect enough, so Heal had another attempt and produced 'Viscountess Doneraile'. This was used as a second parent to create *B. x* 'John Heal'. Heal later succeeded in creating the large, prolifically flowering 'Winter Cheer' and finally, best of all, *B.* 'Elatior' with reddish-pink semi-double flowers – an instant hit for winter colour. Heal produced several more successful crosses, including one named after his wife, *B. x* 'Mrs John Heal'.

Winter-flowering begonia hybrid *Begonia* x 'Mrs John Heal'

CHARLES MARIES IN CHINA AND JAPAN

Charles Maries was still travelling and had returned to China in the spring of 1878 where he suffered an attack of sunstroke so severe that he was incapacitated for two months. It made him tetchy with the 'natives' whom he did not trust and found 'rather troublesome'. The Chinese responded with sullen non co-operation, aggression and even robbery. This may explain why, despite orders to collect primarily in China, Maries spent most of his time in Japan or on the island of Formosa (Taiwan) where he collected seeds of various rhododendrons.

In December 1878 Harry sent him instructions to make another stab at collecting in central China. Maries took a steamer 1,000 miles inland up the mighty Yangtze River ascending into the famous gorges, as instructed, until he reached the town of Ichang (Yichang) where he found the pretty *Primula obconica* (see colour-plate section). Above Ichang the Yangtze runs for almost 200 miles through five narrow gorges with difficult and treacherous currents where few large boats would venture. West-bound junks and sampans had to be hauled upstream against the churning current by teams of fifty or more men pulling tow ropes along narrow footpaths etched into the precipitous canyon-like walls of the gorges. Rapids and the swift current made travel extremely hazardous and required skilful navigation. Nevertheless, it was the vital trade link between the fertile plains of the Red Basin of Szechwan, the salt mines and mineral deposits of western China and the commercial ports on the coastal plain of eastern China. The region was busy with travel and trade as well as containing several magnificent gardens owned by the wealthy salt barons.

But Maries was terrified of the dangerous river. He reported that the locals were hostile and that he had been badly beaten and robbed by bandits. Whether or not this was true, Maries headed back to Japan. He had become so disillusioned by his experiences in China that he claimed that all Chinese plants of horticultural merit had long since been introduced into cultivation in the west. But even he did not come away empty-handed; he introduced some enduring and beautiful garden plants from China, including his treasured *Daphne genkwa*, found growing abundantly in the wild, several species of spiraea, hypericum, deutzia, weigela, forsythia, lonicera and some wild cherries. He also collected the very beautiful lily *Lilium speciosum* var. *gloriosoides* with white and flushed-rose flowers spotted with crimson and scarlet, and the small ash, *Fraxinus mariesii*. Indeed, for gardeners today, Maries's most important discovery was from China, the winter-flowering Chinese witch hazel, *Hamamelis mollis*, from Jiujing (Kiukiang) in Jiangxi province (see colour-plate section). Owing to an oversight at Coombe Wood *H. mollis* did not find its place in the English garden for a further twenty years.

When Harry heard that Maries had abandoned China, he became disillusioned with him and, in a fit of frustration, declared that while Maries may have had enthusiasm he 'lacked staying power'. Later collectors proved what Harry had long suspected, that had Maries pressed on for another two or three days, he would have discovered undreamed of botanical riches.

Maries' collecting activities in Japan, however, showed neither lack of endurance nor enterprise. He discovered, collected and returned to the Veitch nursery a wonderful collection of over 500 living plants, plus quantities of seed of many new species of great merit, including several shrubs now commonly grown in European gardens. From Japan, Maries is remembered for introducing a number of fine new firs, such as the sturdy Nikko fir, *Abies homolepis*, with its long, purplish cones, and the Maries fir, *Abies mariesii*, which is said to have a scent like ginger. During his travels, Maries also discovered the Japanese lace-cap hydrangeas *Hydrangea hortensia* var. *mariesii*

(*Himacrophylla* 'Mariesii') and *H. hortensia* var. *'Veitchii'* (*Himacrophylla* '*Veitchii*'), plus several climbers, including *Actinidia kolomikta*, with pink, creamy-white and green leaves, the first of the 'Kiwi fruit' species to be grown in England and still popular in gardens today. Maries returned home in February 1880 and, on the recommendation of Sir Joseph Hooker, went to India where he remained, working as superintendent of gardens to the Maharajah of Durbhungah and later for the Maharajah of Gwalior, until his death in 1902.

COLLECTING IN MALAYSIA

Harry continued to send out a steady stream of collectors, including Charles Curtis, another of his talented young nursery gardeners, who in 1878 was put to work in Mauritius and Madagascar. From there, he sent back a variety of tropical plants and some handsome new nepenthes, including *Nepenthes madagascariensis*. Curtis was a Devon boy, the youngest of four brothers who all trained in a nursery near Barnstaple. He had worked and studied hard in the New Plant Department at Chelsea to prepare himself for his dream of becoming a plant collector and he soon proved his worth. On losing some of his plants when a native servant treacherously cut the rope of the raft carrying his plants downriver, Curtis held his nerve and re-collected.

He made further explorations into Borneo, Sumatra, Java and the Mollucas in search of orchids, rhododendrons and nepenthes. Curtis was asked to track down a nepenthes which the great botanical painter Marianne North had seen whilst botanising and painting in Sarawak. A friend had found some trailing specimens of this huge plant in the mountains and brought it down to her bungalow where it was 'festooned round the balcony by its yards of trailing stems' so that she could 'paint the portrait' of *Nepenthes northiana*, one of the largest of all pitcher plants. But several years later no one could recall its exact location. Marianne North asked Harry Veitch if his collector would try to find it again and Curtis successfully traced it. Harry sent David Burke, a young Veitch-trained gardener, to assist Curtis in Sarawak and Burke then returned home with a fine collection, including large quantities of orchids such as *Cypripedium stonei*, many vandas, the beautiful foliage plant *Leea amabilis* and some tropical rhododendrons from Sumatra, among them the golden-yellow *Rhododendron javanicum* var. *tubiflorum (R. teysmannii)* and the rich crimson *R. multicolor* var. *curtisii*. Both became prize-winners and were later used with some of Thomas Lobb's older rhododendrons from Java to create new hybrids.

Curtis meanwhile continued on to Dutch Borneo where he found the lovely and rare *Phalaenopsis violacea* but then lost this collection along with his clothes, instruments and nearly his life in a boat accident. Once again the stoical Curtis went back and re-collected, adding *Paphiopedilum curtisii* and *Nepenthes curtisii* to his name. After he had completed his contract with Veitch early in 1884, he became Superintendent of the Botanic Gardens in Penang from where he continued to send plants to the Veitch nursery as well as incomparable herbarium specimens to Kew Botanical Gardens and the British Museum. Eventually poor health forced Curtis to retire to Devon where he cultivated his collection of peach trees, carnations, orchids and sweet peas in his beautiful garden just above the Barnstaple railway station until his early death in 1928.

Like many collectors, Curtis is remembered through a number of plants which bear his name; one in particular was *Cypripedium curtisii*. Years after Curtis had finished hunting for orchids, *C. curtisii* continued to claim high prices in the auction rooms, but its original whereabouts remained a secret which Harry kept to himself until he could find another suitable collector to send out for replacements. As this orchid became rarer, prices soared and attracted the interest of the irrepressible Sander. He commissioned Ericsson, a Swedish collector, to do nothing but find the 'lost' cypripedium. Ericsson spent years wandering up and down the island of Sumatra, even bravely

Cypripedium curtisii. Discovered growing in the mountains of Sumatra by Curtis in 1882

entering an area notorious for cannibalism where, being 'fat and slow moving', he would have been particularly vulnerable, but he found no sign of *C. curtisii*. Suffering recurring bouts of malaria, he ended up in the sanatorium in Padang, his feverish eyes wandering over the wood panels of the walls where previous patients had scribbled verses and drawn caricatures to amuse themselves. Suddenly the sun struck on a particularly lively and colourful drawing of a flower – an orchid. Ericsson sprang out of bed, for it was none other than *Cypripedium curtisii*: 'Its faded colours shone brightly for a moment, green white margin, vinous purple.' Underneath was an inscription: 'C.C.'s contribution to the adornment of this room'. Ericsson, with help from the local people, finally found *C. curtisii*. Greedily he gathered up 3,000 plants and sent them back to Frederick Sander.

Young David Burke was one of Harry's strangest but most productive collectors. Born in Kent in 1854, Burke was trained at Chelsea and, after successfully bringing home Curtis's collection from Borneo, he demanded to be allowed to go out on his own. According to *Hortus Veitchii*, the solitary Burke crossed a greater area of the earth's surface and covered more miles in search of plants than any other Veitch collector, with the possible exception of the Lobb brothers. Over sixteen years he made numerous epic journeys, concentrating solely on orchids, nepenthes and rare tropical plants, through South America, Upper Burma, the Philippines, New Guinea, Celebes and the Moluccas. He would disappear for long periods when nothing was heard from him. But Harry remained patient, knowing that Burke would eventually deliver something worthwhile. In 1881 he sent Burke to British Guiana where he re-discovered the strange insectivorous plant *Heliamphora nutans* which had not been seen since 1839. He found several new and rare orchids, including *Zygopetalum burkeii* and the handsome *Amasonia punicea (A. calycina)* with its brilliant scarlet bracts which made such a cheerful effect in stove-houses during the winter months. He searched the Philippine Islands for more phalaenopsis and, ten years later in 1891, he was still searching for orchids in the newly-annexed provinces of Upper Burma. In 1896, having spent a short time in England, he left for the Celebes Islands and the Moluccas. It is said that before leaving for the tropics which he loved so much, Burke cheerfully declared, 'I'm off again, and if I make a good meal for someone I hope I shall give full satisfaction.' He was aware of the dangers he faced in unexplored

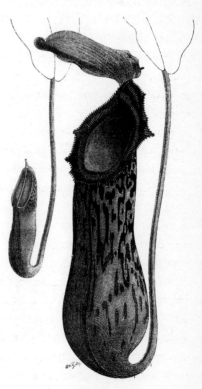

Nepenthes burkeii

regions but he was unlikely to have been eaten, or indeed killed, by the natives since he more often preferred to live like them, and even with them. Increasingly eccentric, he died alone aged forty-three in a hut in a far remote corner of the island of Amboina in the Moluccas in April 1897. A chance visit by a passing German commercial traveller, the only other white man in the island, sent out the news of his death. Otherwise Harry Veitch might never have known of the ultimate fate of his strangest, longest-serving and most adventurous orchid collector. By the early 1880s, the Veitch nurseries had more than enough new plants to work on and, apart from the wandering Burke, it was to be another fifteen years before the Veitches employed another collector.

OLD MONEY, NEW MONEY

In the very early years, John and James Veitch had served the needs of aristocratic landed families while they improved their country estates. Later, James Junior's attentions were most in demand from wealthy plantsmen and women who kept exclusive collections. Over the years, the Veitch nurseries in London had been supplying trees and plants to many of the greatest gardens in England, Scotland, Wales and even Ireland, and their new trees had contributed to some of the finest arboreta. Robert Stayner Holford's arboretum at Westonbirt and that of his friend and neighbour, the 3rd Earl of Ducie at Tortworth Court in Gloucestershire, kept up a continuous order of specimens of every new tree introduced by Veitch collectors. Harry was a regular visitor to Holford's home with its extensive conservatory and nine-span roof range of glasshouses filled with amaryllis, azaleas, fuchsias, foliage plants, camellias and rare orchids. Large orders of plants were sent down by regular rail van from the Royal Exotic Nursery.

Harry was also finding that increasing numbers of new patrons were asking for help and advice with creating suitable gardens for themselves. The Chelsea nurseries, however, had never supplied designers and, in a neat arrangement with his Devon cousins, Harry recommended them for the layout while the Chelsea nursery supplied the plants. Robert Veitch retired with Sarah to Torquay, where he died in 1885 aged sixty-two, leaving Peter to run the Exeter business. He was better trained than his father, and after his travels, more aware of what was going on outside the West Country. He continued his partnership with Meyer, designing rockeries and water features, and they gradually moved into the wider field of formal bedding and topiary work. The first flush of interest in bonsai, encouraged by reports from Japan by John Gould and Robert Fortune, inspired many gardeners to experiment with dwarfed conifers trained as carpet plants for geometric beds. At Minley Manor in Hampshire, Peter and Meyer's most innovative geometric garden, miniature conifers were used as bedding plants in a complex parterre laid out in the form of a family crest. Young cypresses were arranged in a scroll pattern against a groundwork composed of 80,000 seedling yews with panels of variegated dwarfed hollies. The foliage was supposed to shine under electric light and provide a strange, nocturnal effect. Now, Harry and Peter Veitch were finding themselves increasingly on call to a rather different kind of client. A new breed of *nouveaux riches* were moving up the social ladder ready to spend fabulous sums to achieve the most ostentatious, most talked about and admired house and gardens.

In the late 1870s, a series of poor harvests had hit the landowners' pockets and with the repeal of the Corn Laws, cheap American wheat was allowed in. Agriculture slumped and farmers could not pay their rents. A number of large country houses that had been reliant on income from rents and produce from the land were gradually sold off, their woodland cut down for timber and the estates split up. As old landed money hit trouble, the wealth of industrialists, merchants and bankers was increasing through expanding international markets. They started buying up country houses as rural retreats where they could entertain with weekend house parties. The 'green swards' of the Home Counties were particularly sought after, where good rail services allowed busy city gentlemen to be whisked out to their estates for weekends of sporting, shooting and socialising. Owning a country house was not merely a sign of status and wealth, it was also vital to show one had taste and sophistication, and these new country 'squires' relied heavily on the skills of their head gardener and nurseryman to create a garden of fashion and taste.

Fortunately there were a few notable exceptions for whom gardens were more than just a showcase but also a focus of genuine interest and pleasure. For them gardening and exotic plant collections became an absorbing passion and they were prepared to spend huge sums of money in their horticultural pursuits. For example, Ludwig Messel, one of the first-generation Jewish immigrants to make a fortune in the City, bought the Nymans estate in Sussex in 1890. His neighbours were all landowners with city-made wealth: Wilfred Loder at High Beeches, his elder brother Edmund at nearby Leonardslee, Lord Wakehurst at Wakehurst Place, Frederick Godman at South Lodge and Stephenson Clark at Borde Hill. This Sussex clique were all passionate and knowledgeable gardeners; they bought lavishly from the Veitch nursery and even supported their plant-hunting expeditions. In the course of creating their dream gardens, they turned to Harry Veitch and other top nurserymen for advice, landscaping, planting and supplies of plants. Messel built a conservatory which he filled with orchids, planted a pinetum based on the collection at Wakehurst Place, and copied the rhododrendron woodland at Leonardslee. He also created the first heather garden in England as well as a Japanese garden. Messel acquired great skill as a horticulturist which brought him social acceptance among his neighbours in the Sussex gentry and Nyman's became one of the most important gardens in late-Victorian England.

Like his great-great-grandfather, Harry enjoyed visiting patrons around the country but he was on more equal social terms with his customers, many of whom were already family friends through long association with James Junior. Harry often went to Groombridge to meet the garden designer Edward Cooke and when Cooke visited the nursery at Coombe Wood he was taken there in Harry's own phaeton. Harry loved to visit his clients' gardens and was taken on a grand tour of Cooke's garden in 1869. Cooke recorded in his diary; 'After breakfast went with Harry Veitch all round by Arboretum and stumpery, Ward's Rock and Mount Glen, Eagle Rock, Scotland, Crinkum Crankum, Wilderness, Bello Quardo, lawn and back to lunch at 1 p.m.'.

Several members of the hugely wealthy banking family, the Rothschilds, were passionate gardeners, and their vast and lavish Buckinghamshire gardens at Gunnersbury, Ascott, Waddesdon, Exbury, Tring and Halton were filled with Veitch plants. The patriarch, Lionel Rothschild, who once described himself as 'a banker by hobby but a gardener by profession', was a long-time customer and friend of the nursery. He was very taken with the idea of Japanese-style gardens and he had one created at his estate based on a photograph of a 'Japanese' garden he had seen in Italy. Not surprisingly, when the Japanese ambassador visited the garden, his comment was, 'We have nothing like it in Japan.'

Lionel's son Leopold was another keen gardener and passionate orchidist. He asked Harry to advise him on laying out a new garden at Ascott. He loved growing the latest novelties and delighted in extravagant displays of flowers, which had to be bigger, brighter and more scented than anyone else's. Leopold liked to see planting *en masse* and his carnation house was crammed with blocks of brightly coloured blooms. He employed over eighty gardeners to keep the flower beds in perfect condition and to clip his extraordinary topiary garden of golden yews into the shapes of animals, birds, tables, chairs and other strange objects, including a huge sundial of cut yew and box. Harry also helped Nathaniel 'Natty' Rothschild plant rare conifers and fill his glasshouses at Tring with magnificent orchids. Lord Ferdinand and Alfred Rothschild both had over fifty greenhouses in which they grew enormous quantities of plants in their gardens at Waddesdon Manor and Hatton. The Rothschilds always wanted instant maturity in their gardens and twenty horses, specially bred and selected for their exceptional strength, were used to drag large trees to their planting positions. Most members of the family were passionate horticulturists and spent many hours poring over their greenhouse novelties. Amazingly, however, according to Miriam Rothschild, author of *The Rothschild Gardens* and eminent ento-mologist, none of them ever actually handled a spade or pruned a bush. The amounts spent by the Rothschilds is staggering: in 1879, a fairly routine bill for Leopold totalled £237.5.9. One of the Rothschilds' numerous gardeners recalled years later, 'I once heard it say that rich people used to show their wealth by the size of their bedding plants list: 10,000 plants for a squire; 20,000 for a baronet; 30,000 for an earl; and 50,000 for a duke.' The gardener noted that Alfred de Rothschild, a baron, had 40,418 plants, 'which put him well above an earl'.

THE MECCA OF GARDENERS

Head gardeners of these vast and lavish gardens ordered seed and plants in enormous quantities and they expected prompt delivery. As planting was seasonal, orders tended to come all at once and thousands of young bedding plants, shrubs, roses, bulbs and newly introduced plants had to be available in pristine condition at the right time. Through Harry's management and personality the Veitch nurseries in London had built up loyal, hard-working and highly skilled gardening and administrative staff who were able to respond to increasing demands and ensure the smooth running of the busi-ness. The Royal Exotic Nursery had become the largest and most impor-tant nursery in the capital if not the country. But if it was to continue on its current trajectory, Harry knew that it would have to expand.

In 1882 he bought four acres of land close to the Fulham fruit nursery, on which a seed warehouse and other buildings had been erected, and he also rented a further twenty-one acres of farmland called Southfields which lay to the south of the King's Road where fruit and vegetables were to be sold. (Now the site of South Park, this is the only surviving bit of the Chelsea nursery not built over.) When the Great Western Railway

company required the land on which the Fulham nursery stood, Harry
decided to move more of the business to the outskirts of London. He
bought fifty acres at Middle Green Farm in Langley, conveniently near
Slough railway station. The Fulham stock of fruit and vegetables was
moved to Langley where Veitch nurserymen built up a new fruit tree and
rose nursery and concentrated their seed production of vegetables and
flowering annuals. For the customers wishing to visit the new nursery by
train 'past the dingy brickfields . . . from Southall to Slough, a peep at
the rich and varied colours in the grounds of Langley Farm affords a
change at once agreeable and refreshing'. Mr Newby, the Veitch
superindendent, changed the dull fields into a 'sparkling mass of colour,
all neatness and regularity', while ruthlessly removing any plant that
showed itself less than perfect in size, colour and health. Acres of different
kinds of parsley grew alongside fields of broccoli, Veitch's 'Red Globe'
turnip, Nutting's selected beet, seakale, dozens of varieties of potatoes and
other vegetables all grown for seed.

The soil at Langley, which was light and open, was perfect for seed-
growing, not just vegetables but acres of flowers as well. For their beds and
borders as well as for cut flowers, customers could select 'delightful blooms'
of exceptional size and richness of colour in almost every shade. Great
squares were filled with mignonettes, carnations, larkspurs, clarkias,
Canterbury bells, candytuft like drifting snow, lobelias, carpets of pink
saponaria, purple malope, delicate sweet peas and other showy annuals.
There were splendid beds of double-flowered Indian pinks, ten-week stocks
with huge flowers, rich scarlet nasturtiums contrasted with blue and yellow
bedding violas, multicoloured antirrhinums and *Vesicaria oculata.* Along one
path William Lobb's best-selling *Tropaeolum lobbianum fulgens* were trained
up four-foot stakes and nearby was a plantation of new Japanese irises.
Harry bought another sixty acres in Feltham in Middlesex which he used
for specialising in hardy trees and shrubs.

James Veitch & Sons now had three major nursery grounds and a number
of smaller sites. Their advertisements claimed that at the King's Road show
houses in Chelsea, customers could purchase the finest in rare and specialist
stove and greenhouse plants, in particular orchids, azaleas, tree ferns, palms,
camellias, ericas, ferns, vines, and so on. There was also a seedhouse which
sold (both retail and wholesale with discount) vegetable, flower and
agricultural seeds as well as garden tools and 'other requisites'. At Coombe
Wood in Kingston Hill, customers could walk through the beautiful and

extensive grounds admiring and choosing from a huge selection of rare and unique hardy trees, shrubs, herbaceous plants and roses. At Langley there was also a wide choice of roses as well as vegetable and flower seeds which could be ordered in huge quantities, while Southfields and Fulham nurseries sold fruit trees, as well as fresh fruit and vegetables.

The Veitch nursery was now the most dominant force in the nursery trade, the 'mecca of gardeners', a vast concern covering hundreds of acres, growing thousands of plants of every description from the commonest annual to the rarest orchid, and employing and training a huge army of skilled gardeners, specialist nurserymen and a range of staff working from packaging to finance and management. It was like a vast and complex ship steaming seemingly effortlessly towards even greater goals of profit, public approval and scientific recognition: a liner of class, of taste, even of beauty, calmly and very competently navigated and captained by Harry Veitch. With a combination of business acumen and sound judgement Harry 'had the control of a tremendous business, and unquestionably, he controlled it'.

The headquarters at the Chelsea nurseries extended from the King's Road to the Brompton Road, bounded on one side by Gunter Grove and on the other by St Mark's College. It was not a large site and most of it was covered with ranges of glasshouses housing the different plant depart-ments which had their own propagating sections. There was a service entrance from the Brompton Road for the cartage of coke, loam, manure, pots and other materials. The roomy packing sheds which were presided over by Mr Black, who was also timekeeper, opened on to Gunter Grove. At the King's Road end were a seed warehouse, library and herbarium, plus spacious offices. Here too was the grand entrance and Show Rooms with some 'handsomely furnished' rooms where wealthy customers, botanists, foreign visitors and returned collecters could be entertained by Harry or Mr Manning, the tall and imposing general manager. Any staff coming into contact with patrons were required to wear frock-coats and white gloves. Their manners were expected to be exemplary, their horti-cultural knowledge without question and their patience endless. Not all customers were easy. Some asked silly questions, had no idea what they wanted, did not know plant names and could not make up their minds or make intelligent choices. As the ladies swept through the displays and narrow places in the glasshouses their crinolines snapped off flowers and damaged plants. Gentlemen brushed glowing cigars in the foliage, grabbed delicate orchids and nepenthes to sniff and peer at, and wrenched blooms from

Photographs taken at Chelsea c.1900 show the new show front
and offices (above), and the cramped glasshouses (below)

their branches, loosening the roots. But the customer, however maddening,
was always right and every Veitch employee knew it.

Life at the nursery during this golden age was described by William
Camp who remained for five happy years in a 'most exacting job' and
watched the business grow and flourish under Harry, its new director.
Another nurseryman was the young Charles Curtis, a nephew of the Veitch
collector. His father had been a schoolfriend of John Heal's and both had
had training in a nursery in Barnstaple in Devon. Curtis wrote in detail
about the Veitch nursery, its organisation and its hard-working but
colourful-sounding staff at Chelsea.

Each of the many plant departments had a distinct and independent entity working under a capable and experienced foreman who was responsible only to Harry Veitch. Charles Canham, who presided over the large and important 'Orchid Department', was a rather short, Falstaffian man, so fat in fact that during his later years he could not squeeze himself through the doors of the smaller house but could only look in to give orders. John Heal was in charge of the equally important 'New Plant Department' which consisted of two long ranges of glasshouses plus the big Amaryllis House. The glasshouses of these departments were so secret and private that there were no handles on the outer doors. The head of the 'Fern Department' was George Schneider, a Frenchman, author of the three-volume *Book of Choice Ferns*, a very knowledgeable man, kindly and softly spoken, who presided in genial and fatherly fashion over the horticultural students from abroad who were training in the nursery. The head of the 'Tropical Department' was the 'tall and alert' George Tivey, 'a past master in the cultivation of nepenthes, anthuriums and codiaeums'. The 'Greenhouse Department' was controlled by Mr West who grew gloxinias, ixoras and many other decorative flowering plants. Mr Minns, known as 'the Doctor' and his deputy, Mr Weeks, were kept busy in the 'Soft-wooded' and 'Hard-wooded Departments' propagating summer bedding, which occupied such an important place in the annual routine of Victorian gardening. The foreman of the 'Vine Department' was Mr Wilkins, who grew wonderful vines (but only planting vines, not grapes). 'Perhaps,' Curtis wrote, 'it was the thought that others reaped the fruits of his labours [which] had something to do with his acidity and hermitic retirement from the company of his fellows.'

John Seden, now Veitch's most senior and valued hybridiser, was a 'bright-eyed, humorous and altogether kindly person'. But he was rarely seen, as his specialist 'Propagating Department' was tucked away in a corner, behind the corridor entrance from Brompton Road. It was here that the famous early hybrids and new orchids, nepenthes and other rare species were raised. Harry Veitch's great friend, the nurseryman Henry May, who was once 'fellow lodger' with Seden in their youth at Chelsea, recalled that Seden's career was an illustration of 'dogged does it' – no doubt the best qualification in the 'Propagating Department'.

Mr Davison, who presided over the 'Seed Department' at the other end of the establishment, looked more like a professor than a seedsman and he never used two words when one would suffice. His deputy was the tall and gentlemanly Alfred Dawkins and together they may have seemed a formidable pair for the unwary customer who did not know what he or she wanted. The 'Decorative Department', close to the 'New Plant Department', was run by Mr Archer, a 'man about town', alert and clever, who kept his men working at high pressure in the London season. In those days, the town houses of the nobility and the more important hotels were decorated 'in prodigal fashion' for all social functions and unbelievable quantities of potted and cut flowers were ordered from the nursery.

Royalty, nobility, gentlefolk and gardeners of every description and background strolled through the nursery grounds, full of curiosity and admiration for the extraordinary displays of fabulous plants. Gentlemen in morning suits with top hat and gloves and ladies, tightly waisted and bustled, took leisurely perambulations up and down the nursery paths, pausing to indicate with their parasols a colourful bloom or new leaf shape that caught their eye. Before he died, the Prince Consort, an 'ardent patron of horticulture', was frequently seen in the grounds with his children. One day an appointment was made for the Princess of Wales and the Crown Princess of Prussia to visit the nurseries. Elaborate preparations were made, a special tea service was bought and the German Ambassador was to be present to receive the royal ladies. William Camp recalled that the general manager, Mr Manning, told him to deal with two ladies who were in the nursery and get them out of the way before the royals arrived. Camp duly escorted the ladies around the ground, they seemed very pleased with everything and spent a happy half hour in his charge until someone came up in a great state and revealed that the ladies were indeed the royal princesses who had walked in unaccompanied, having sent their page boy away in the chaise. Such was the confidence and good humour that underlay the strict discipline and rigorous duties of all the staff that no one, least of all the royals, seems to have minded.

It was through the prince that the Veitch nurseries were permitted from time to time to present the bouquets at royal weddings. The first time the firm received the royal command was for the marriage of the Princess Royal to the Prince of Teck at Kew. The newspapers reported that 'Messrs Veitch of Chelsea had the honour of presenting, by special permission of H.R.H., the Princess Mary's bridal bouquet' which was composed of orange blossoms, stephanotis, white roses and a variety of orchids including *Odontoglossum pulchellum*, all tastefully held together with Honiton lace. 'The bride looked pale but radiant with beauty though it was easy to perceive the tremulous motion of the large bouquet of orange-flowers which she carried.'

A NURSERY FOR GARDENERS

Harry, like his father and grandfather, believed strongly in the education of gardeners and nurserymen and would not accept that they were merely 'labourers with plants'. All his heads of departments were highly trained and experienced men and their loyalty to the firm was unswerving; for them Harry Veitch 'inspired the complete confidence of the working gardeners, who saw in him not only a great plantsman and a trustworthy dealer but a sincere well wisher to their craft'. A large amount of the nursery work was done by men 'in for a job' or 'young fellows desirous of training' and engaged for a period of two years at 12 shillings per week during the first year and 15s in the second year, plus a slightly higher rate for Sunday duty – usually once in three weeks. The hours were 6 a.m. to 6 p.m. and 'discipline was splendid, though a trifle irksome on occasion'. A man fifteen minutes late in the morning might be sent back until after breakfast and would then 'lose a quarter'. Men who worked in the nursery while waiting for an appointment used to take things more easily, but the 'young fellows', the two-year men, had to toe the line.

One veteran gardener observed that 'Veitch was not just a nursery garden, it was also a nursery for gardeners'. Many generations of head gardeners were of Veitch origin and over the years hundreds of trained gardeners were sent to appointments thoughout the country and abroad. An average of 400 young men each year entered the nurseries to be trained and placed in situations. 'I wish I knew the names of all those who have gone through our place,' said Harry, who could certainly recall most of them. Veitch nursery apprentices were moved from one department to another, acquiring knowledge and skills as they went. They learned the whole process, from germinating the seed or striking a cutting through to maturity of flowering and setting seed. They would learn about different plant structures, diseases and how to combat them, the functions of different parts of plants, roots, leaves, flowers and how different soils and climates affected them. They were kept busy stoking fires, carrying loads of fuel for the boilers and manure and lime for the beds, scrubbing pots and sorting and cleaning spades, hoes, rakes, brooms, baskets and barrows. Nurserymen, they learned, had to have eyes everywhere; in the seed trays, watching the temperature of the glasshouses, for the right amount of watering, for signs of disease or blight which could decimate young plants, or the invasion of insects which could rip through a house of tightly packed stock in a matter of days.

Training was rigorous and thorough and life was tough for the young

Apprentices working in the nursery

apprentices. The heated greenhouses were often a more welcome place to
spend time than the draughty, damp bothy which the younger ones called
home. The older lads lived out in lodgings and while some had financial
help from home, many did not. Charles Curtis lived above a grocer's shop
in West Brompton at 10s. per week, which left 2s. for his fares and for the
'pleasures of life'. Those who were not 'remittance men' often walked many
miles to save on bus and rail fares. Veitch's always encouraged trainees to
study as widely as possible; a proficiency in reading, writing, arithmetic,
botany, plant physiology and design drawing were essentials. If a man was
aiming for head gardener on a large estate, he would also need management skills to cope with a large staff, a good head for figures to keep within
budget, plus good manners and diplomacy in his relations with master and
mistress of the house.

Some of the brighter trainees took evening courses in botany and biology
at the Birkbeck Institute which, to save fares, meant a long walk from Chelsea
to Chancery Lane. The lads would take a rest at Victoria Station, where, in
the corner of the station yard, they could buy the largest cup of coffee and
the biggest Bath bun for a penny each. Those who needed to increase their
wages could do so by working overtime in the seed warehouse packeting
seeds, or in the office making out the bills from marked copies of the order
sheets. The money earned was paid in a lump sum at the end of the season
and enabled them to buy clothes – a good overcoat could be found in

Lambeth Marsh for a pound. As Curtis recalled, 'We were busy, keenly interested, poor but happy, those were the days.' Amongst them was the day John Seden called everyone along to the Propagating Department to see the first flowering Brassocattleya.

One story related by Charles Curtis is reminiscent of John Veitch, Harry's great-great-grandfather, from whom Harry had inherited his rather racy, teasing humour. Secrecy and security were paramount and it had been impressed on young Curtis when he arrived that he was not to permit any unauthorised person to enter any part of the New Plant Department or he would suffer instant dismissal. Although there were no door handles to the houses, the spindle had a filed notch into which the edge of a penny could be thrust deeply enough to lift the latch. On his first morning, to Curtis's horror, the outer door of the range burst open and a burly, bearded figure entered and shouted for Heal. Curtis rushed towards the intruder and berated him for bursting the lock. He informed the man that Heal was in his office in the next range and if he entered it unannounced he would 'hear all about it'. The man with the beard disappeared without a word and closed the door. Sometime later Heal berated Curtis in the severest tones: 'Young man, you *have* done a fine thing for yourself, don't you know who it was you turned out just now?' Of course it was Harry Veitch himself and Curtis waited for the axe to fall. But Harry loved this kind of spirit and had said to Heal, 'He's a sharp lad, we shall have to keep our eyes on him.'

The following afternoon, Curtis heard the soft click of the latch and very quietly 'Mr Veitch' entered and slowly walked up the range, inspecting plants until he came to Curtis who was potting seedlings. 'Good afternoon, Curtis, have you a plant of *Begonia froebelii*?' he enquired. Despite his nerves, Curtis found the plant and bravely expressed the view that it was a small specimen and not an easy subject to grow. As Curtis turned to go and find Heal, Harry said, 'Curtis, I promise not to steal anything while you are gone!' They became great friends and years later Harry enjoyed introducing Curtis as 'the only man that ever turned me out of my own nursery'.

For all Veitch staff standards were high and men who went out with the Veitch warranty took with them something special. The departing graduate was presented with a knife and an apron, the insignia of his craft, and a promise that if the post proved unsatisfactory, he would be welcomed back on the old terms, and another post found. Veitch's always stood by its opinion of a man, whatever an employer might say.

CHAPTER TWELVE

A NEW GENERATION

'It is no unworthy aim to reveal what God has planted in the lost mountains, since thereby may also be revealed what he has hidden in the hearts of men.'

F. Kingdom Ward,
From China, 1924

O N A SUMMER evening in 1889, in the glittering banqueting rooms of the Grand Hotel, Charing Cross, sixty-two guests were seated at two long tables laid with snowy white linen, fine crystal glass and sparkling silver. The Veitch clan was assembled to celebrate the coming-of-age of James Herbert, eldest son of the late John Gould, and of Arthur James, son of the late Arthur. Family guests included the boys' widowed mothers Jane and Emily, James Herbert's younger brother John G. and Arthur's five brothers and sisters, their maiden aunts Constance and Pauline, and numerous cousins, including Peter and his family up from Exeter. Presiding over this happy occasion was the head of the family, Uncle Harry and his wife Louisa. There were plenty of guests who were close friends of the family, many of whom were also horticultural worthies – Sir William Thiselton-Dyer, Director of Kew, Dr Robert Hogg, the RHS Secretary and great pomologist, the Reverend William Wilks, discoverer of the Shirley Poppy, Sir George Holford of Westonbirt, and Veitch's 'friendly European rivals', the botanists and nurserymen de Graaf of Leydon and de Smet of Ghent, and, of course, Baron Sir Henry Schröder.

James Herbert Veitch (1868–1907)

As ever, there were Harry's close friends, nurserymen George Paul and Nathaniel Sherwood, whose son had recently married Arthur Veitch's daughter Mary Isobel.

The rooms and entrances were beautifully decked out with pots of palms, tree ferns and anthuriums. The tables were decorated with masterly but tasteful displays of Veitchian flowers. The Decorative Plant Department of the Royal Exotic Nursery, daily providing lavish and extraordinary floral displays for society functions, had made a special effort for this dinner; down the centre of the tables snaked garlands of flowers twined with sprays of apple blossom, circlets of evergreens and coloured leaves such as dracaena and coleus. There were intricate chains of different myrtle studded with bright hybrid begonias, while hanging in great loops were wired garlands of *Ampelopsis veitchii* interleaved with blooms of gardenia, *Lapageria rosea* and some of Veitch's finest and rarest orchids wafting their lovely scent on to the guests below. In front of each guest was a tiny glass which held a small spray of maidenhair fern, a single orchid as a button-hole for the gentlemen and a small bouquet for the ladies.

The splendid feast was almost over and bowls of Veitch's finest fruits were set out, cigars lit and the port started on its journey. Baron Schröder stood up and made a toast to the 'capacity and skill which had brought the House of Veitch to a position second to none in the world' and was now reaching the 'fifth generation of a family, so intimately connected with the progress of horticulture in this country'. The Baron invited the assembled guests to raise their glasses and welcome the two young gentlemen now making their entrance into horticultural life. He expressed the hope that now that 'they were called to the helm of affairs' they would follow the excellent example before them, which would assuredly lead them to a 'like honourable position'. More speeches of congratulation followed, toasts were drunk, and the memorable evening was rounded off with Miss Marie Belval and her company entertaining the guests with 'some charming singing'.

Expensive banquets held in public hotels with mixed company were a far cry from those learned, intimate and sometimes volatile dinners that had once carried on into the late hours at Stanley House. Many of those who had enjoyed James Junior's energetic hospitality regretted the passing of those times. The 'Old Dwelling House' had been demolished after Harriott Veitch's death in 1879 to make way for new offices in the cramped Chelsea nursery grounds. Meanwhile Harry and Louisa still lived in Redcliffe Gardens. His two unmarried sisters, Constance and Emma Pauline, lived close by in Cathcart Road where the younger generation of Veitches from Exeter and elsewhere were encouraged to stay on their visits to London. Harry's eldest sister, Anna Harriott, had married Charles Scorer, a solicitor from Lincoln, and another sister, Agnes, had married Reginald Vining, a son of the Veitch family solicitor. It was a tight-knit family, held together by religion. The Chelsea Veitches were regular churchgoers at St Luke's Episcopal Church in Redcliffe Gardens where Harry was church-warden. Throughout his life he kept up his charitable work, funding two London Church missionaries in Chelsea and working on behalf of the Gardeners' Royal Benevolent Institution and the Gardeners' Orphan Fund which he helped found in 1887.

Throughout his adult life Harry, who had no children, had had to act as surrogate father to numerous nephews and nieces, paying for their educa-tion as well as providing financial support for their widowed mothers. Considerable sums from the business went on the upkeep of several house-holds. James Herbert's younger brother John Gould Junior, a very intelli-gent boy, was sent to Westminster School and Trinity College, Cambridge. He suffered from increasing deafness which made him shy and retiring but Harry brought him into the firm on the business side where he proved a loyal and diligent worker. There is no record of young Arthur ever working for the firm, he married and had a daughter and predeceased his uncle. But it was on James Herbert that Harry had set his ambitions for the future of the business and it was he who was causing Harry the most concern.

James Herbert grew up in the house at the Coombe Wood nursery where he was steeped in plants and in the horticultural business. He was educated at Crawford College in Maidenhead and then, as was the family custom, sent for training in nurseries in France and Germany. Although he never knew his father, James Herbert seems to have inher-ited the same restless, enquiring spirit and, like John Gould, he was cheerful and plain speaking. However, he seemed in no hurry to settle down

John G. Veitch (1869–1914)

and join the family firm, nor to set to and work his way up through the departments at Chelsea and Coombe Wood. Perhaps taking a trip abroad, as his father John Gould and his Uncle Peter had done, would give the boy a chance to see a bit of the world and give him a sense of purpose. It was something for Harry to think about.

HARRY AND THE RHS

Harry's concern about a successor to help run the nursery was understandable. He was in danger of being overwhelmed with the demands of the nursery business as well as his responsibilities to the RHS Council with its endless committees, sub-committees, conferences and shows. Nearing fifty, he was still fit and healthy. His generosity was characteristic of his open-handedness which had made him so respected and liked. Despite secrecy in business, Harry always believed in sharing horticulture knowledge not just with fellow horticulturists but with ordinary gardeners and he sometimes felt torn between his relationship with the grand names on committees and with the general public. He believed that he and his friend George Paul, a fellow council member, were 'connecting links between practical gardeners of the country and the amateur element'. People would come up to him at shows with all kinds of questions which he thoroughly enjoyed and he would often spend hours in discussion with individuals and small groups of people.

Like his father, who had started the idea of plant committees, Harry served on several during his long life. His favourite was the Orchid Committee for which he was chairman for many years. It was in May 1885 at the RHS Orchid Conference at South Kensington, where the largest and most varied collection of orchids ever seen was staged, that Harry decided to share the secrets of hybridising orchids. Harry's father and grandfather had always kept to themselves the details of the nursery's methods as had other nursery businesses and it was still a carefully guarded trade secret. But he was determined to share his firm's knowledge with ordinary gardeners and he shocked the horticultural world by giving a paper on the hybridisation of orchids in which he revealed the entire process. The result was electric and from that single lecture dates the widespread raising of hybrid orchids and a more egalitarian approach to horticulture generally. Harry's readiness to share the technical knowledge and skills acquired by Veitch attracted much criticism from the more secretive and conservative members. He never accepted the idea of a horticultural elite, believing that gardening was for everyone, as was the knowledge that went with it. Curiously Harry seems to have felt no qualms about hybridising, despite his own strongly held religious beliefs. Indeed he was puzzled by Bateman's reaction to hybrids. During his speech at the famous orchid meeting Harry said; 'Mr Bateman is such a kind-hearted, genial gentleman that many a time I have asked myself why, when he came into my [green]houses, he used to act in such an extraordinary manner when he saw a hybrid.' After Harry's paper, Bateman was called upon to propose a vote of thanks and his views appeared to have mellowed, as he explained how he had come to hold them. 'I am sure that he [Veitch] and Mr Dominy also, will know and appreciate the effort it costs me to make this proposal, for I have been brought up with the very strongest abhorrence of hybridisers . . . my first orchid-growing friend was Mr Huntley, when I paid him a visit at his snug rectory in Huntingdonshire, he pointed out to me his cacti and his orchids, and said "I like those plants, in fact they are the only plants I grow, because those fiends [the hybridisers] cannot touch them' Bateman carried on: 'but, however strong my prejudices were, I must confess that when I saw such plants as the cattleya downstairs, if I was not converted, I was at all events, what amounts to the same thing, shut up . . .' and he sat down to cheers and applause.

Harry was increasingly finding he was spending too much time on committees and too many hours on the business. He was now also under critical fire, his wife Louisa was unwell and the strain had become too much. By 1888 Harry had come to the difficult decision to resign from the RHS Council, 'simply because I have not the physical strength to do all that is required of me besides attend to my business which must of course have the first consideration . . . I am not,' he wrote to his friend Thiselton-Dyer, the Director at Kew, 'one of those who having joined in any undertaking can only give occasional attention to it' and he expressed his frustration with other less dedicated council members. He even complained about the lack of effort shown by some of his own closest friends such as Dr Hogg and Colonel Beddome, but reserved his fiercest criticism for Dr Maxwell Masters who 'wouldn't even lend his name but is always ready to have a rub at us in the *Gardener's Chronicle*' (of which Dr Masters was then editor). Ending the letter rather testily, Harry declared that: 'The Council gets very spare credit for all their work and anxiety whilst there is never any diffi-culty about getting up an attack on us.'

Fortunately for the RHS, its President, Sir Trevor Lawrence, persuaded

Harry to withdraw his resignation. Indeed, it seemed a curious time to be thinking of backing out, just when things were starting to go so well for the RHS. 1888 was a turning point in the Society's fortunes and the beginning of a long period of prosperity and success. Having made its escape from the disasters of Kensington, the RHS was now settling into its new headquarters in Victoria Street, Westminster, while the fortnightly meetings and shows were being held in the Drill Hall of the London Scottish Volunteers nearby in Buckingham Gate. Only a few days after Harry's letter to Thiselton-Dyer, the first of the Society's Temple Shows was held in the gardens of the Inner Temple on the Embankment. The weather was appalling but, a journalist wrote: 'This departure . . . is so remarkable and the circumstances are so peculiar, that a few superlatives are more than admissible. Altogether the display is one which shows convincingly that the Society is amply worthy of that extended support which we heartily hope it will get in the shape of new subscribers.' Despite the expense and the rain, the first of the annual Temple Shows – the forerunner of the Chelsea Flower Show – was hailed as a success.

Fruit and vegetables continued to be as important a part of the Veitch nursery business as orchids and garden plants. In 1888, John Seden was moved from Chelsea to oversee the introduction of improved strains of vegetables and fruits in the Langley Nursery. Some amazing and enormous vegetables were the results, including Veitch's 'Autumn Giant' cauliflower, 'Red Globe' turnip and a cos lettuce called 'Self-folding Chelsea Imperial'.

A typical floral fête, this one in Covent Garden

The Fruit and Vegetable Committee, first started by James Junior, continued with its work and the RHS garden at Chiswick became, despite its restricted size, the venue for many well-attended conferences, such as the Vegetable Conference in 1889 at which the Veitch nursery assembled an impressive non-competitive display of its own vegetables. Though expensive to stage, these conferences were greatly praised for their educational and scientific value and, as Harry wrote, 'The promotion of the profitable cultivation, uses, and improvements of all kinds of roots, tubers, leaves, flowers, and seeds, by the reading of papers, discussion of propositions, and demonstrations of practice, they bring together, for the purpose of reciprocal information and fellowship, all those interested in the growth of vegetables.' And, of course, all the many other groups of plants – roses, dahlias, grapes and chrysanthemums – on which these conferences were later held.

Harry was also busy supervising a number of important Veitch publications being prepared by the nursery foreman, Adolphus Kent. *A Manual of the Coniferae* published in 1888 included beautiful engravings by the firm's artist, J. Page. Many of Harry's papers appeared in the *Journal of the Royal Horticultural Society* including 'Orchids Past and Present' and 'Deciduous Trees and Shrubs of Japan' and a description of twenty years' work by Seden and Heal on the hybridisation of South American hippeastrums. His greatest work was the two-volume *Manual of Orchidaceous Plants Cultivated Under Glass in Great Britain*. Published in ten parts between 1887 and 1894, it was praised by the orchid writer Frederick Boyle as a 'model of lucidity and a mine of information'.

Gooseberry 'Golden Gem'

In 1891 the Society held a Conifer Conference, bringing together cones, timber and 'fruiting and vegetative branches from all parts of the British Isles'. It proved how widespread and successful had been the introductions of conifers by the Horticultural Society collectors, David Douglas and Theodor Hartweg, and the Veitch collectors, William Lobb, John Gould and Charles Maries. Harry gave a paper on 'The Coniferae of Japan' describing the development and success in Europe and North America of introductions made by his brother in the 1860s. He also paid tribute to Charles Maries's introductions as well as the collector's extensive knowledge of Japanese conifers in their native country 'which enabled us to give in our Manual much interesting information respecting them not previously known'. The following year there was a Begonia Conference and again Harry gave a paper, this time about the extraordinary work done by Heal and Seden in hybrids created from Richard Pearce's begonia introductions.

During one conference Thiselton-Dyer remarked to Harry that Kew was having problems with its antiquated and inadequate hothouses. A few days later Harry visited Kew Gardens to inspect repairs to one stove-house and was horrified by what he saw: 'I have been quite haunted by the sight of men repairing the stove, so much timber in the roof, the superintendent should turn his attention to shipbuilding – he is evidently not aware that plants require *light*.'

In October 1897 on the sixtieth aniversary of their patron Queen Victoria's accession to the throne, the RHS created a new medal, the Victoria Medal of Honour. In the historic ceremony at the Drill Hall, sixty medallists, one for each year of Her Majesty's reign, stepped forward for the presentation. They included Veitch hybridists John Seden and John Heal, one-time Veitch collectors Frederick Burbidge and Charles Maries, and fellow nurserymen George and William Paul and Nathaniel Sherwood. Other eminent friends of Veitch's who received the VMH were Lord Rothschild, Baron Schröder and Sir Joseph Dalton Hooker. There were only two women medallists, Gertrude Jekyll and Ellen Ann Willmott.

Harry could not receive the VMH because he was on the committee recommending names of medallists, but his turn came later. He was also responsible for the Veitch Memorial awards in which he seems to have had free rein. Harry chose to award three Veitch Memorial Medals to orchidists for their contribution to the discovery, cultivation and nomenclature of orchids. One went to the Rev. Charles Parish for the large number of new species he had sent back from Burma, one to John Seden for raising so many beautiful hybrids for the Veitch nursery, and the third, fittingly, to Professor Reichenbach for his lifetime's work in describing and naming new species and hybrids.

In 1889 Professor Reichenbach died in Hamburg and all the talk was about who would get the professor's priceless collection of dried orchids. Everyone had hoped – even assumed – that Reichenbach would leave his famous and jealously guarded herbarium to the Botanic Gardens at Kew. Over the years thousands of rare plants had been sent to Reichenbach by collectors, from individual enthusiasts and nurserymen, especially Veitch's, but Harry knew that there were many plants in the hands of amateur orchidists who had been intimidated by Reichenbach and his inaccessible private collection in Hamburg 'around which was such an aura of mystery'. He believed that these people would be happier sending their specimens to the herbarium collection at Kew. Replying to a letter from Thiselton-Dyer enquiring if he knew anything about Reichenbach's will, Harry had written that since Veitch had begun publishing its own orchid manual and had started to use Kew for naming its plants, the Professor had 'felt hurt at the proceedings' and they had heard nothing from him 'despite a long and close association'. Harry had 'long felt the inconvenience of and drawbacks of having to send our specimens to Germany for naming'. 'However,' he wrote, 'as long as R occupies the position he cannot be ignored, but he is getting now so advanced in years and it needs a younger man to take up the subject.' Harry described to Thiselton-Dyer a recent visit to the Botanic Gardens in Zurich where he had discussed the Veitch relations with Reichenbach with the director, Mr Ortgies, who had told Harry how 'sore' Reichenbach was with the Veitches. Unaware that the professor had just died, Ortgies expressed his confidence that the herbarium would be left to the Royal Botanic Gardens at Kew, particularly 'as the German government had never properly recognised the professor and there was no one in Germany who was capable of properly caring for it'.

But the horticultural world fell into a state of shock when Reichenbach's will revealed that he had left everything to the Imperial Hof Museum in Vienna (now the Naturhistorisches Museum), stipulating that it was to remain in sealed cases and not be permitted to be seen for twenty-five years from the date of his death. 'Disgust was universally felt,' wrote the Gardener's Chronicle. Reichenbach's explanation was that this would prevent the destruction of his valuable collection which, he believed, was inevitable as a result of the 'present craze for Orchids' – which seemed to imply a lack of integrity at Kew. The professor had often warned of the destructive activities of orchid collectors in the wild, but there were many people, including Harry Veitch, who did not believe that this was the real explanation. Here was a man who, since John Lindley's death, had reigned supreme as the orchid authority. His devotion to orchids amounted to a consuming passion: 'To him meals and clothes were necessary evils, but his herbarium was a prime necessity of existence.' His impetuous temper and biting sarcasm had kept many friends at bay, yet he himself was very sensitive to insult; indeed it may well be that Harry Veitch was – as he seems to have suspected – one of those whose innocent activities had been instrumental in creating this extraordinary act of spite. In fact, the value and quality of Professor Reichenbach's orchids would not to be judged until after the First World War – more than thirty years after his death.

The Veitch nursery had no collectors travelling during this time, apart from the wayward and solitary Burke. This was not for lack of interest nor of funds but because the Coombe Wood nursery was still processing the fruits of earlier expeditions. Harry was biding his time, waiting for the right moment, the right place and the right man. He had particularly admired the sumptuously produced first volume of *Plantae Davidianae*. Published in Paris in 1884, it was a botanical treatise describing more than 1,500 new plants which, over a thirteen-year period, had been found in China by Abbé Armand David, the French missionary and botanist. Included in this remarkable collection were new cotoneasters, astilbes, rhododendrons, roses and scores of other plants, including some entire new genera. By then much of the coastal flora of China was known to botanists, but the remote regions of the interior and Tibet and Mongolia were still unknown to the West. Along with David's discoveries were those of another extraordinary botanist from China, whom Harry met one day in 1889 at his welcoming party at Kew.

Dr Augustine Henry was home on leave from his post as medical officer and assistant in the Chinese Imperial Maritime Customs Service at Ichang, in the province of Hubei. For some years Dr Henry had been sending copious quantities of beautifully prepared herbarium specimens of the local flora to Thiselton-Dyer at Kew. Dr Henry, an amateur naturalist, had made several botanising trips, penetrating the lush, undisturbed forests, home to hordes of golden monkeys, in the no man's land on the Hupei–Sichuan border. The amazing botanical diversity astonished Dr Henry and he set about making dried specimens of new maples, viburnums, cotoneasters, hollies, rhododendrons, lilacs, lilies, honeysuckles and much more, including nearly 500 new species, twenty-five new genera and an entirely new family of plants, the *Trapaceae*, comprised of two species of aquatic plants from China and Japan. Dr Henry's infectious enthusiasm aroused interest on both sides of the Atlantic. Botanists at Kew were almost overwhelmed as they rushed out articles in the science and horticultural journals describing these exciting new discoveries.

IN HIS FATHER'S FOOTSTEPS

Meanwhile James Herbert was finding the routine work in the Veitch nurseries rather irksome. Like many young people who have grown up without a father, particularly one as well-known as his, James Herbert was anxious to go in search of his father's memory, to make contact with the man and his achievements. His dream was to trace his father's footsteps through Autralasia and Japan. A frequent visitor to his uncle Peter in Exeter, he cross-examined him about his own travels and adventures. But Harry had no great need for a collector to go to Japan since there were by now several very good Japanese nurseries who could supply him direct, plus plenty of contacts who would send him any new introductions that appeared. After a couple of years, it was clear to Harry that if he wanted James Herbert to settle down and take over the business, he would have first to let the young man go on a voyage of study and adventure to the Far East.

A detailed itinerary was planned with arrangements for James Herbert to visit botanical and private gardens, nurseries, correspondents and some ex-Veitch collectors. His instructions were to carry out detailed botanical research and to report on plants not yet known in the regions he visited, the conditions in which interesting plants lived and, most importantly, 'to ascertain whether our gardens could be enriched by further additions from the wealth of vegetation with which those regions are favoured'. James Herbert sailed from Naples at the end of October 1891, stopping off in Ceylon before travelling to southern India, where he travelled around comfortably by train visiting various gardens.

He proceeded in a leisurely fashion, calling on sultans and maharajahs and staying with British officials who smoothed his route for him. He stayed with the district judge in Kandy – 'better than the noisy tourist-filled Grand Hotel' – and mixed easily with the Anglo-Indian communities in the hill stations where he toured the coffee and cocoa estates. Conditions were sometimes uncomfortable but not intolerable; he likened the languid, muggy heat to diluted marmalade. In Bombay he saw the Victoria Gardens, visited temples and holy sites and toured some magnificent Palace gardens, 'doubtless the result of European management, with the Maharajahs' money behind them'. He noted the considerable English and Italian influence in many gardens and the heavy Victorian planting designs, such as scroll bedding with statuary, sometimes showing peculiar perspectives and unusual arrangements of topiary. He was amazed by the variety of plants introduced from other countries, palms brought by the Arabs, a vast *Araucaria cunninghami* and, among English vegetables being grown, Veitch's very own 'Autumn Giant' cauliflower with heads growing up to two-and-a-half-feet in diameter. He watched a new garden being created using prisoners chained together to do the digging while women carried away the earth in baskets on their heads.

Despite describing himself as a 'learner', James Herbert seemed to have had an encyclopaedic knowledge of plants and their names and he recorded in mind-numbing detail every plant in every garden. He certainly knew his botany yet his disposition leaned more towards an interest in social interaction and the study of people and their culture rather than in the cultivation of plants. He loved the romance of the ancient cities of India and feared the changes being brought by progress. Jaipur he described as 'a pink city on a blue lake' which was being spoiled by the erection of a corrugated iron railway station, a school of arts, a water supply and a huge cotton press with massive engines lighted by gas. 'I suppose such things indicate progress,' he wrote, 'but I agree with Kipling, it is a pity.' He stayed with Charles Maries who was by then in charge of the Maharajah's gardens near Gwalior. Maries complained that he was frustrated with not being allowed to make changes and improvements and having to cope with problems such as the elephant stables nearby – 'When one breaks lose there is sad havoc in the gardens.' James Herbert, who was always ready to be kind and cheerful, tried to soothe Maries by admiring his English roses and special collection of ferns, 'so fresh and green despite being grown in the dusty plains of Central India'.

In January 1892 James Herbert arrived in Penang where he stayed with another ex-Veitch collector, Charles Curtis, in his bungalow overlooking the public gardens he had created. Curtis showed his experimental garden for native fruits and introduced fruits as well as spice groves and nut forests. After taking his leave of Curtis, James Herbert moved on to Hong Kong where he toured various gardens and again expressed surprise at the number of newly introduced plants thriving in alien surroundings, such as *Pittosporum tobira* from Japan, the fragrant Madagascan *Stephanotis floribunda*, the spectacular rose-red passion flower from Brazil, *Passiflora racemosa*, and a bed of blissfully cool-looking white azaleas from China. James Herbert loved the bustling city of Canton where he was described by the locals as 'the red-headed barbarian'. He strolled along the city walls looking at nursery gardens stretching along the riverbank below. All the plants were set out in porcelain pots of varying shades of blue in which Chinese privet was trained into many extraordinary shapes – fishes, dragons, sampans and even men and women whose heads, eyes, hands and feet were made of porcelain and attached to the plant.

By April James Herbert arrived in Yokohama. At last he was in Japan where his father had been over thirty years before, but things were now very different indeed. Japan was busy transforming itself into a modern industrialised power. More confident and at ease in its trade with the western world and looking for its own expansion, Japan was infiltrating Taiwan and Korea and shaping up for a confrontation with China. James Herbert travelled to many parts by train with only occasional forays by bone-breaking rickshaw. He noted that the better-educated classes had successfully adopted many western ways while 'the great mass of people look goodhumouredly on'. He enjoyed visits to several gardens where he was interested to see many kinds of European flowers such as petunias, mimulus, pansies and primulas, then much admired in Japanese gardens. He was turfed out of his hotel in Kamakura when the Empress was expected and had to eat and sleep Japanese-style in an inn. He quoted from a new guidebook: 'Many who view Japanese food hopefully from a distance have found their spirits sink and their tempers embittered when brought face to face with the unsatisfying actuality.' But he

A Japanese garden. Illustrated by James Herbert
in his journal *Traveller's Notes*

seemed happy enough to live on rice, fish, bamboo and soup, plus 'a few things of one's own'.

While in Tokyo, he was invited to the home of a wealthy silk merchant where everything in his garden was laid out on a miniature scale: 'Little hills, little forests, very little summerhouses, little paths wind round the hills and by little bridges over the little river. Most curious.' Like his father, James Herbert was very taken with the Japanese people and with their love of gardening, especially the classic gardens with their tea-houses where they sit and 'moon away their idle hours'. He made one memorable dawn visit to admire the Morning Glory, *Convolvulus*. He also loved the night fairs held around different parts of the city where the stalls sold plants and produce from the peasants living in outlying areas.

> Along each side of the street were arranged booths, in front of each flaring lamps giving a strange colour to the pines, pinks, Ardisia berries and delicate tea roses. On a low seat sat the owner . . . One saw an old woman, bent with age, carefully bearing off an old dwarf pine as bent and crooked as herself; or a young girl with a child strapped to her back, carrying in her hand a porcelain tray, holding a piece of stone resembling a rock which had on its sides a stone lantern or two, at its base a small house, and around it pebbles to be covered with water to represent a lake on its summit, a clump of fresh green *Acorus gramineus* − a toy and a plant, nature and art in one, reduced to the space of a dozen square inches.

James Herbert's colourful and energetically written account of his travels in Japan was privately published as *Traveller's Notes*. His description of Japanese gardening doubtless further fired the fascination for it in England. The significant event that John Gould, Robert Fortune and Maries had been unable to witness on their expeditions to Japan was the extraordinarily beautiful spring blossoming of thousands of cherry trees. James Herbert was utterly enchanted by the clouds of soft pink and pure white blossom that flowed along the streets and riverbanks, around the temples and filled private and public gardens visited by thousands as part of the annual cherry blossom parties. James Herbert had no doubt that these trees would delight and astonish English gardeners with their spring blossom and autumn colouring. Confident that they would grow well in Europe, he ordered large quantities of different varieties of flowering cherries from

Japanese nurseries to be sent to Coombe Wood in London, including the
'large fruited Winter cherry', *Physalis franchetii*, and a pseudo-cerasus then
known as 'James H. Veitch' (see colour-plate section). When the Japanese
cherry trees first blossomed in Coombe Wood, the Veitch nursery was inun-
dated with orders. James Herbert might not be a disappointment after all.

He went on to make a short trip to Korea which was still very isolated.
Here he became more adventurous, travelling over 600 miles in great heat
and discomfort through areas rarely seen by Europeans except for a few
unpopular missionaries who rarely 'summoned up the moral courage to
leave the hole where fate has placed him'. He was welcomed everywhere
as a very important person, though his 'hosts' consumed his stores of French
prunes, Huntley & Palmer biscuits, coffee and all his whisky and assured
him that the hair of foreigners was red because they drank sheep's milk.
He found the country botanically rich and made a considerable collection,
including an introduction of his own, the Korean rhododendron
Rhododendron schlippenbachii (first discovered by a Russian collector on the
Korean coast forty years earlier) which he saw growing in profusion on
the Diamond Mountains. But the 'filth in the streets, reek of cesspits, torture,
violence, disease and squalour' were a far cry from the pleasant life in Japan
and he was glad to return to Tokyo where he had promised himself an
ascent of Mount Fuji. Perhaps here more than anywhere, James Herbert
would find some affinity with the father he never knew.

Even the Sacred Mountain was changed; it was now a tourist attraction
with huts for resting on the way up where one could drink 'straw-coloured
water, a compound the Japanese affectionately call tea!' and where one slept
head to toe under thick quilts 'rich in animal life'. He chose to walk alone
with just a guide, admiring the cloud effects: 'Truly a most impressive sight
– several thousand feet below a sea of cloud, nothing else and nothing
more, the only land in sight, the peak on which you stand – the only island
in the world.'

As he climbed, holding his father's map of tree zones, James saw forests
of *Abies veitchii*, towering groves of *Pinus thunbergi* with *Ampelopsis veitchii*
(*Parthenocissus tricuspidata* 'Veitchii') clinging to their stems and John Gould's
famous tiger lily growing out of the thatched roofs of the houses. One
might imagine, had his father been with him, that the two would have
been deep in animated conversation and argument. As James Herbert wrote:
'I do not understand my father not having met with *Platycodon mariesii*,
Rodgersia podophylla or *Clerodendrun trichotomum*. Presumably with the first

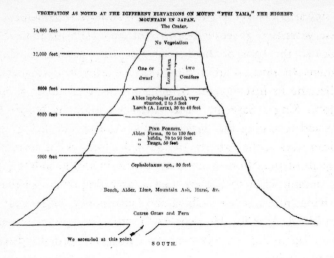

VEGETATION AS NOTED AT THE DIFFERENT ELEVATIONS ON MOUNT "FUSI YAMA," THE HIGHEST MOUNTAIN IN JAPAN.

and last named, he did not leave Yokohama during the flowering season; and with Rodgersia, it is probable he ascended and descended the mountain at the south side, where I did not meet with it.' As if gently scoffing at his father, James stated that the platycodons were 'as common as dandelions round the base of the mountain, tons of Rodgersia could be collected on the East side and handsome flowering bushes of the Clerodendrun were common on the hillsides'.

Happy and satisfied with this trip, James Herbert returned to Tokyo where a letter from Uncle Harry was waiting with the news that Professor Sargent of the Arnold Arboretum in Boston was on a tour of Japan. Harry instructed James Herbert to travel to Aomori, the northern port of Honshu, where he was to meet up with the American professor.

AMERICAN ALLIES

When John Gould and other pioneering collectors were making their first forays into Japan in the 1860s, the United States was collapsing into civil war. No one had time for botanising, except for Thomas Hogg, the son of a Scottish-born nurseryman, who had emigrated to New York and set up business there. Hogg was sent to Japan by the government where he spent many years travelling and meeting with high-ranking Japanese officials, many of whom shared his love of plants and horticulture. Hogg was able to send several valuable collections of plants to the family firm in New York. Trees such as the lovely Japanese Snowbell, *Styrax japonica*, and the

Japanese stewartia became popular in North American gardens.

In these years two generous bequests of land were made near Boston, which formed the basis of the Harvard Botanic Garden in Cambridge, Massachusetts. In 1872 an arboretum was established and Charles Sprague Sargent became its first director. Sargent, a cousin of the great American painter John Singer Sargent, made extensive tours of North America collecting and recording the flora; he built up a unique living collection of American trees at the Arboretum and had a long list of correspondents sending seeds of trees from many parts of the world, including Japan and China. It became clear to Sargent that a large proportion of the woody plants arriving from northern China and Japan could survive and flourish in eastern North America. He decided that the Arboretum should send a collector to Japan and possibly even to China. He also decided that he would be that collector.

He sailed for Japan in August 1892, taking with him his nephew Philip Codman. From Tokyo they headed for the northern island of Hokkaido where they visited Professor Kingo Miyabe of the Imperial Agricultural College in the city of Sopporo. With one of Professor Miyabe's students as guide, Sargent was soon collecting in the rich forests of Hokkaido. When James Herbert arrived by steamer in Aomori he was met by Sargent and Codman. Sargent, who was about the same age as John Gould would have been, seems to have got on well with James Herbert and they established the basis of a long friendship. Sargent wished to see Maries's Fir *Abies mariesii* so they set off up Mount Hakkoda, spending several miserable nights shivering in straw huts. There was plenty to see and collect, with large stands of Maries's Fir near the summit, 'acres' of holly *Ilex crenata*, the Plum Yew, *Cephalotaxus harringtonia* var. *drupacea* in fruit, magnificent specimens of *Magnolia hypoleuca* covered with long, scarlet fruits, rigid above the immense foliage which James thought was unequalled by any other Japanese forest trees, and a 'lovely little *Acer capillipes* covered with golden samaras' which he particularly admired.

There was also plenty to talk about, especially Sargent's desire to send a collector into China. He grilled James Herbert about Charles Maries's travels, the problems he had encountered and his discoveries. James Herbert was so won over that he too became infected with the desire to penetrate the Chinese interior and discover some of its botanical treasures. Here perhaps was his chance to emulate his father's achievements. The young man enthusiastically offered to try his luck, sure that he could succeed where a previous Veitch expedition had failed. Sargent for his part was pleased with the idea

of a joint venture with an English commercial nursery which was so admired
for its plant and tree introductions. The Arnold Arboretum would benefit
from herbarium specimens and could take a share of seeds and living plants.
The three men took the steamer back to Hokkaido, again following in
Maries's footsteps and making excursions into the woods where they found
seeds of a sumach, *Rhus tricocarpa*, with its striking autumn foliage and the
large-leaved vine, *Vitis coignetiae*, which James took home to the Coombe
Wood nursery. Returning to Sapporo, they found a new maple which was
named *Acer miyabei* in honour of Professor Miyabe.

When they parted, Professor Sargent and James Herbert agreed to keep
each other informed about their plans for an expedition to China. Sargent
and Codman sailed for America laden with a collection of seeds of 200
species of plants and over 1,200 dried botanical specimens. James Herbert
remained in Japan, his head swimming with excitement An expedition to
China could prove to be hugely important for science and hugely profitable
for the Veitch nursery: he sat down to write to his uncle Harry to inform
him of his plans for mounting an Anglo-American expedition to China.

Professor Sargent also wrote to Harry Veitch expressing his confidence
that Harry's impressive (and impressionable) young nephew would make a
fine collector in China. But Harry had no intention of allowing James
Herbert to extend his absence from the nursery and in January 1893 replied
to Sargent that he wanted James Herbert home to experience the more
practical, if less romantic, aspects of running a nursery. He pointed out that
his wandering nephew had already been away for nearly two years and
another journey would extend this by a further two:

> It would be taking him out of the business for about *four years* and
> this would be a very serious matter indeed . . . too much travelling
> is apt to unfit a man for settling down again to the routine of work.
> My nephew even before leaving home found routine work irksome
> & I am desirous that this feeling should not overpower him. It was
> partly in the hope that he would overcome this feeling that induced
> me to let him go abroad . . . if he is to become one of us here he
> must come and take his place.

But James Herbert was not quite ready to take his place. His itinerary
included an exploration of Australasia where both his father and cousin
Peter had travelled. However, he too found Australia disappointing and

wrote that it was easier to collect seed in Japan where there was cheap labour; in Australia 'no one will help'. He complained that the seed of many plants was so tiny he did not know if he was collecting seed or dust. Perhaps, after all, the arduous task of plant collecting in harsh conditions was not for him: 'Stooping on the hard-baked earth . . . in a blazing sun, is not a pastime to be chosen', especially with the ever-present danger of poisonous snakes and insects. Nevertheless, James Herbert sent to Kew an exceptional collection of dried specimens of 250 species from Western Australia. Later he visited the North Island of New Zealand where he was disturbed to see vast areas of forest burned and felled to make way for the settlers and their 'endless sheep which pay', destroying the 'bush trees which did not'. He went to Lake Taupo which Cousin Peter claimed to have been the first botanist to visit, now just a two-day trip where James Herbert lazed in the hot thermal springs. By July 1893 he was ready to go home and he boarded a ship bound for England where Uncle Harry was waiting for him to 'take his place' and settle down to the business.

Harry went to considerable lengths to encourage James Herbert to take his responsibilities seriously. In 1894 he appointed him managing director of the firm. James Herbert's younger brother, the shy John, had already made his mark in the offices and so Harry promoted him to secretary in charge of the administration of the company. Harry wisely retained a majority holding himself. James Herbert settled down with his wife Lucy in a large house in Richmond which he crammed with artifacts and souvenirs brought back from his 'Grand Tour' until it was more like a museum than a home. Apparently resigned to giving up the idea of going to China, he hung the large maps showing the routes of his travels and the colourful passports to Korea and Japan on the walls of the director's office and turned his attentions to the nursery business. Now 'equipped with a wider view of life than falls to the share of most men on the outset of their career', James Herbert, for a while at least, proved himself more than worthy of his uncle's generosity and confidence in his abilities.

His writing talent was put to good use in producing nursery catalogues, helping with the conifer and orchid manuals and papers and articles, including papers and talks on Japanese trees. One project that he started and which demanded much of his attention was *Hortus Veitchii*, a record of the Veitch family, their collectors, the plants they had introduced and the horticultural achievements of the hybridists and nurserymen. It was to be a 'compendious account', beautifully illustrated and privately published and

circulated. Adolphus Kent was again employed to do most of the horticultural and botanical work and Harry was persuaded to do some research
into the family history. A letter written by Harry to John Veitch's abused
and orphaned grandson, Thomas Beatty, then a very old man, enquiring
about early Veitch family history, resulted in the surviving letters that give
so much information about those early days in Devon. There was, however,
one witness from the past who was still alive whom Harry could never
bring himself to approach – Thomas Lobb, whom Harry held responsible
for his father's death.

For thirty-four years the man who had introduced to England some of
the finest tropical orchids ever seen had shut the door of his house – which
significantly he had named 'Stanley Villa' – in the Cornish village of Devoran.
Thomas Lobb had become a virtual recluse, tending his garden and relying
on his nephew to bring supplies to the door (he was rewarded with a white
camellia to wear in the parish choir on Sundays). One villager recalled that
Thomas could be seen every morning stumping through the village to visit
his sister but 'none of us knew he was a great man'. The lonely old collector's
house was described as 'spick and span', the walls covered with drawings
and paintings of orchids growing on trees in Java, 'but what Lobb did with
his time remains a mystery . . . since orchids were one of his few topics of
conversation'. Many reports, including *Hortus Veitchii*, state that Thomas lost
his leg 'as a result of exposure' during his last expedition to Borneo. But
he had in fact hung on to the badly damaged leg for some time after his
flight from Chelsea. He had suffered terribly for years until it was finally
decided that the leg had to be amputated. The operation under anaesthetic
was carried out on his sister Jane's kitchen table, not unusual in those days,
and Thomas seems to have recovered completely from the operation.

Most likely when Thomas Lobb died in May 1894, he did so without
a single member of the Veitch family having made amends, either privately
or publicly, to recognise the value and enormity of one of their finest plant
collector's achievements. The Lobb brothers had been the Veitches' first and
arguably the best of their many collectors.

Five years after Thomas Lobb's death, Harry Veitch was preparing to send
out another plant collector. He was to eclipse them all.

CHAPTER THIRTEEN

'CHINESE' WILSON

'E.H.Wilson from James H.Veitch, 1899–1902:Well done!'

CHINA IS A vast country, so vast that it is almost impossible to imagine its distances and enormous differences in climate, topography and vegetation. The idea of looking for a single species of plant in just one region would be extremely daunting; to search for one specimen of one species would be worse than looking for the smallest needle in the largest hay-stack. Yet that is precisely what Ernest Henry Wilson was sent to China to do. The scale of the operation and its dangers were compounded by China's frequent eruptions of violence and its dislike of everything foreign. After the opium wars in the 1840s, Britain held four treaty-ports and the island of Hong Kong. France, Russia, Japan, Germany and the United States also held 'spheres of influence' along the coast and at customs posts in a few larger cities in the interior. But travel inland continued to be risky. China was still essentially a feudal country, divided by tribes and dialects as well as geographic barriers. Travellers and explorers into the hinterland and missionaries who set up bases there did so at their peril and as late as 1905 Tibetan monks tortured and killed the plant-collecting missionaries Père Bourdonnec and Père Dubernard.

However, by the 1890s increasing numbers of westerners were living and working in China and many had become more familiar with some of the languages, traditions and the rich flora and fauna. Dr Augustine Henry, after being fêted as a celebrity at Kew, had returned to his post in China from where he continued sending back herbarium specimens. One in particular which arrived at Kew had intrigued Daniel Oliver, the Keeper of the Herbarium. After a search through *Plantae Davidanae*, he was able to identify as a specimen of the new genus, a flowering tree, *Davidia*, named after Père David, the French missionary and naturalist, who had discovered it in Boaxing (Mupin) in China in 1869. Dr Henry, however, had found his specimen nearly a thousand miles away. He had been so impressed by the beauty of this one spectacular tree that he had sent two servants to collect fruiting specimens which had not previously been studied. As Daniel Oliver sat at his bench in the Kew Herbarium studying dried specimens of the curious large white bracts that cover the tree in May, he became convinced that it would be of inestimable value to both science and horticulture. He wrote an article describing the tree and declaring that 'Davidia is a tree almost deserving a special mission to western China with a view to its introduction to European gardens' (see colour-plate section).

Since embarking on his 'amateur botanising' Dr Henry had become concerned about the increasing depletion of rare plants and trees in many regions of China and, in a letter to Thiselton-Dyer at Kew, suggested that as so many plants in China were fit for the European climate an expedition should be mounted as soon as possible, covering two seasons, around the mountain area above Ichang. (This is the area where Charles Maries had failed and which Harry Veitch had rightly believed would prove to be a botanical treasure-trove.) Dr Henry never regarded himself as a trained plant collector, claiming to have only a 'smattering of botany'. He was essentially a part-time collector of herbarium specimens, and although he collected some seeds he claimed that it was 'really a difficult matter collecting seeds – one arrives on the ground too early or too late'. Voicing a view shared by generations of the best collectors, he wrote: 'Money is not what is wanted, but time, oceans of time. Nothing astonishes people at home so much as the fact, that in countries like China, you cannot do everything with money. Patience is more valuable.' Despite his enormous contribution to botanical science he was a modest man and bemoaned his own lack of training and experience: 'If you ever come across a budding collector like what I was when we began corresponding some years ago, please insist on him being more than a mere collector: and perhaps you will help to develop a naturalist.'

When Professor Sargent had heard of Dr Henry's work he too started badgering him for duplicate herbarium specimens and requesting seed for trial in the Arnold Arboretum. Dr Henry repeated to Sargent the same advice he had given to Thiselton-Dyer in England – set up an expedition. But when Sargent invited Henry to head it, he refused. Nevertheless he was generous with advice and ideas for an expedition and continued to encourage both Kew and the Arnold Arboretum to raise funds and find a suitable man for the job. As he wrote to Sargent in November 1899:

You will be sure to find a man. I trust that you will do so, and that you will have many years to live to devote yourself to the flora of China. It is by far the most interesting one on the globe & to an American must offer even more than to a European – as China in so many ways, its great rivers, mountains, climate, etc, seems to be a counterpart of the United States.

And to rub home his argument: 'The *Davidia* is worth any amount of money. I only saw one tree of it, but doubtless there are others in the district.'

But Kew decided it was unable to afford the expense and asked Harry Veitch for help. Harry was by then looking forward to his retirement and leaving everything to his nephew James Herbert, but together they decided that the nursery should fund an expedition to China. In later years, James Herbert wrote that it was not Dr Henry's work which had drawn Veitch's attention to collecting in China but that it was he and Sargent, whilst they were in Japan, who had discussed his going on a joint China expedition which Uncle Harry, his 'Chief', had forbidden – 'The expedition was long determined on in my own mind, before Henry appeared on the scene.' This is not quite correct since Dr Henry had shown his plants at Kew in 1889 and James Herbert and Sargent were not in Japan until 1892. He also appears to have forgotten one of his own nursery collectors, Charles Maries, who was in China even earlier.

Thiselton-Dyer wrote to Veitch recommending a promising young student who had been training at Kew. He was to be a new breed of collector, not just an enthusiastic garden boy, but a properly trained and educated plant collector, just the kind of man that Dr Henry had been calling for. Ernest Wilson was born in 1876 in Chipping Campden in Gloucestershire, part of large family with not much money and a father who drank. Wilson was a clever, determined and ambitious young man. After four years working in the Birmingham Botanical Gardens and studying botany at the city technical school where he won the Queen's Prize for botany, Wilson was then taken on at Kew and continued his spare-time studies. He did so well in the newly created RHS Higher Grade exams in horticulture that he left Kew and concentrated on full-time studies at the Royal College of Science in South Kensington. His ambition then was to become a teacher of botany but when Kew recommended Wilson to Harry Veitch, his life took a very different turn.

Ernest Wilson (centre) while an apprentice in the Birmingham Botanical Gardens

The Veitches were busy making preparations for the expedition. They had decided to pay Wilson £500 per annum for a three-year expedition – a mere £100 salary for Wilson (rising to £150 in the third year) and the rest for expenses. Meanwhile, Wilson spent six months under George Harrow at Coombe Wood, studying the Japanese introductions and training in all aspects of plant collecting. In the Botanic Gardens at Kew he learned to make herbarium specimens. Professor Sargent wrote to James Herbert offering to help Wilson and enquired whether Veitch would supply the Arboretum with dried specimens of woody plants from the expedition. Now head of the firm, James's relations with Sargent were rather changed from the young man idolising the older in Japan, but a mutual agreement was reached.

Veitch's exclusive contract with Wilson could not have been more clear, nor, as always, were his instructions more secretive: 'The object of the journey is to collect a quantity of seeds of a plant the name of which is known to us. – In furtherance of this you will first endeavour to visit Dr A. Henry at Szemao, Yunnan, and obtain from him precise data as to the habitat of this particular plant and information on the flora of Central China in general.' The plant was, of course, *Davidia*.

Soon after celebrating his twenty-third birthday in early spring 1899, Wilson left for Boston where he was instructed to meet the great Professor Charles Sprague Sargent. 'My first meeting with Sargent took place in the shadow of the large pig-nut hickory on Bussey Road in the Arboretum ... After formal greetings he pulled out his watch and said, "I am busy now,

but at 10 o'clock next Thursday I shall be glad to see you. Good morning!"'
Undaunted, Wilson wrote: 'I voted him autocrat of the autocrats, but when
our next interview took place I found him the kindliest of autocrats.' Indeed,
the Veitches were also finding that working with Professor Sargent was not
going to be easy for the Arnold Arboretum and the Veitch nursery had rather
different priorities: science and commerce were once again at odds. James
Herbert's brother, John Gould Junior, on behalf of his brother, wrote to
Wilson enclosing a letter from Sargent to James Herbert:

Read the letter carefully and ask any questions on any point therein
that may appeal to you. You will see that the Professor suggests your
going to the North first and next year to the South. Your instructions are of course to go to the South this year and then to the North
and in spite of what the Professor says, we think this plan preferable
and would prefer your following it ... The Professor is a very dogmatic
and strong man but you must not let yourself be too impressed by
what he says about collecting dried specimens. On this point, however,
we all know you will be careful, and understand what we want.

By June, Wilson had reached the Crown colony of Hong Kong where
there was an outbreak of bubonic plague. Eager to find Dr Henry, he set
off into French Indo-China without an interpreter because of quarantine
restrictions. The French were inhospitable, the Chinese wary. Yet despite
speaking neither language, Wilson managed to reach Hanoi. The journey
ahead was looking increasingly dangerous, with murderous attacks on any
foreigners, and Wilson was obliged to sit it out until things settled down.
After a hair-raising boat journey through rapids in which his boat capsized
and he was rescued by a friendly Frenchman, Wilson arrived at the Customs
House of Mengtsz (now Mengzi) where he saw the ghastly wreckage of
the rioting and wooden cages hanging in a tree containing the heads of
rioters. 'Later,' he wrote, 'I met a posse of soldiers bringing in another grue-
some looking head.' Wilson was learning fast: he acquired a servant to act
as guide and interpreter and joined a caravan of mules and muleteers and
some armed soldiers to protect him and his fellow travellers from armed
robbers. 'With these picturesquely clad but grotesquely armed soldiers our
caravan looked like a small punitive expedition.' He also discovered that
the easiest way to climb a mountain was to 'hang onto the mule's tail and
let him drag you up'.

After seventeen gruelling days travelling westwards, seven or eight hours a day up one range and down another, on crumbling cliff-edge tracks, through vast forests full of monkeys, orchids and ferns, covering both tropical and temperate regions, crossing the wide Red River and the Black River and climbing high over mountain ridges, Wilson finally arrived at the customs post in Szemao (now Simao) where he found Dr Augustine Henry. Henry had just been ordered back to Mengtsz, so together they made the journey all over again. Wilson's trials were not completely wasted, however, because he made his first introduction, the primrose-yellow *Jasminum primulinum* (now *J. mesnyi*), which when successfully raised by Veitch nurserymen, won Wilson his first RHS First Class Certificate.

Dr Henry gave the young novice much valuable advice and information about the local flora and he handed Wilson a map showing the location of the only specimen of *Davidia* that he had seen. It was not much of a map, more a scrap of paper torn from Henry's notebook marking the position of one tree in an area of some 20,000 square miles of barely populated country, covering the borders between the Hubei and Sichuan provinces. Barely able to contain his fears about such an impossible challenge, Wilson returned to Hong Kong to replenish supplies, despatch his collections and report back to Veitch.

James Herbert was a man of considerable charm and warmth, and having travelled himself and talked with many Veitch collectors about their experiences, he felt able to offer wise counselling and much-needed support to his worried new collector. He wrote regular cheerful letters with well-meant expressions and homilies of support and encouragement, warning Wilson of the loneliness he would feel and assuring him that his friends and employers were thinking daily of him: 'Do not worry but steadily stick to it day by day . . . stick to the one thing you are after and do not spend time and money wandering about.' Whatever happens: 'Keep up your courage – never lose faith or drink Whiskey – both are fatal and both grow on one,' and even less helpfully: 'Are you dressing as a Chinaman? I think it better.' Unlike some collectors such as Robert Fortune and David Burke, Wilson never adopted native dress and, despite never learning the language, relied entirely on an increasingly effective ability to communicate and get on with the Chinese, something few plant collectors managed to achieve. Sometimes he travelled with other Europeans, sometimes with his small and faithful team of Chinese servants whom he trained to collect; he was usually accompanied by several dogs who often appeared in photographs with him and of which he was very fond.

Unfortunately James Herbert did not always take into account the stress and exhaustion that affected plant collectors and often made them short-tempered and paranoid. In one letter he suggested that Wilson might make regular accounts of his expenses; 'I quite trust you and wish for no details.' Wilson misunderstood the letter and replied furiously that his agreement had stipulated annual accounts and he was disgusted that James Herbert should impute his honesty by only 'quite' trusting him. James hastily sent a very long letter of apology:

> I hardly know what to write to you when you take one to task for telling you I 'quite trust you'. I especially put in those words lest you might have *no* doubt of the point, yet apparently it had more the contrary effect . . . well, dear friend, believe me that what I say and write, I mean . . . and you need never look for double meaning . . . absolutely no offence was intended . . . I fear you have been a little too sensitive on the matter.

And he offered to send more funds to cover the extra costs needed for the early stages of the expedition.

The costs were indeed considerable and Wilson went way over budget. After steaming a thousand miles up the Yangtze River, he arrived at Ichang,

Wilson's team whom he described as 'my Chinese collectors faithful and true'

by now a busy commercial city with a large European community where he set up base and started to organise his search for the *Davidia*. He was forced to carry quantities of Chinese coins as well as silver bullion to pay his bearers who would be carrying considerable loads of equipment and supplies, including a medicine chest stocked with insect powder, quantities of opium pills, quinine sulphate, Epsom salts, permanganate of potash and brandy. On many of his expeditions Wilson took his huge cameras and photographic plates as well as his watch, compass, barometer, pedometer, pocket altimeter, his journals and a vasculum (a japanned metal box with a hinged lid, for safely transporting plant materials back to camp). Considerable equipment was necessary in the preparation of dried speci-mens: masses of drying papers and plant presses which Wilson had specially made in China, tags and rubber date and numbering stamps for cataloguing the plants, cardboard, paper, string, glue and ink for mounting and labelling specimens. Also needed were oiled paper for wrapping prepared specimens and bottles of distilled rice liquor which Wilson called 'Chinese spirits' to keep fleshy plant material which could not be dried. Two sedan chairs, taken everywhere for Wilson and his 'head' boy, were rarely used but were important indicators of Wilson's status – equal to a 'mandarin' and 'more useful than a passport'. Wilson bought a native houseboat which he believed would give him more independence, security and mobility in the unset-tled state of the country and he engaged a crew. By April, when the tree would be in flower, Wilson was ready to search for the *Davidia*.

A hazardous journey up the rapids above Ichang brought Wilson and his large party to Badong where he was warned not to continue his travels because of rioting between anti-Christian and Christian villagers. A Roman Catholic priest had been brutally murdered and the flames of hatred for all things foreign were being fanned by the Empress Dowager and her supporters who feared the rapid changes being brought about through foreign interference in China. Secret societies and sects were encouraged to roam the countryside causing terror and bloodshed, and the city streets were filled with cries of 'kill the foreign devils'. The most infamous group was known as the Boxers (because of their prowess in martial arts), instigators of the bloody Boxer Rebellion in June 1900, which swept through the northern provinces and laid siege to several foreign legations in Peking.

Wilson believed that he could remain safe if he kept to remote and barely populated regions and so he left the houseboat and went on foot across the wild, mountainous country, following little-known tracks once used by salt smugglers. Miraculously, he found the house where Dr Henry had been staying when he had found the one *Davidia* tree in flower. The villagers remembered Henry and the tree and so, full of excitement and expectation now that he was so near his goal, Wilson followed a villager who guided him to a clearing. There he saw a small, newly built wooden house and, to his horror and despair, the fresh stump of a *Davidia* tree. It was 'one more little cup of bitterness to drain', he wrote in his journal: 'I did not sleep during the night of April 25th 1900.'

But Wilson was made of tough stuff. He returned to Ichang where he spent a few months making some valuable collections from around western Hubei. Upriver from the city, the Yangtze tributaries had carved miles of gorges, and on their cliffs and ledges grew an extraordinary abundance of plants, many of them spectacularly beautiful. In his *Leaves from My Chinese Notebook* Wilson described some of the more interesting flora growing in the rocks and limestone cliffs. It was the home of the Chinese primrose, which in March covered the cliff face with masses of delicate mauve-pink flowers and delicious fragrance. Also found there was the lovely *Lilium henryi* as well as an astonishing variety and quantity of trees and flowering shrubs, many already known to English gardeners. He found

Wilson in China.

Azalea indica (Rhododendron indicum), Deutzia scabra, Jasminum floridum, Vitex negundo, Anemone hupehensis var. *japonica, Aspidistra punctata* and some varieties of crataegus and pyracantha, to name just a few. In the spring Wilson noted the 'lovely' densely flowered, lilac-coloured *Daphne genkwa* which had so captivated Charles Maries but wrote, 'It is a thousand pities we cannot succeed with the Daphne in England'. *Wisteria sinensis* scaled the highest trees, smothering them with blossom, and flowering *Loropetalum chinense*, resembling a white witch hazel (*Hamamelis*), formed an impenetrable scrub on the tops of the cliffs, 'looking like patches of snow'. 'Messrs Veitch,' he later wrote, 'show the plant very well, but there is an enormous gulf between the best grown pot-plants and the plants in a state of nature.' Other native plants were *Sophora viciifolia (S. davidii)*, commonly used as a thorny hedge to protect fields and vegetable plots, its masses of bluish-white flowers, Wilson wrote, 'ought to be acceptable in gardens where it proved hardy'. There were abundant varieties of rose bushes and on the cliffs, the loquat tree, *Eriobotrya japonica* and *Chimonanthus fragrans* (*C. praecox*) which both flowered around Christmas time and were both wrongly thought to be natives of Japan.

Wilson kept busy collecting, making up dried specimens and taking notes of plants to return to later for seed. He was also re-collecting his thoughts, and decided he was prepared to travel another thousand miles, to an area in the west, and search for the *Davidia* specimens reportedly found there by Père David over twenty years earlier.

But good fortune smiled on Ernest Wilson: when he was exploring in the south-west of Ichang he came across a *Davidia* tree fifty feet high and in full flower. It was the most unexpected, dramatic and beautiful sight he could have dreamed of and it was love at first sight: 'The most interesting and most beautiful of the trees which grow in the North temperate regions.' He climbed into the branches with his camera to take photographs and 'drank in the beauties of this extraordinary tree' with its large snow-white bracts – 'stirred by the slightest breeze they resemble huge butterflies or small doves hovering amongst the trees'. For other, less romantic types, they resembled the fluttering of freshly laundered, white pocket handkerchiefs and the tree acquired the popular names of both the Dove and the Handkerchief tree. In the following days Wilson found about a dozen trees bearing abundant crops of flowers which he was able to collect seed from in great quantities to ship home to England.

The newspapers in London and Boston were by now full of news about the bloody rebellion in China and James Herbert wrote urging Wilson to return home. But by the time his letter reached Wilson, the situation was settling down, the siege had been broken, the ringleaders executed, and in the remote regions where Wilson was working, little seemed to have changed. He decided to stay put and continue collecting. Now that he had achieved his principal objective, he could concentrate on the vast botanical riches which lay all around him. He found a new *Actinidia*, a vine-like climber similar to the one Charles Maries had found in Japan. This variety, however, produced delicious fruits which created great excitement among European friends in the foreigners' settlement in Ichang. They quickly called it 'Wilson's Chinese Gooseberry', later named *Actinidia chinensis (C. deliciosa).* (Commercially grown in New Zealand, it is now commonly known as Kiwi fruit.) Aware that Veitch required hardy plants rather than tender hothouse ones, Wilson headed into the mountains where plants that would suit cool, temperate conditions would be growing. He found various abies, including *Abies fabri* and *A. oliverianum,* the curious peeling Paperbark maple *Acer griseum,* the fragrant, evergreen *Magnolia delavayi,* several rhododendrons such as the large trumpet-shaped *Rhododendron decorum, R. auriculatum* and *R. vernicosum* (see colour-plate section), *Camellia cuspidata* and two viburnums, the large-leaved *Viburnum rhytidophyllum* and the popular *V. utile.* Among the choice of wonders that Wilson brought home, the most memorable are the evergreen *Clematis armandii* with scented, creamy-white flowers and the vigorous *C. montana* var. *rubens* which clambers over so many garden walls. Wilson also amassed a herbarium collection of nearly 2,600 plants and a seed and bulb collection numbering many hundreds of species.

Two of Wilson's herbaceous introductions. (left) *Senecio clivorum (Ligularia dentata)* and (right) *Rehmannia angulata*

Wilson returned home to England early in 1902 with a rich harvest. At Coombe Wood he found George Harrow in charge of all his plants and seedlings: the evergreen *Magnolia delavayi, Rhododendron fortunei* subsp. *discolor, Malus hupehensis, Abies fargesii* and two species of maple had all germinated and were growing strongly. But there was not a sign of a *Davidia* seedling, not one had yet germinated. The 'nuts', having arrived safely in England in the early spring of 1901, had been sown using a variety of methods as was the practice: 'Some were soaked in hot water, some in cold, others were filed down – in short, everything that a skilled resourceful propagator could think of was put in operation,' wrote George Harrow as he and his nurserymen patiently waited and watched nervously for *Davidia* to show signs of life. Some seeds were put in the stove-house using different temperatures, a few were planted outside, exposed to the English climate – but the seeds took their own time. Eventually the outdoor seedbeds showed signs of germination and by May thousands of tiny plants had poked through the ground. Wilson and Harrow were ecstatic and James Veitch & Son heaved a corporate sigh of relief. (Successful germination of *Davidia* seed requires a warm period followed by a cold one which can be done in greenhouses before planting outdoors. In controlled conditions the seeds can be made to germinate within six months.) Ten years later, in May 1911, one of the outdoor seedlings produced the first flowers ever to be seen in England.

The Veitch nurseries had triumphed once again. Even before its first flowering, *Davidia* was a huge commercial success and became all the rage in English and American gardens. Yet, like William Lobb and his *Sequoiadendron*, Wilson was to be denied the triumph of being the first to introduce *Davidia* to Europe. In 1898 the French nurseryman Maurice de Vilmorin had already successfully raised a young tree from seed received from the missionary Père Farges. Despite knowing this, the Veitch family did not tell Wilson until his return because they did not want to 'dampen his enthusiasm'. When Vilmorin's specimen flowered in 1906 it produced smooth leaves and was named *Davidia involucrata* var. *vilmoriniana*. What Wilson had found a thousand miles away was a hairy-leaved version which was named *Davidia involucrata*. Although the expedition cost over £2,000, the Veitches were so pleased and impressed with Wilson's achievements that they presented him with a gold pocket watch on which they had inscribed 'E.H. Wilson from James Herbert Veitch 1899–1903 "Well Done!"'.

In June, Wilson married Nellie Ganderton. But if Nellie expected Ernest to settle down she was in for a disappointment. Hugely encouraged by his success, James Herbert and Harry Veitch had more ambitious plans for Wilson. His expedition had shown that previous collectors had only scratched the surface of China's floral goldmine. Within six months he was to set off again for the Far East and again with instructions to find one particular plant. This time it was the alpine yellow poppywort, *Meconopsis integrifolia*, which he was to search for in the

high, snowy mountain ranges on the China–Tibet border.

In an agreement similar to the first, Wilson was ordered to 'get a quantity of seed of a plant – the name and general locality of which is known – *this object is the object* – do not dissipate time, energy and money – on any other'. In addition, James Herbert wrote – in increasingly wild handwriting – that Wilson should collect 2,300 bulbs of *Lilium henryi* 'packed as before' and 1,200 seeds of *Davidia* 'if obtainable'. Wilson was ordered to return 'with all speed' to England by 30 January 1905, having reaped the benefit of the previous year's autumn crop. 'The last trip was a success – let not this damp your ardour or lessen your energy – to rest on reputation means certain failure.' Furthermore, as the Veitches had always warned their collectors, he was never to write to his friends about his activities or to send them plant material: 'the most friendly queries of friends are the most harmful.'

In the spring of 1903 Wilson was back in China. He called together his trained and trusty men, bought a new boat which he called *Ellena* after his wife, and headed once again upriver towards the dangerous and spectacular Ichang gorges. Here he could forget the Veitches and their obsession with profits and secrecy and get back to doing what he loved best – especially in these areas which afforded 'such wild and wondrous scenery that neither pen, pencil, brush, nor camera can adequately portray them' in the breathtaking gorges which were 'alive with lovely flowers, shrubs and herbs in the wildest profusion. Truly a sight for the Gods.'

Wilson and his crew set out towards Szechuan and into the heart of China. They travelled over 13,000 gruelling miles, hauling, pushing and steering their boat through some of the most difficult and treacherous waters, up the infamous Yangtze rapids and shallow, boulder-strewn torrents where they saw many boats come to grief and one of their own men drowned. They fought their way in driving rain and fierce headwinds through the Mitsang Gorge with its towering cliff walls, twice nearly losing their boat and their lives. Wilson's crew frantically tried to appease the angry water gods: 'My captain chin-chinned, joss crackers were exploded, a little wine and rice were thrown over the bow, joss sticks were burnt, together with candles and some paper cash – in short, every rite necessary to appease the terrible water-dragon was strictly observed.'

The gods thus satisfied, calmed down, the weather improved and Wilson stood happily on deck, lost in admiration at the abundance of flowers around and above him and which

> gladdened the heart – a grassy bank one mass of the lovely *Primula obconica*; a cliff, in every niche of which nestled *Corydalis thalictrifolia*, with its erect racemes of green-tipped yellow flowers; a waterfall, beneath which hundreds of *Iris japonica* luxuriated; the rocks, drenched in spray, were green with maiden-hair fern, *Adiantum capillus-veneris*; even the crags themselves were alive, with masses of *Caesalpinia sepiaria, Rosa moschata, Spiraea dasyantha, Wisteria sinensis, Polygala mariesii* and other such favourites.

In one day alone Wilson recorded some eighty-four distinct species of plants belonging to seventy genera, while every hundred yards or so revealed some 'fresh aspect'.

They sailed on past the French naval station to the city of Chungking (Chongqing), where Wilson enjoyed a brief rest before pressing on until they tied up in the prosperous trading town of Kiating (Leshan), which lay on the main route into Tibet. From his base Wilson ascended the massive, flat-topped mountain of Wa Shan where he found himself surrounded with numerous varieties of rhododendron:

> Their gorgeous beauty defies description. They were there in thousands and hundreds of thousands. Bushes of all sizes, many fully 30 ft

in height and more in diameter, all clad with a wealth of flowers almost hiding the foliage. Some had crimson, some bright red, some flesh-coloured, some silvery pink, and others pure white flowers. Their huge rugged stems, gnarled and twisted into every conceivable shape were draped with pendent mosses and lichens.

Wilson also collected two diminutive rhododendrons, only a few inches in height, one with deep purple and the other with pale yellow flowers. He scaled a cliff by wooden ladders with his dog struggling in terror under his arm; he nearly fell over a precipice but was saved by a sharp-eyed coolie, and he survived nights in dark, insect-infested, filthy inns. He spent four days botanising on the mountain and collected 220 species, including *Paeonia anomala, Rubus xanthocarpus, Clematis pratii (C. pogonandsa), Ribes pachysandroides*, as well as various species of styrax, anemone, pyrus, berberis and primula. High up on one cliff he found an edelweiss, *Leontopodium alpinum*, and several species of the 'everlasting' Anaphalis, while on dripping, shady rocks and trunks luxuriated the filmy ferns *Hymenophyllum*.

After three weeks of arduous travelling, the expedition arrived at Tachienlu (Kangding) on the borders of China. Here they crossed into Tibet towards Lassa (Lhasa) over the Ya-chia Pass, a region almost unknown to westerners. The whole party suffered severely from altitude sickness and the cold and damp was miserable. But Wilson had not lost sight of his goal and one morning at dawn, after a breakfast of ship's biscuit and cheese, they set out and climbed even higher to an altitude of 11,000 feet, where Wilson saw his first specimen of *Meconopsis integrifolia*. Higher still, at 12,000 feet, an alpine meadow spread out before them awash with a fluttering, paper-yellow lake of poppies as far as the eye could see.

Like many hardy plant collectors, Wilson always understated the horrors of his travels. With typical

Meconopsis integrifolia

stoicism he described this extraordinary journey in his search for the yellow poppywort as 'not so bad' and '. . . having found it rather more easily than I had anticipated, I went out on some information that I had about a red one.' While examining dried specimens of the yellow poppywort at Kew, Wilson had noticed a reference to a red species, *Meconopsis punicea*. The label had read 'Potanin (G N. Potanin (1835–1920), Russian explorer and plant collector in China) China borealis, Prov. Szechuan Septentrionale, '85'. It was all he had to go on, but he was now determined to go in search of the scarlet poppy.

Wilson scoured the mountains surrounding the town of Sungpan but the people were reluctant to share any knowledge of the habitat of *Meconopsis punicea*. Eventually he took a posse of soldiers and climbed again to 12,000 feet where he found both *M. punicea* and *M. integrifolia* in abundance. He also discovered a prickly blue-flowered *M. horridula* and a violet-blue species, the *M. heurici*. Seeds were just setting and he was able to collect a rich harvest.

The journey had been harder than anything Wilson had experienced before; he was suffering from exhaustion and had lost over three stone in weight. After a short rest, however, he was on the road again, this time to explore the sacred Mount Omei (Emei Shan). Three days of hard climbing took him through a variety of different species which he noted – mainly evergreen trees and some giant Banyan trees. Higher up were stands of Silver Fir, *Abies fabri*, with their striking blue-black cones, bushes of willow birch, five species of berberis, the Himalayan *Viburnum coriaceum* (*V. cylindricum*), and some species of rhododendron with huge *Clematis montana* trailing over everything. Wilson emerged from a dense thicket on to a narrow ridge 6,100 feet above sea level, and was confronted by the most magnificent view: 'Above, gigantic limestone cliffs, which ultimately culminate in the Golden Summit; below, valleys and plains filled with a dense cumulus of fleecy clouds, the higher mountain-peaks jutting out like rocky islands in the ocean; to the west, the mighty snow-clad ranges of the Tibetan border, 80 miles distant as the crow flies, stretching north and south as far as the eye can range.'

The contrast in vegetation was equally startling; below was a mass of 'rich sombre green' and above were autumnal tints of viburnum, vitis, pyrus and acer together with the Silver Fir, *Abies fabri,* and *Enkianthus himalaicus* (*E. deflexus*) creating a palette of pale yellows through to the richest crimson. Everything was bathed in sunlight with 'gorgeous butterflies flitting around'. The awesome silence and sight of the world set out far below him was a stunning and memorable moment. Wilson went on to climb several formidable stone staircases to reach the summit where he sat on the edge of a precipice and took tea with the priests, listening to the myths and legends of the sacred mountain.

Wilson spent Christmas on his houseboat in Ichang where he found his mail waiting and arranged for his collections to be shipped to England. In the spring he received a letter from Herman Spooner who worked for Veitch and was responsible for examining Wilson's herbarium specimens, giving him the identity and commercial value of individual plants, and adding that his *Meconopsis integrifolia* was doing well at Langley. But then he dropped a bombshell. As with the old orchid wars, the findings in China had awakened the competitive spirit among nursery businesses and Arthur Bulley of Bee's Nursery in Chester now had a man, George Forrest, exploring in China. And somehow Bee's had managed to get credit in the *Gardener's Chronicle* for producing the first flowering specimens of *M. integrifolia*. Spooner reassured Wilson that James Herbert had immediately wired the *Chronicle* to point out that the Veitch nursery plants had flowered at the exactly the same time. This 'took the wind out of Messrs' Bee's sails' and perhaps lessened the blow for Wilson. But competition was tightening and James wrote to Wilson: 'I see Vilmorin must have got quite a lot of plants – and there is no doubt we are only just in time.'

The letters Wilson received from James Herbert were increasingly full of excitement about his achievements: 'We are to fill a centre table in the [RHS] Hall with all your specimens – it will make a most interesting show.' An exhibition of Wilson's herbarium specimens had 'created considerable interest and an immense amount of jealousy'. In one letter James Herbert suggested that Wilson write more often to Sir William Thiselton-Dyer at Kew: 'It is always well to keep in touch with such gentlemen . . . everybody likes a little attention especially those beyond their first youth and in the so-called high places of the world.'

And despite the fact that Wilson had been sending descriptions of his travels to the *Gardener's Chronicle*, James Herbert cautioned him to make notes and to use them 'for his own sake' as well as warning him to keep his journals for his own future use: 'Do not fritter away your information by writing scrappy information to injudicious friends, who, with the best of intentions in the world, send it on to the papers and thus forestall you.'

Wilson returned to Kangding the following spring and explored the high mountains with a small party comprising three mounted soldiers, half a dozen porters a cook, three horses, four pack animals and Wilson's missionary friend, Mr Moyes of the China Inland Mission, who spoke Tibetan. They travelled into eastern Tibet, where the cold was terrible and they nearly lost two men in a snowstorm. But they had many rewarding times such as one 'bountiful' day when Wilson found *Meconopsis henrici, Incarvillea principis (I. lutea), Cypripedium tibeticum* and *Lilium lophophorum,* plus some unusual specimens of primula, saxifraga, potentilla, veronica, fritillaria and, best of all, the orchid *Cypripedium guttatum* with its striking flowers blotched with dark reddish-pink and white.

Wilson made his last trip from Kangding in November when he hoped to find *Dipelta floribunda,* a beautiful flowering shrub found only in the most inaccessible places on mountainous cliffs – nothing new to Wilson, only this time the plant in question rarely produced fertile seed. Yet in two weeks he had achieved his objective and was ready to return home. 'As soon as you have the result of the autumn of 1904, come right home,' wrote James Herbert, 'I know I can trust you not to leave until you have these – but stay not a moment longer.' He sounded just like his great-great-grandfather, James Senior, just as keen not to miss one single plant but equally anxious to get them home as soon as possible.

Wilson set out for home on 5 December 1905, after buying some souvenirs requested by James Herbert for his collection: 'A few good pieces of lacquer, porcelain or bronze, not much silk, something quaint but good.' He arrived back in England in March 1906. This expedition had produced over 500 different seeds, including some more of his most memorable plants – *Primula pulverulenta, Viburnum davidii, Rhododendron calophytum, R. lutescens* and *Rosa moyesii,* plus nearly 2,500 herbarium specimens. Wilson had earned every penny of his pay and this time James and Harry presented him with a gold pin in the form of *Meconopsis integrifolia* with five solid-gold petals encrusted with forty-one diamonds. A year later Harry ensured he received a Veitch Memorial Award with the citation 'to E H Wilson in recognition of his great services to Horticulture by his discovery and introduction of new plants from China'. Wilson declared that he would not travel to China again, and so it was the end of Veitch's employment of their greatest plant collector.

CHAPTER FOURTEEN

LAST INNINGS

'Be sure that if a man is fond of a garden he has got a soft place somewhere.'

Sir Harry Veitch, 1913

A

FTER THE NATION had mourned the death of Queen Victoria, life settled down to business as usual, but now it was allowed to be a bit more fun. Travel to the continent and to the seaside was becoming popular and the wealthy could now avoid the bleakest months of winter with tours by steamships and railways to distant, warmer regions of the world where they stayed in fashionable hotels. The Veitches, who were as happy to follow fashions as they were to influence them, enjoyed cruises in Egypt and holidays in popular coastal resorts in the south of France. Although many of his colleagues might be forgiven for not realising it, Harry Veitch had officially retired in 1900. He had long since handed over the seat of director to his nephew James Herbert, but had been loath to give up all his horticultural and business interests and his RHS committee work. His only concession to retirement was to buy a 'country seat', East Burnham Park in Buckinghamshire, a Victorian gabled house built in 1837 by the Greek historian George Grote. Here Harry and Louisa created a large and beautiful garden which they filled with a fabulous range of their favourite 'Veitchian' plants. He was very proud of his 'gardener's hands', and seemed to have the 'spirit of eternal vigour'.

Time and distance were shrinking and with them went many of the old values. Reassurance in a world that was moving so fast might be found in gardening where, in place of the gaudily coloured artifices of high-Victorian bedding, gardeners were trying old-fashioned approaches such as cosy cottage gardens, or romantic 'medieval gardens'. Simplicity and restraint was preferred by the new brand of skilled and dedicated lady gardeners inspired by the planting schemes of Gertrude Jekyll. William Robinson launched a campaign, through his book *The Wild Garden*, against 'ostentatious Victorian bedding and the costly artificialities of the hothouse and conservatory'. He called for a softer, more natural kind of gardening with hardy herbaceous plants, alpines, delphiniums and English roses. George Gissing's *Henry Ryecroft* echoed the growing dislike of trim, scentless and symmetrical beds: 'Most of the flowers that are put into them – hybrids with some grotesque name – Jonesia, Snooksia – hurt my eyes.' Even the Veitch collector Frederick Burbidge turned against the plants he had discovered in Borneo. In his book *Gardens of the Sun* he compared flowers of the tropics to

> a lovely woman, jaded by over-enjoyment, the whirl of a whole season's gaities! . . . During a year's rambles in one of the richest and most fertile of tropical islands, I saw nothing really fresh and spring-like; nothing like the 'green and gold' of daffodils and the tender young grass of April, or the royal glory of a summer iris, or an autumnal crocus on its mossy bed.

Harry's own extensive country garden was refreshingly eclectic and informal, a sort of diplomatic middle way between Victorian and Edwardian styles. It was laid out with formal flower beds near the house and with herbaceous beds in the lawns. The real attraction was an area of woodland, rockery and water gardens which was designed and created by F. W. Meyer and Peter Veitch, who were still running a successful business in garden design and rockwork. Lord Rothschild's head gardener at Gunnerbsy, James Hudson, who was famous for his Japanese garden, reported that Harry's garden was 'another excellent example of fitting in with the surroundings . . . At the wild garden everything is quite informal and the utmost use is made of the woodland' where bamboos and other shade-loving plants thrived. A special feature in the rock garden and accompanying pools were the naturalistic planting of small alpines in clefts and among the surrounding paving stones. Hudson, who was an advocate of the use of tubbed plants and planting on walls and in the gaps between paving, commented on this arrangement that 'this is quite unlike anything I have ever seen, in every way most picturesque and charming'.

The growing passion for fresh air and exercise and a new interest in games and sports to entertain visitors in the country garden led to a rash of tennis courts, croquet lawns for the ladies and, if there was room, a cricket pitch. In those warm, languorous summer days in the gardens of Edwardian England the thwack of wood on leather was an increasingly familiar sound. It became a custom at the beginning of July for members of the RHS standing committees to visit East Burnham Park to play cricket and to make a critical but appreciative tour around Harry's gardens. In these congenial surroundings council business was often discussed. Here differences might be settled, ruffled feelings smoothed, ideas mooted. The intense negotiations once held in the dining room at Stanley House had given way to a more relaxed style where, as on today's golf course, business could be done. A correspondent later wrote that both gentlemen and their gardeners were brought in to take a sporting part in cricket matches at East Burnham Park: 'Turn back the scorebooks of country house cricket and find the names of today's head gardeners, then mere striplings, figuring among the ennobled names.'

By the turn of the century the Royal Horticultural Society was approaching its own centenary, to be held in 1904. Having achieved a decade of steady progress with a growing list of active members and, for almost the first time in its long and difficult history, no debts, RHS council members began discussing ways to celebrate. It was typical of the Society that this would lead to years of rows and disharmony. Harry, despite his retirement, continued to play a wise, patient and diplomatic central role; initially he was invited to set up an Exploratory Committee to replace the experimental garden at Chiswick, now considered to be too small and too near London. After a long and arduous search, Harry and his team reported back to the council who inspected the recommended site in Surrey. At a particularly acrimonious meeting in April 1900, deep rumblings of discontent and fears about the proposed changes were voiced and friends took opposing sides.

The bone of contention was whether the RHS should celebrate its centenary with a new garden or a new hall – both of which were urgently needed. The argument hotted up as Harry attempted to explain the council's proposal to a meeting of Fellows. 'But,' he wrote, 'the scheme had no chance against the torrent of criticism poured upon it.' After thanking the council for the trouble they had taken in seeking a site for the new garden, Dr Masters put his spoke in the wheel with an amendment that 'this Meeting is of the opinion that the proposed site is not the best means of celebrating the forthcoming Centenary of the Society'. It was carried with a 'very large majority amid enthusiasm!' After further interminable wrangling, it was agreed in principle to move the Chiswick garden, but not to Harry's choice in Surrey where the land was considered to be too heavy and waterlogged. Harry swallowed his pride and irritation and, with his customary professionalism, reconvened the Exploratory Committee to start a new search.

The general consensus was, however, for a new hall. The Drill Hall was proving to be too small and the lighting inadequate for showing displays to their best advantage. Baron Schröder had for some time been pressing for the creation of a purpose-built horticultural hall in Westminster and he made generous contributions to a fund to build the Society's own 'central metropolitan hall'. Whether Harry preferred to support the move for a new garden or for a new hall is not known but, since his services were always valued for their impartiality, he was now asked to join another committee chaired by Baron Shröder with the Rev. Wilks, Sir Trevor Lawrence, and Harry's fellow nurserymen, Nathaniel Sherwood and Harry May. This time the task was to explore the practical and financial possibilities of a new hall and to find a suitable location. The committee found an ideal site in Vincent Square, Westminster. Despite increasing ill-health, Baron Schröder was determined to see a new hall created in his lifetime. Well aware of how conservative and slow the deliberations of the society were, and fearing that the inevitable wrangling would lose it, he secretly went ahead and took a 999-year lease on the site. Fortunately approval was soon given and the long, hard business of fundraising and building began.

The dream of a new garden also persisted and in 1903 Harry found himself on yet another committee, again in search of a suitable piece of land. This time they struck lucky when Sir Thomas Hanbury, then owner of the famous Italian garden La Mortola, bought sixty acres of garden owned by a former society council member, George Fergusson Wilson, at Wisley in Surrey and presented it to the RHS. Everyone was delighted and for once there was no dissent. There was no longer any need for dispute between a new hall or a new garden – they could have both. Such was everyone's enthusiasm that when Harry Veitch proposed increasing the entrance fee to the Temple Shows in order to help raise funds for the new garden, it was carried 'by practically the whole Meeting'.

On 22 July 1904, King Edward VII and Queen Alexandra, joint Royal patrons of the Society, opened the New Hall in Vincent Square (now known as 'Old Hall'). The Queen was presented with a bouquet which included the orchid *Odontoglossum crispum*, discovered for the Society over sixty years earlier by Theodore Hartweg, one of its first collectors. Four days later, the first of the regular fortnightly shows was held in the New Hall and a magnificent display of Veitch fruits was awarded a Hogg Medal. It represented the culmination of John Seden's extraordinary achievements with fruit and vegetables during fifteen years of work in the Langley nursery.

Soon after this crowning glory, Seden retired to Worthing on a generous pension from the nursery.

Meanwhile at Coombe Wood, George Harrow and Ernest Wilson were proving so successful in raising Wilson's Chinese introductions that they were in danger of flooding the market, so much so that James Herbert felt he could no longer afford to employ Wilson. On 2 October 1906 he wrote to Thiselton-Dyer at Kew that 'After five years most satisfactory service Wilson's engagement is terminated with my firm . . . Very shortly there will be no work for him here . . . and I am taking the liberty of troubling you in the hope that during the next few months some suitable position may be open.' Kew took Wilson on a temporary basis and he later accepted a post as botanical assistant at the Imperial Institute of Science in London, cataloguing collections from Asia. His wife was glad to settle at last in London where their daughter was born in May 1906, the same day one of Wilson's primulas flowered for the first time at Coombe Wood. The girl was christened Muriel Primrose and the plant was named *Primula wilsonii*, the first of his introductions to be given his name.

But if Ernest Wilson thought he had finished with China, Professor Sargent did not and he brushed aside all Wilson's refusals until he succeeded in getting him to agree to undertake a further two-year expedition to China for the Arnold Arboretum, this time primarily for science rather than commerce. 'So you have captured me after all,' Wilson wrote to Sargent. 'Twelve months ago I would not have believed it possible for anyone to have persuaded me into revisiting China on any terms.' Before he left Wilson received training from the well-regarded photographer, E. J. Wallis, who prepared the plates for *Hortus Veitchii*. Wilson mastered the high-quality whole-plate camera and the smaller, folding Kodak with its recently intro-duced roll film, and during his later travels proved to be a fine photographer.

In 1906, at the age of sixty-six years, Harry Veitch was awarded the Victoria Medal of Honour. He and Louisa had recently celebrated their silver wedding anniversary and begun to indulge themselves with long days of gardening and hosting cricket and tennis parties. They spent more time and money on their favourite charitable works, including picnics for poor orphans in their garden. As an 'ardent churchman of the old Evangelical school', Harry's liberal generosity and religious and philanthropic preoccupations had never ceased. For nearly a quarter of a century he served as chairman of the Gardeners' Royal Benevolent Institution to which he gave very large sums; he was a generous supporter of the Royal Gardeners' Orphan Fund, the British Orphan Schools, and was a patron to the United Horticultural Benefit and Provident Society and treasurer and chairman of the Horticultural Club.

Nor did Harry ever truly give up his involvement in the nursery, keeping a careful and constant watch on all that was going on. With characteristic tact, he continued to advise James Herbert and his brother John Gould Jnr. from the wings. But some of the nursery's most trusted and valued staff were increasingly seeking Harry out to express their concerns about the way James Herbert was running the business and about his 'alert' and 'rather fiery' behaviour which antagonised both staff and customers. Perhaps he had inherited some of his grandfather's irascible temperament, but there seems also to have been some kind of 'nervous affliction'. While his brother retreated into an almost silent world, James Herbert became 'nervy' and excitable. It was seriously affecting his health and his ability to meet the huge responsibilities of running the business.

The nursery staff came close to revolt and, after the publication of *Hortus Veitchii* which had proved excessively taxing to produce, James Herbert suffered a complete nervous breakdown and was compelled to retire from the firm in November 1906. With his wife Lucy he retreated to Exeter. In November 1907, aged only thirty-nine, James Herbert died of 'paralysis' – a medical euphemism used to record the deaths of increasing numbers of middle-aged, middle-class men from neuro-syphilis, usually contracted some ten or fifteen years earlier. Whether James Herbert had contracted the then fatal disease on his travels, as William Lobb had done a generation earlier, can never be certain but he manifested many of the classic symptoms of this terrible affliction which caused so much misery and shame in 'respectable' families where it was quietly covered up and never referred to. Many wives were infected and their lives ruined by it. Lucy Veitch lived to an old age, but there were no children.

BACK AT THE HELM

James Herbert's death was a shattering blow to the Veitch dynasty. Apart from James Herbert's delicate brother, Harry had no one to take on the mantle of inheritance (Peter Veitch was ensconced as director of Robert Veitch & Son of Exeter). Now sixty-seven years old, the 'great-hearted leader' was forced to come out of retirement. His return to the director's office at Chelsea was hailed with relief and enthusiasm. It was a credit to Harry's loyal nursery staff, especially George Harrow, John Heal and the recently departed John Seden, that the business under James Herbert's erratic leadership had survived and remained productive and profitable. But Harry was concerned to discover that much had been left undone or unattended to. For example, nothing had been done with the development of hybrid winter-flowering begonias. A new man, C. J. Gleed, was appointed as foreman of the 'New Plant Department' at Feltham and was 'charged with improving potentially good strains'. John Heal was still doing brilliant work in the glasshouses at Chelsea, hybridising and propagating many varieties of houseplants such as streptocarpus and clivias from South Africa and the succulent kalanchoes from eastern Africa. His first very successful kalanchoe hybrid *Kalonchoe x kewensis* had recently won an RHS Award of Merit and was described by the Floral Committee as 'quite remarkable for its pink or rosy purple flowers borne in large branching corymbs. The leaves are . . . of a beautiful metallic or glaucous green colour.'

George Harrow at Coombe Wood was meanwhile successfully raising such a glut of Wilson's introductions that Harry decided to issue special 'China' catalogues between 1909 and 1913 in order to reduce some of the stock. As a result, a number of Wilson's original plants found their way into private gardens where they have flourished to this day. Lord Aberconway of Bodnant in Wales bought a selection of Chinese rhododendrons, including *Rhododendron davidsonianum* collected by Wilson in west China which Aberconway drily noted his head gardener 'could not say they would not grow, because he had never tried them'. So many new species were arriving in English nurseries from abroad, especially from China, through new collectors such as George Forrest and Frank Kingdom-Ward, that one nurseryman recalled: 'Many thousands of new plants that had never been seen before were arriving by the barrowload. We were overwhelmed. It wasn't just an ounce or two of seed of each new plant, but pounds of it in many cases. You sowed what you could; pricked out what you could and the rest went on the tip. Such terrible waste, but it was far too much material for us to handle.'

The Veitch nurseries were particularly lucky to have George Harrow who, despite being almost overwhelmed with so many historic plants, was a brilliant nurseryman and propagator and it is arguable that some of the credit for Ernest Wilson's successful introductions should be attributed to him. As the parcels of seeds arrived at the Chelsea headquarters, they were sorted, and all those of trees, shrubs and primroses were sent for Harrow's attention at Coombe Wood. (Seeds of most of the herbaceous plants were sent to Langley.) Harrow's orders were to sow everything, and to obtain anything in the way of frames, pits, lights, etc. that might be needed and not to stint on the cost. He was to report regularly with news of germination, growth, flowering and so on. As the seeds arrived, Harrow's men planted half the quantity and kept back the other half for a second sowing, so nothing was lost. The seeds of many species failed to germinate, and of those that reached maturity, a proportion regarded as commercially worthless was sent to Kew, Edinburgh, Glasnevin and Cambridge Botanic Gardens.

So many new introductions were arriving, some with no more than a tagged number and description of habitat and character, that mistakes were inevitable while some plants were mislaid or misnamed. Years later, George Harrow confessed that he did not realise that he was growing Charles Maries's *Hamamelis mollis* at Coombe Wood until one day George Nicholson, who had recently retired as Curator of Kew, noticed during one of his visits something unusual about one of the larger plants of *Hamamelis japonica* var. *arborea*. 'What have you here?' he asked and Harrow suggested that it was another variety grafted on. Nicholson whistled through his teeth and said, 'Yes, and a very scarce and valuable plant.' Harrow immediately had every piece cut up and grafted for stock, and the following year it was distributed as a new plant, becoming one of the most popular winter-flowering plants of all time.

Harrow also recalled having had particular difficulty with some seeds such as *Davidia involucrata* and *Meconopsis punicea*. Some of the poppy seeds germinated quickly while others in the same pan lay dormant for eighteen months or more. Patience, as ever, was the greatest virtue of the successful nurseryman. Harrow kept a register of everything he received, noting the date of receipt of the seeds, the particulars of the field tickets, the germination, date of flowering of the plants and a description of the flower. As the plants came into flower, he took them to Kew for illustration and identification. Altogether he handled about 1,864 packets of seed sent home by Wilson from his first two expeditions – all the lilium seed and part of the collection of *Astilbe davidii* (*Astilbechinensis* var. *davidii*) as well as *Iris chrysographes, Rheum alexandrae, Senecio clivorum* (*Ligularia dentata*) and *Paeonia veitchii*. There were several rhododendrons, scores of cotoneaster plus several roses, among them *Rosa moyesii*. Many batches of seeds from Wilson's third expedition made for the Arnold Arboretum were also sent to Coombe

Wood, amounting to another 1,474 packets, all of which had to be processed and evaluated.

Friendly rivalry between Coombe Wood and Chelsea kept everyone on their toes. George Harrow relates how when Harry Veitch decided that the Camellia House at Chelsea was to be cleared out to make way for new plants, he instructed John Heal to have the plants sent down to Coombe Wood where they were to be burned. Harrow chose to ignore the instructions and to see if camellias could be grown outside. He had the plants cut back hard and planted in a well-prepared border sheltered from north and east winds where they were syringed overhead morning and evening for a month. The following spring Heal came out to the nursery one Sunday afternoon to have tea with Harrow. They took a stroll round the grounds and came upon the camellia border, now filled with healthy plants covered with blooms. 'Hello,' he said, 'where did your camellias come from? I thought they would not do out of doors.' After Harrow had told him what he had done, the two nurserymen laughed heartily and congratulated themselves on yet another experiment that had overturned the horticultural conventions of the day.

In spite of the long hours and the enormous responsibility which he carried while James Herbert was failing, George Harrow stayed at Coombe Wood for over twenty years. He grew to love the place and got great pleasure watching the 'individual ways of different plants'. He met every horticulturist of note who visited. Sir George Holford once brought King Edward VII to the nursery where 'His Highness greatly admired the wonderful variety of stock, in particular *Rhododendron souliei* which was in bloom for the first time in Britain'.

THE LAST VEITCH COLLECTOR

Despite Coombe Wood and Langley nurseries experiencing difficulty in coping with Wilson's introductions, when Harry received a letter from Professor Sargent in Boston in 1907 outlining his idea for a new expedition into northern China, he agreed to co-sponsor it and furthermore to find a suitable collector. Harry knew of a young, rather rebellious horticultural student at Kew who had recently taken part in a protest over training and conditions. William Purdom came from Westmorland where his father was head gardener at Brathay Hall and he had trained at Low & Co. and also with Veitch's at Coombe Wood. Harry admired William's intelligence and spirit, and decided to take him back and train him up as the new Veitch collector in China.

William Purdom (1880–1921)

Early in 1908, after a period working under George Harrow at Coombe Wood where he gained a good knowledge of Chinese plants from Wilson's collections, Purdom sailed for Boston to meet his other boss, Professor Sargent. Sargent was particularly interested in obtaining conifers and shrubs, especially the Moutan peony as well as seeds of the wild peach, pear, chestnut and walnut trees. By the beginning of 1909, armed with a thorough training and specific instructions from his two masters, Purdom had landed in Shanghai where he met up with the great Wilson himself, still collecting for the Arnold Arboretum and not particularly pleased to see him.

Although Wilson feared that another trip would have 'completely broken up my wife', he also confessed to 'a slight feeling of chagrin at being passed over so completely in favour of another and without a word of warning'. He was especially concerned that his reputation would suffer since others might see Purdom as a successor to him and a reflection on the quality of his own work. Nevertheless, he gave Purdom valuable botanical and practical advice – including how to obtain cash payments from the Hong Kong and Shanghai Bank. Purdom was very generously financed, being paid £500 a year and a bonus for good results, plus £400 in travelling expenses (considerably more than Wilson had ever received). As Wilson packed up his plants, including a huge quantity of lily bulbs carefully encased in clay for the return to the United States, Purdom proceeded to Peking where the British Legation helped him with passports and travelling equipment and engaged an experienced *mafu* or head muleteer who remained loyally with Purdom throughout his travels.

Like all Veitch collectors, Purdom was instructed to write regularly. Few of them ever did but Purdom was better than most. He sent regular shipments, to Harry in London and Sargent in Boston, of the plants and information that each most desired. His first expedition was to Jehol and across the Great Wall of China to the town of Weichang near the Mongolian border. Although it was still too early to collect seeds, he noted oaks, maples and ash bearing 'sweet-scented flowers' which lined the roads and a variety of conifers growing in temple grounds. He crossed into Mongolia by mule where he saw many interesting plants, including a free-flowering deutzia, an anemone and a blue iris which he planned to collect on his return. He wrote to Harry from Weichang and described seeing two beautiful primulas, one pink and 'very pretty', another brick-red. Also a 'fine cream white anemone . . . I have had six flowers in a glass for one week and they are still very fresh' – clearly a potentially valuable new addition for the London florists. The ravines were filled with peonies about to flower and large clumps of a daphne with vigorous shoots growing from a thick root stock, while the hillsides were covered with a deep rose-purple rhododendron which the locals used for firewood. Like Wilson, Purdom got on with the local people wherever he went, though some were more friendly than others. He seemed to have a knack of finding the right level of relationship, whether they were peasant, official or priest: 'You will be pleased to hear that the people are very good to me.'

After resting in Peking and packing off his first collection, Purdom headed out again south-west by train and then climbed high into the Wutai mountains where he found cones of the Dahurian Larch, *Larix gmelinii* var. *principis rupfrechtii*, which grew very well both at Kew and Boston. Higher up, he found three wonderful clematis for which every gardener can still thank him: *Clematis aethusifolia* with pale yellow bells, the blue clematis of the Alpina persuasion and the similar but far more popular *C. macropetala* which produced its first delicate violet-blue flowers in Coombe Wood in 1912. Purdom also sent back seed of campanulas, aconitums, a scabious, *S. fisheri*, and a number of potentillas, including a shrubby *P. fruticosa* 'William Purdom' which was raised in the Langley nursery where many of Purdom's seeds were sent.

Back at his base in Peking a letter from Harry was waiting with a list of names given by Kew for Purdom's discoveries. Primula No. 27 found near Weichang was identified as *P. geraniifolia*; No. 10, a new primula found in the mountains, was named *P. maximoviczii*; No. 80 *Trollius ledebourii* (*T. chinensis*) and No. 112, a campanula, *Platycodon grandiflorum*. Later in the year Purdom retraced his steps, retrieving seed and cones from locals whom he had organised to collect for him. Purdom wrote to Sargent about the many kinds of trees he had seen and collected from, including elms, limes, wild peach, ash, larch, poplars and conifers from around the temples. But winter was fast approaching and he faced freezing temperatures, the dangers of predatory wolves, jackals, and wild cats, as well as fighting off highwaymen in the northern mountains who regularly raided the local villages for their scant grain stores.

In January Purdom was preparing for another expedition. He sent Harry a shopping list: balls of string, an axe, some sealing wax and an extra water-proof groundsheet. Like Wilson, Purdom was issued with a camera but, unlike his predecessor, he had little liking for its bulk and fragility and struggled unwillingly to make it work. He asked for replacements for the many plates which were smashed on the journey, noting that anyone consid-ering travelling the rough roads of China should carry the newly intro-duced film camera instead of plate ones, especially as films could now be processed in Peking.

In the spring of 1910 Purdom was ready to start his search for the Moutan or tree peony, a glorious plant which was so highly regarded in China that it was known as the 'King of the Flowers'. Ranging in colour from white, pink, red or purple with maroon marking at the base, it was grown in pots in the Imperial Gardens. There is a seventeenth-century description of vast areas of the Moutan Shan hills in Shensi province glowing red and scenting the air for miles around. But when Purdom arrived there he could find no trace of them and was told by local woodmen that every plant had been grubbed out for medicine or firewood. There had been several unsuc-cessful attempts to establish the peony in European gardens until, in the 1840s, Robert Fortune had discovered a large source in north-east China.

Peonies in the wild

Purdom eventually located a large number of the Moutan peony growing wild and he made dried specimens and arranged for a missionary to collect seeds later in the year. Whilst exploring 'off the map' and without official permission, Purdom made specimens for Sargent of a wild pear in flower, a sweetly-scented *syringa*, an abelia, the violet shrub *Leptodermis oblonga* which later did well in Boston, two indigoferas,

I. potaninii and *I. amblyantha* which Veitch sent to Kew in 1913, and the lace-bark pine, *Pinus bungeana*. For Harry there was seed of the Bead tree, *Melia azedarach*, with fragrant pinkish-lilac, star-shaped spring flowers and a yellow rose, *Rosa xanthina.f.spontanea*.

Purdom crossed the slopes of the Taipei mountain, following in the footsteps of the French collector Père Giraldi, collecting gentians, primulas and two pretty daisies, *Anaphalis modesta* and the pale, rose-violet flowered *Aster flaccidus*. But in attempting to reach the summit, Purdom found himself in trouble. An unseasonal downpour was preventing the annual pilgrimage to offer food, opium and silver to the priests, who were unhappy at their loss. They blamed the presence of the foreigner Purdom and threatened him so much that he was forced to send a message to the British legation in Peking asking for protection. As soon as help arrived, things calmed down and 'what a change took place . . . each man who was hostile before could be seen carrying a few nuts as a present to my tent, or a few flowers or anything.' Whilst on the mountain he had found more primulas as well as a white potentilla, a 'showy' rodgersia and a variety of the Himalayan birch, *Betula utilis*, with a 'rosy-red bark which peels off like paper'. His most exciting find was an unusual yellow daphne, *D. giraldii*, which was raised at Coombe Wood but did not produce flowers until 1916 at Wakehurst Place.

Purdom went on to explore the lower Tao River where he found the small blue *Allium cyaneum* and two startling meconopsis, one a lavender-blue, *Meconopsis quintuplinervia*, and yet more primulas. His most important discovery in this region was the still popular winter-flowering viburnum, *V. fragrans* (later renamed *V. farreri*), which he found growing in temple grounds (see colour-plate section). Purdom explored along the Chinese-Tibetan border within sight of the snow-covered mountains but was disappointed to be refused entry to the monasteries. By then the situation in China was again becoming hazardous and Purdom was instructed to get out while he could. It was not that simple, however, and for three months he had to travel across China, facing several dangerous encounters, including rioting soldiers and murderous robbers: 'I had a very narrow escape from the brigands. They attacked me, shooting down two of our horses, but thanks to a rifle I had, a stand was made, and although I'm sorry to have had to shoot three Chinese to get clear . . . this was the saving of my life.'

Purdom reached Peking in March 1912 where he cabled Harry to say that he was safe. After a 'last-minute' search in the gardens of forty temples around Peking, Purdom found 'an imposing grove' of the Chinese Horse

Chestnut, *Aesculus chinensis*, which Professor Sargent had particularly requested. Carrying six tiny plants, he boarded the Siberian railway and steamed comfortably home to London.

Purdom had worked hard and conscientiously but Professor Sargent and Harry Veitch expressed disappointment with him. According to Purdom, few new species were found because the northern flora was too similar to the regions already visited by Wilson – a view refuted by Sargent who described Purdom's collections as 'unremarkable' – despite his having found the Moutan peony. Harry criticised him for waiting too long to send his shipments and for packing them carelessly as they had often arrived in a poor or useless condition. Sargent also complained that Purdom was far too keen on collecting and adventures and not on the tiresome task of pressing and drying specimens, making lists and sending carefully packed seeds. To be fair, Wilson was not keen on the onerous business of making herbarium specimens either and he too had had his failures.

Wilson had shipped thirty-two cases of lily bulbs to Boston from his first expedition for Sargent which had rotted on the journey as a result of being stowed too near some raw hides. Whilst Purdom was busy in northern China, Wilson was also making his second expedition for Sargent and his fourth journey into China. He was searching for conifer seed and was also attempting to replace the disastrous shipment of lily bulbs. In the arid Min valley near Sungpan, where the summer heat is intense and the winter freezing cold, Wilson had found the Regal lily, *Lilium regale*, one of his most important contributions to western gardens. He gazed in awe at thousands of lilies, their huge, lustrous white flowers wafting their fragrance on the cool morning and evening breezes: 'For a brief season this Lily transforms a lonely, semi-desert region into a veritable fairyland.' This time Wilson wanted no mistakes and he and his team marked out the position of thousands of plants to be lifted in October when they would return and pack each bulb in clay. But catastrophe struck when, on the journey out, they were hit by a landslide and Wilson's leg was badly broken. With a crude splint made from his camera tripod, Wilson was carried to a nearby town where a doctor operated on the leg. Wilson was lucky that both his life and his leg were saved, but for the rest of his days he walked with a cane and suffered from what he called his 'lily limp'. After his 'faithful, intelligent, reliable and cheerful team' had harvested the lily bulbs for him, Wilson cut short the expedition and returned to Boston with his precious consignment of *Lilium regale*. He never returned to China.

On 11 April 1913, after the return of both Wilson and Purdom, Harry Veitch wrote to Kew asking for identification of some of Purdom's primulas which he wished to exhibit at the forthcoming Primula Conference. They included the purple *P. maximowczii*, yellow *P. szechuanica* and the lavender-coloured *P. purdomii*. They drew admiration from everyone attending the conference, especially from Reginald Farrer, an amateur gardener and botanist who specialised in rock and alpine plants. Farrer, who had collected in the European Alps and wrote *The English Rock Garden*, was so impressed by Purdom that he invited him to return to China with him on a private expedition. Their two years of travels in Kansu region and the Tibetan borders were described by Farrer in his book, *On The Eaves of the World*, which he dedicated to William Purdom, his 'absolutely perfect friend and helper'. If Purdom had been a less than rigorous collector for Sargant and Veitch, he clearly made a brave and entertaining fellow traveller, and the two made an ideal team, returning with a rich collection of plants, including a variety of the increasingly popular alliums, *Gentiana farreri*, the alpine pink geranium *G. farreri*, and the gorgeous and entirely new *Buddleja alternifolia*. This became a favourite in European gardens because, as Farrer described, 'It sweeps in long streaming cascades . . . like a gracious small-leaved weeping willow when it is not in flower, and a sheer waterfall of soft purple when it is.' At the end of the expedition, Farrer went home and Purdom was appointed to the Chinese Government Forestry Commission. He spent the last five years of his life living in a railway carriage in some of the most remote regions of China. He died in the French Hospital in Peking in 1921, following an operation, the last of twenty-three Veitch plant collectors.

THE GARDEN KNIGHT

The successful opening of the New Hall and the transfer of the Chiswick garden to Wisley was followed by a long round of congratulations and honours. The RHS president, Sir Trevor Lawrence, in recognition of twenty-one years of service, was commemorated with a new medal, the Lawrence Medal for the most outstanding exhibit of the year. The eminent Victorian painter, Sir Hubert Herkomer, was commissioned to paint Sir Trevor's portrait which was duly hung alongside that of Sir Joseph Banks in the Council Room. Baron Schröder, now popularly known as the 'Father of the Hall', was also painted by Herkomer in gratitude for his services to the Royal Horticultural Society.

One evening Harry and his friend Henry May were on the train returning home from one of many regular committee meetings at Wisley. Harry alighted at Clapham Junction and stood on the platform talking through the open window of the train to May. He remarked somewhat wearily, 'I suppose we shall meet again on Tuesday.' 'Why yes,' replied May, 'all being well.'

'You know, Mr May,' Harry said, 'you and I do a good deal of work for the RHS.'

'Never mind,' replied May, 'you will get your reward some day.'

'I don't suppose I shall get my portrait by Herkomer,' said Harry, half wistfully, half in jest. 'Oh, you might do that,' said May as the train moved out of the station, leaving Harry suddenly looking and feeling his sixty-nine years.

Indeed, the idea had already occurred to May and his fellow council members and while Harry and Louisa were away on holiday in the south of France, the Rev. Wilks sent out a circular to ten amateur members while Henry May sent one to ten trade members to test the response. The warmth of feeling for Harry Veitch was so great that subscriptions rolled in from around the country until they had collected nearly £800. When asked to

Louisa Veitch's copy of her husband Harry's portrait by Hugh Riviere, now in the Royal Albert Museum, Exeter

select an artist, Herkomer was not available, so Harry chose Hugh Riviere, son of another eminent portrait painter. So generous was the response that there were sufficient funds for two copies of the portrait to be painted, one to be hung in the RHS Council Chamber and one for Louisa Veitch to display in the drawing room at East Burnham Park. A grand presentation dinner was held on Tuesday, 24 January 1910 in the New Hall in Vincent Square.

During the dinner the pair of portraits stood on easels for all to admire. Harry stands with his long white 'Father Christmas' beard and famous twinkle in his eye, holding his favourite orchid, *Masdevallia veitchii*, in one hand and a microscope in the other. Nathaniel Sherwood presided as chairman and sat between Harry and Louisa at the high table in the large and draughty New Hall. But the atmosphere of good humour soon warmed everyone, even the ladies shivering in their gowns. Sir Trevor Lawrence drew applause when he told them that they should 'regard themselves as hardy herbaceous plants'. The menu for the dinner was characteristic of Harry's sense of humour and he must have chuckled over its witty associations with all things Veitchian.

MENU

PETITE MARMITE DE FELTHAM
★ ★ ★ ★ ★ ★
SUPRÉMES DE SOLES À LA RUE DU ROI
TOURNEDOS ÉCOSSAIS
★ ★ ★ ★ ★ ★
SELLE D'AGNEAU DE BURNHAM
ÉPINARDS DE LANGLEY
POMMES AUX JARDINS DE REDCLIFFE
★ ★ ★ ★ ★ ★
SORBET DE L'EXE
★ ★ ★ ★ ★ ★
FAISANS AU BOIS DE COMBE
SALADE AUX HERBES JAPONAISES
★ ★ ★ ★ ★ ★
PODDING LOUISE-MARIE
BOMBE DE LA CHINE NORD
FRIANDISES DES ORCHIDÉES
★ ★ ★ ★ ★ ★
FILETS D'ANCHOIS DE CHELSEA
★ ★ ★ ★ ★ ★
CAFÉ
★ ★ ★ ★ ★ ★
DESSERT
FRUITS DE VEITCH

There was magnificent vintage port and choice cigars for the gentlemen and chocolates for the ladies, recitations and music and plenty of speeches.

Sherwood read out telegraphs of congratulation. In his speech, Sir Trevor Lawrence praised the Veitch Nursery for its long history in which, under the guiding hand of five generations, the nursery had stood foremost as the most thoroughly honourable, straightforward, enterprising and successful horticultural firm of all time, 'proving that honourable dealing in every form brought its natural and legitimate reward'. It was a day of of celebrating and of acknowledging the enormous achievements of a century of the Veitch horticultural business, over half of which had been masterfully managed by Harry Veitch – a man who loved horticulture with an unparalleled knowledge of the business, a man who had made himself loved everywhere for his generosity, not just to charities but to gardeners and science. Harry, basking in so much affection and praise, might have felt that this was the finest moment of his life.

The 1866 International Horticultural Exhibition and Botanical Congress, which had been such a defining occasion for Harry in his youth, was to be repeated forty-five years later. Despite his age, Harry was invited to play a leading role which he took up, as one journalist wrote, 'with the same buoyant and genial energy that has characterised him throughout his life. Age has not quenched his ardour, nor curbed his breezy humour.' The 1912 Royal International Horticultural Exhibition was held in the grounds of the Chelsea Hospital; the tents, the largest ever erected, were lit by electricity with special ventilation for the orchid and cut-flower tents. The 1912 Exhibition was such a big event that the RHS had agreed in advance to cancel its own Great Spring Show, then traditionally held in the grounds of the Inner Temple, which were too cramped. The phenomenal success of the International Exhibition proved that people were prepared to travel 'out to Chelsea', which had always been thought of as too far from the centre of town. Harry, however, whose own nurseries lay nearby, had long dismissed these objections and believed correctly that the Royal Hospital grounds would be the ideal venue for future RHS shows. And so they were. In 1913 the first Chelsea Flower Show was held and has continued (with the exception of wartime) ever since.

The Exhibition was a huge success and at the opening banquet, Harry made a speech. The occasion, he said, was a very solemn one for him, for he well remembered the 1866 Exhibition and its importance, and he was thankful that he had been spared, as so many had not, to take part in this present one. Harry was awarded a knighthood to mark the occasion and a life-time's achievements. This honour, 'the greatest moment of my life', was the first ever to be conferred for services to horticulture, then still considered the 'Cinderella' of the sciences.

Sir Harry, the 'Garden Knight', had still not finished. He remained chairman of the RHS Orchid Committee for many more years, continued his charitable works and sat on numerous committees, including horticultural education, an interest that had always been particularly important to both the Acland and Veitch families. The 140-year relationship between two families of gentlemen and gardeners culminated in December 1911 when a Diploma Committee, presided over by the Rt Hon. A. D. Dyke Acland with Sir Harry Veitch, recommended a national diploma to be incorporated into the National Diploma in Horticulture; it was launched in 1913.

A journalist from the *Daily Mail* visited Harry at East Burnham Park: in his study, Sir Harry took down his huge copy of *Hortus Veitchii* with its descriptions of over 2,000 new plants contributed by his 'great family' to English gardens. 'We had six travellers at one time touring the world,' Harry recalled and added with a sigh, 'that was in the good old days when men faced every sort of danger from climate and man, including the use of a pistol by one collector escaping from China.' He recalled how 3,000 of

Sir Harry (left) chairs the RHS Orchid Committee, March 1920

William Lobb's *sequoia* seedlings were sold in one day, and with his usual twinkle, added, 'I must not tell you what they were sold for.' The journalist reminded Harry of his controversial lectures on orchid hybridising when he had been highly criticised for 'letting the cat out of the bag'. 'But,' said Sir Harry, 'if you really love your work you do not keep things dark. I do not believe in that way.' As they finished their tour of the garden and crossed the tennis lawns, Sir Harry remarked: 'I do not play games, I do not shoot, I hate the water as a recreation. But I work and have always liked my work, which brings me into contact with the most charming people. Be sure that if a man is fond of a garden he has got a soft place somewhere.'

But if men and women would always remain fond of gardening, their ability to do so on the scale seen during the Victorian age was slowly in decline. By 1909, the Liberal prime minister Lloyd George had introduced taxes and death duties which hit the wealthiest the hardest. Hereditary political power and landed wealth were under threat. The repercussions would inevitably have profound effects on the horticultural nurseries which had made their fortunes selling to their richest patrons. The first half of the twentieth century was a period of enormous social and economic change, as England's upper crust was beginning the slide from vast wealth and consumption towards more modest lifetyles.

Meanwhile, improved communication – the railways, fast steamships, telephones and now cars – which had once benefited the business by moving nursery stock quickly and efficiently around the country, was now perceived as a threat. It was becoming increasingly hard to compete in a world of commerce and trade that extended way beyond the old protected routes and markets of the British Empire. Exotic fruits and out-of-season vegetables once produced in the glasshouses of large estates by armies of gardeners could now be brought in from the Caribbean or the Continent. High-street florist shops stocked imported flowers such as carnations which arrived in London fresh from the commercial forcing houses of the Riviera. Gentry and middle classes alike could afford to shop for these luxuries and the huge estate kitchen gardens and expensive glasshouses gradually shrank away.

People were travelling abroad and seeing the wider world and its natural treasures for themselves and had less inclination to create romantic and imaginary ideas of the world in their gardens. Japan, China and South America were sending plants direct from their own nursery stocks of plants. It seemed that the pioneering plant collector had had his day in all but the most remote and unexplored regions. Gradually gardens developed more natural, personal styles and women gardeners emerged as a powerful and creative force. As social life and values changed and became more fragmented, the country weekends and dinner parties were scaled down, as were the great show gardens and exotic hothouse collections. The wild passions for rare plants had lasted over half a century until the men and the money which fed them were consumed in the Great War.

Gardening never seemed so unimportant as in 1914 – truly the beginning of the end. Harry's nephew, John Gould Junior, died, the lease on Coombe Wood was due to expire and could not be renewed, war loomed on the horizon and gardeners were laying down their tools and taking up arms. Sir Harry Veitch was seventy-four years old and there was no one to inherit the 'House of Veitch'. With a heavy heart he decided to close down the business rather than sell the goodwill of the name and its unrivalled reputation. The great sale began on 10 November 1914 and continued for several weeks.

Many acres of nursery land, and all the glasshouses and nursery buildings at Chelsea, Langley, and Feltham came under the hammer. Middlesex County Council bought forty acres of the Feltham land for building and allotments, leaving four acres containing greenhouses which were taken over by Wills and Segar, the long-established South Kensington florists. Suttons, the famous seed merchants, bought most of Langley nursery (although Harry gave his fruit foreman J. C. Allgrove some of the land on which to set up his own business, trading in fruit trees). Over 5,000 lots of fruit trees went along with 1,300 yards of box hedging and 2,900 flowering plants in pots for forcing.

The auctioneers took ten days to sell the plant stock at Coombe Wood, for many a far sadder occasion. However, for countless plant enthusiasts, it was the opportunity of a lifetime. Gardeners travelled from all over the country, even from abroad, to attend the sale in the hopes of finding a bargain or obtaining an historic or rare Veitch introduction. They came by rail, some with special rail vans, in cars, trucks, horse-drawn carts. The Veitch-trained nurseryman Edwin Hillier pedalled his bicycle all the way from Winchester and filled his basket with several rare things, including *Cladrastis sinensis* and *Emmenopterys henryi*. Every day the large, stooping figure of Sir Harry, wrapped up in his greatcoat against the cold weather, could be seen walking around the paths stopping to inspect a plant or exchange a few words with a prospective buyer.

With loyal nurseryman George Harrow and John Heal at his side, Harry recalled the history of every specimen, the name of every tree, shrub and plant, the story of every man who travelled the world to find them and all the nurserymen who had laboured at the benches to raise them. Together they remembered the day each one first 'bloomed', its colour, the shape of its flowers and leaves, its hardiness and particular seasonal attractions, its potential commercial appeal and, in many cases, the awards it had won. In George Harrow's nursery record book was the official description and name of every new introduction, in John Heal's were the records of every hybrid created by Veitch nurserymen. The production of hundreds of 'false' or 'mule'plants had sometimes been vilified by the more conservative, but they had been praised and purchased by thousands of grateful gardeners.

There were 6,000 named rhododendrons to be disposed of and hundreds of still-unnamed Chinese species. Many of Wilson and Purdom's seeds had successfully germinated but the plants had still to flower and show their true characteristics so that they could be named: many simply carried Wilson's or Purdom's original number. It was a sad parting for old friends as nurserymen handed over their precious charges to others: Purdom's *Viburnam fragrans* (*V. farreri*) which had still not flowered, went to gardeners employed by the Loder family, one to Wakehurst Place where in 1920, W. J. Bean saw the first fragrant flowers to appear in England.

Before the sale, Harry had invited a number of close friends and colleagues to choose some special specimens; he had to use considerable care and diplomacy not to offend old customers. He wrote to Sir David Prain that he was very sorry that the original plant of Pearce's *Eucryphia pinnatifolia* (*E. glutinosa*) was already presented to Leopold Rothschild for his garden at Leighton Buzzard, 'a kind client and good friend for many years . . . and gives a good home to a souvenir from Coombe Wood'. He instead offered a *Magnolia macrophylla* and later, after the sale of Feltham, he also sent Prain a large collection of Veitch 'winter-blooming' begonias. Sir Frederick Moore, another old friend, chose many kinds of foliage plants for his glasshouses in Glasnevin in Ireland. The Loder family took on huge quantities of Veitch specimens. R. B. Loder bought a selection for his 'Veitch' bed in his garden at Maidwell Hall in Northamptonshire, including several deutzias, a large *Dipelta floribunda, Sorbus folgneri* and a *Prunus serrula*. Colonel Giles Loder filled two trucks with plants for High Beeches in Sussex, including *Cornus kousa*, the Japanese tree *Kalopanax pictus*, and *Deutzia longifolia* 'Veitchii', of which a few still survive. J. C. Williams bought a fine pink-flowered magnolia, then named *Magnolia denudata* for his Cornish garden, Caerhays. Major Stern and his wife wrote that they bought a number of Veitch's Chinese introductions: 'We thought we must try and get some of these plants' despite having a chalk garden in Sussex.

Some shrubs and trees had become so large they could not be sold and were left in peace. George Harrow recalls a fine specimen of *Magnolia acuminata* which had reached fifty feet in height; other mature magnolia specimens included *M. hypoleuca (M. obovata)* at twenty-five feet, *M. macrophylla* at twenty feet, *M. x watsonii (M. x wieseneri)* and *M.parviflora (M. sieboldii)* each at twelve feet, and a *M. kobus* which, Harrow wrote, had shown no sign of flowering until it had been in the ground about thirty years 'and then, one morning, I discovered about twelve pure white blooms on it, each about the size of a pullet's egg'. In other parts of the grounds stood a large *Berberis hakeoides* and *Daphniphyllum glaucescens (D. macropodum)*, a remarkable *Viburnum plicatum 'Mariesii'* which many visitors admired for its huge height and spread, and a lovely specimen of *Stewartia pseudocamellia*, by then twenty feet high. John Gould's *Sciadopitys verticillata* and *Acer nikoense (A. maximowiczianum)* and several other acers had grown up to considerable heights while the Monarch Birch *(Betula maximowicziana)*, a *Quercus acuta*, *Cornus macrophylla* and *C. nuttallii*, all grown from original seed, were now too mature to be moved. One or two *Sequoidadendron giganteum* towered over everything but William Lobb's original avenue of 120 specimens of *Araucaria araucana* had grown so old and 'unsightly' that most had already been grubbed up. Perhaps the most famous of Coombe Wood's entire tree collection, already rising to respectable heights of nearly twenty feet, were a number of Wilson's *Davidia involucrata* which had produced their first lovely flowers in Coombe Wood in 1911.

When all the stock was sold, the land at Coombe Wood was put on the market. The nurseryman Arthur Luff put in a bid but failed. Lady Paget appealed to the landowners who agreed to sell her the two acres of nursery land adjoining her Japanese garden where the stream and bottom pond lay, and all the Chinese and Japanese trees and plants. Thus many original plants and numerous other rare shrubs and trees were saved, including Wilson's original Davidias. When the sale was over, John Heal, now in his seventies, locked the last greenhouse door and retired to a small house in Fulham where he died in 1925. Walter Davis, one of Harry's most loyal and adventurous collectors who had stayed with the firm to the end, died in 1930. George Harrow retired and died in 1926. Harry had ensured that all his staff were either found new posts or were helped to set up in business and the older men were given generous pensions.

The Great War took its massive toll. Thousands of gardeners and nurserymen who went to the front never returned. Across the country hundreds of country houses were taken over as military hospitals or were mothballed, the gardens abandoned, untended and unwanted. In 1916, Paxton's conservatory at Chatsworth was allowed to go cold. Four years later that vast and arrogant symbol of all that was achievable through wealth and ambition was blown up. Out of the mountains of fallen masonry, massive wood beams and smashed glass 'two withered palm trees raised their forlorn heads', victims of the changing times. One old gardener cried 'a national calamity' – the end of a garden era.

Like most families, the Veitches had suffered losses: Harry's nephew Arthur's nineteen-year-old grandson, Lt Dick Sherwood, had been killed serving in the RAF, and Peter's younger son, Major Leonard, was killed while fighting with the Devons after gaining the MC.

Despite the end of James Veitch & Son, Harry continued to be active and after the war he became treasurer of the fund which the RHS raised for the relief of the gardeners and nurserymen in Europe whose businesses had been ravaged by the Germans. He raised a total of £45,000 which was used to buy seed, fruit trees and tools to help restore the devastation. For this work and for a long life of eminent services to international horticulture Harry was made a member of the Legion of Honour of France and Chevalier of the Crown of Belgium, and received the French Isidore St Hilaire Medal and the American George R. White Gold Medal. He resigned as chairman of the Wisley Garden committee but the RHS had not quite finished with Harry and, in 1918, he was briefly called out again to serve as treasurer. Louisa died in 1921, leaving Harry to carry on alone for three more years until his own peaceful death aged eighty-four at East Burnham Park, on Sunday, 6 July 1924.

The newspapers and journals published fulsome obituaries recording Harry's and the Veitches' great achievements. Sir Harry, claimed by many as the most outstanding horticulturist of his day, was the last of a great family dynasty whose plant collectors had introduced from around the world some of the finest and most popular garden trees and plants. Their nurseries had filled greenhouses with some of the most exotic plants ever seen, their highly trained and skilled men had pioneered the art of hybridi-

sation and given gardeners new orchids, begonias and amaryllis. Five generations of men whose innovative ideas had created fashions and new ideas
about gardening had influenced the steady progress of British garden history
through their services to horticultural societies, education, charities and the
development of scientific knowledge. But Harry might have preferred a
reminiscence written many years later, in 1958, by one of his old employees:
'When the hands of the Royal Hospital clock move towards noon on the
Thursday of the Chelsea Flower Show an assembly takes place inside the
Main Gate. Serge-suited, fresh-faced, walking sticks in hand . . . the head
gardeners of Britain hold their annual reunion.' Over well-earned pints of
ale, the old comrades compare memories and 'the talk turns towards time
shared with James Veitch & Son':

> Fifty years ago wages were low, the welfare state a mere figment of
> Lloyd George's imagination. But to those whose working hours were
> spent among the odours of potting composts, mulch, and new-mown
> lawns, it was a more satisfying and less complicated world than ours
> today . . . Hours were long, but there was fun to be had in the days
> before the Flanders fields took their harvest.

Training was strict for the 'bright lads of the bothy' and there was rigid
loyalty between men and master but

> Veitch's fulfilled a special role in days gone by and even today many
> of the head gardeners represent a Veitch vintage. Men who have spent
> long years as the rulers of that *sanctorum*, the propagating house, with
> the keys of peach houses and vineries in their keeping. These things
> have a steadying effect. The emergency fiver has long since given place
> to the gold watch-chain, the spade to the secateurs. Times change and
> men change with them, but men now growing old do not forget the
> comradeship which began in the glasshouses of Veitch's.

ENDWORD

SIR HARRY VEITCH'S death and the closure of the London nurseries were not quite the end of the story. Peter Veitch continued to run the Exeter nursery until his death in 1929. Until F. W. Meyer's death in 1906 the pair had continued to design and landscape gardens and public parks all over the country. Their last joint venture was plans for a rockery and alpine garden for the RHS garden at Wisley. Peter's daughter Mildred worked with him, and after his death took over the firm which she moved to new premises and ran for a further forty years until she sold it in 1969, two years before she died aged eighty-two. It would be gratifying to be able to say that after so many men, a woman was at last successfully involved in the Veitch nursery business. But sadly Mildred was not an easy person to work with. A nephew, Douglas, and a great-nephew, Peter, were brought in to try to keep the name going but, as a family descendant wrote: 'Regrettably her strong personality was such that none of them was willing to stay on.' She did create *Camellia x williamsii* 'Mildred Veitch' and she continued to supply plants and trees to the gardens at Bicton, Poltimore and Killerton.

At some point, possibly after the death of her father, who was the main legatee in Harry's will, Mildred is said to have destroyed all the Veitch papers – mountains of accounts, plant records, catalogues and correspondence, all the paraphernalia that we would now treasure as archive material but, to Mildred, was then understandably only rubbish fit for the bonfire. Harry Veitch left his large art collection and the Veitch collectors' museum pieces to the Royal Albert Museum in Exeter for a Veitch gallery. It was never set up and in the 1950s most of the collection was sold. With so little archive evidence of the Veitch family left, we can only be thankful that our gardens, arboreta and national botanical collections remain the best living repository of their extraordinary achievements.

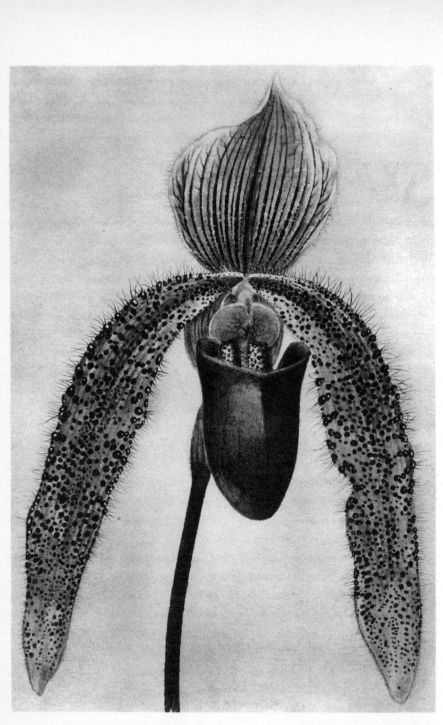

Cypripedium x 'James H. Veitch'. Named after James Herbert Veitch, one of the most striking-looking Veitch orchid hybrids, first produced in 1894

ACKNOWLEDGEMENTS

W HEN I DISCOVERED that there was almost no surviving archive of the Veitch family or their business, I realised that it was going to be necessary to hunt through numerous archives, libraries and private papers and I am indebted to many people who have helped me in this long, but fascinating search.

I should first say that my efforts were facilitated by work already done by a Veitch descendant, Shirley Heriz-Smith, in a number of articles she wrote about the Veitch family and their collectors (1980/90). Information by the late Harold Fletcher in his book *The Story of the Royal Horticultural Society* (1969) also made my life considerably easier. Roy Briggs, author of *A Life of Ernest Wilson* (1993), was very generous with his help

The librarians at the Lindley Library, especially Liz Gilbert, were always enthusiastic and helpful, and Kate Pickard, the archivist at Kew, was another great ally. I would like to thank other librarians at the University Libraries of Bristol and Exeter, the Devon Records Office, the West Country Studies Library, the Hawick Museum and Scottish Borders Archive, the National Library of Scotland, the Bristol Public Library, Kensington and Chelsea Public Library and local history libraries at Feltham, Kingston, Twickenham and Fulham. Thanks also to Richard Schofield at the Rothschild Archive. My special thanks go to the London Library, particularly to the recently retired Alan Bell who entrusted me with the Library's precious copy of *Hortus Veitchii*. I am grateful to St Bridget's Nursery in Exeter for access to their Veitch memorabilia, and to Charlotte Cowe in Edinburgh who helped track down the early Veitch family history. I would also like to thank Toby Musgrave, Bridget Graham and Todd Gray, also members of the Bristol Medico-Historical Society.

I am grateful to Sir John Acland for permission to quote from the Acland archives, and to David Hoare for allowing me to see and quote from his archives at Luscombe Castle. My thanks too to Jocelyn Hemmings for her help with Poltimore, to Isobel Richardson and the National Trust at Killerton and Holnicote and to the National Trust generally for their help with gardens connected with the Veitches now in their care. I am grateful too to many other archivists, head gardeners and garden historians, in particular, Chris Wilkinson at the River Gardens (all that survives of the Coombe Wood Nursery grounds), Steve Martin at Bystock Court, David Mead for information about Bicton, Kate Felus at Stowe, and John Clark of the Devon Gardens Trust.

The need for help, advice and encouragement from specialists in writing a book of this kind is terribly important and I have been really lucky to have found Tim Mowl, lecturer in Garden History at Bristol University, who helped me with garden history, Nick Wray, Superintendent of the Bristol University Botanic Garden, who gave his valuable time to correct my many botanical errors, and most importantly, Roy Lancaster, whose generosity to anyone interested in plants and gardening is legendary. He not only gave helpful advice and information, but also kindly wrote the foreword, in which he was too modest to reveal that he is a holder of both the Veitch Memorial Medal and the Victoria Medal of Honour.

For her continuing enthusiasm and support I want to thank my agent Jane Turnbull; and Matthew Parker and my husband Ben Shephard for their editorial and historical input. For producing such a beautiful book I wish to thank everyone at Bloomsbury, especially Alexandra Pringle, Marian McCarthy, Chiki Sarkar and Polly Napper. In my family I thank in particular my aunt, Angela Lawrence, for her hospitality in Edinburgh and loan of her car. My enduring love, as always, to my husband Ben as we continue our long walks and writing, and to my children Louisa and Joe, for their endless patience, love and support.

AUTHOR'S NOTE

THE NAMES OF plants and places are continually changing and I have used, where appropriate, the contemporary name followed by the most up-to-date one in brackets. Many Veitch plants have passed out of cultivation or changed name several times and I have therefore only indicated new names for those still commonly found. Common or colloquial names of plants, when given, are wherever possible followed by their botanical name in italics. Large numbers of Veitch plant introductions have since disappeared, being too difficult to cultivate in England.

Carl Linnaeus's binomial or two-word system created in 1753, remains the basis for modern taxonomy. It puts the genus first, for example, the oak *Quercus*, followed by the particular species name within the genus, the red oak, *Quercus rubra*. Extra descriptive epithets can be added to convey more information such as size, habit, colour or habitat such as *alba* (white), *supinus* (prostrate), *japonicus* (of Japan), while personal names can be given in honour of a patron or the collector who first discovered or introduced the plant such as *banksia* and *veitchii*.

There are certain terms which can be confusing. For example, the 'discovery' of a plant means the first time it is seen and recorded by a botanist, collector or interested traveller. The 'introduction' of a plant is when seed or living matter is successfully returned to a garden and cultivated. This did not however mean that it entered gardens generally, since many wealthy plantsmen kept new plants within an exclusive circle. 'Commercial introduction' was most usually made by nurserymen who cultivated, propagated and then put on sale new species of plant. Who first discovered a plant is often rife with controversy and so, apart from one or two important events, I have tried to stay only with claims to general introductions.

The word 'amateur' for gardeners in the early days was not as we would use it now. An amateur gardener or plantsman was a member of the wealthy gardening elite which distinguished him or her from the 'professional' or employed gardener and the 'trade' or nursery gardener.

The word 'specimen' was most usually taken to mean a dried specimen of the parts of a plant and its seeds. These were vital for botanists trying to identify and name a plant and were kept in herbarium collections.

Families in the past had a maddening custom of naming their children, especially the boys, with the same names, as were several Veitches. To help the reader avoid confusion, I have given every character a consistent distinguishing name. It may be a combination of their first and second names such as 'John Gould' (the second was often taken from the mother's maiden name), or a nickname such as Sir 'Tom' Acland. A family tree on page viii should be helpful for navigating through the generations of Veitches.

SOURCES

ABBREVIATIONS

AA	*Archive of the Arnold Arboretum, USA*
CGM	*Cornish Garden Magazine*
CL	*Country Life*
DRO	*Devon Record Office, Exeter*
GC	*Gardener's Chronicle*
GM	*Gardener's Magazine*
JGHS	*Journal of the Garden History Society*
JRHS	*Journal of the Royal Horticultural Society*
Kew	*Archive of the Royal Botanic Garden, Kew*
LL	*Lindley Library – The Royal Horticultural Society, London*
WCSC	*West Country Studies Centre, Exeter*

CHAPTER ONE

1 Company of Gardeners' Minute Books. Guildhall Library (London)
2 Stephen Switzer: *Ichnographia Rustica* vol 1 (London 1718)
3 Churchyard records and local history records: Hawick Museum and Scottish Borders Archives, Selkirk
4 *Transactions of the Hawick Archaeological Society* 1898. Scottish Record Office, Edinburgh
5 Dickson's *Day Books*, 1750–66, also Farm Memo Book and Servant's Ledger 1760. National Library of Scotland, Edinburgh
6 E. H. M. Cox, *A History of Gardening in Scotland* (London 1935)
7 William Boutcher, *A Treatise on Forest-Trees* 1775 National Library of Scotland
8 Blanche Henrey, *British Botanical and Horticultural Literature before 1800.* Vol 2 (Oxford, 1975)
9 John Harvey, 'A Scottish Botanist in London in 1766' (*JGHS* 1981)
10 E. J. Willson, *James Lee and the Vineyard Nursery* (Hammersmith Local History Group, 1961)
11 E. J. Willson, *West London Nursery Gardens* (Fulham & Hammersmith Historical Society, 1982)

12 John Harvey, *Early Nurserymen* (London 1973)
13 John Harvey, *Early Horticultural Catalogues* (London 1984)
14 Joseph Lucas, (trans.) *Per Kalm's Account of his Visit to England on his way to America in 1748* (London 1892)

CHAPTER TWO

1 Anne Acland, *A Devon Family* (London 1981)
2 Acland letters, papers and estate ledgers. *DRO*
3 National Trust, The National Trust Archaeological Survey of Killerton Estate
4 Timothy Mowl, *Gentlemen and Players – Gardeners of the English Landscape* (Stroud 2000)
5 Beatty Letters, Sept/Oct 1892. Correspondence between Thomas Beatty and Minnie and Harry Veitch (Private Collection)
6 *Exeter Flying Post* 1785 (*WCSC*)
7 Todd Gray, *The Traveller's Tales – East Devon* (Devon 2000) Rev. Stebbing Shaw, *A Tour of the West of England 1788*
8 Ibid. *The Travels of Mrs Parry Price through Devon in 1805*
9 Todd Gray, *The Garden History of Devon – An illustrated guide to sources* (Exeter, 1995)
10 J. C. Loudon – comments on Shute, Nutwell Court, Luscombe, Killerton, Poltimore etc. *GM* October 1842
11 Luscombe Castle (Hoare Archives)
12 *Luscombe Castle CL* 1956
13 Shirley Heriz-Smith, 'The Veitch Nurseries of Killerton and Exeter' *Pts 1–2. JGHS* 1987–88

CHAPTER THREE

1 Letters from John Veitch to Sir Thomas Acland 10th Bt sent from Killerton to Edinburgh Nov 1808–Feb 1809. *DRO*
2 Acland letters, papers and estate ledgers. *DRO*
3 J. C. Loudon, *GM* Nov 1842
4 Beatty letters
5 Harold Fletcher, *The Story of the Royal Horticultural Society. 1804–1968* (London 1969)
6 Broadclyst Parish records. *WCSC*
7 Richard Polwhele, *The Story of Devonshire 1793–1806. DRO*
8 E. J. Willson, *West London Nursery Gardens* (1982)

9   Shirley Heriz-Smith, 'The Veitch Nurseries of Killerton and Exeter'
    Pts 1–2. JGHS 1987–88

CHAPTER FOUR

1   W. G. Hoskins, *Devon and its People* (Devon 1959)
2   *Exeter Gazette* 1828–40. *Exeter Flying Post* 1828–39. *Exeter & Plymouth
    Gazette* 1830–41. *DRO*
3   James Veitch's handwritten advertisement. Private
4   R. Prothero (ed) *The Letters of Richard Ford* (London 1900)
5   J. C. Loudon on Bicton. *GM* 1842
6   David Mead, *Guide to Bicton* (Exeter, 2000) (The gardens of Bicton
    nr. Buddleigh Salterton, Devon are open to the public)
7   *GC* 1830–1840
8   *Journal of Horticulture & Cottage Gardener* Sept 1871
9   N. D. G. James, *The Trees of Bicton* (Exeter, 1969)
10 Shirley Heriz-Smith, 'The Veitch Nurseries of Killermont and Exeter'
    Pts 1–2. JGHS 1987–88
11 Fortescue-Foulkes, *The Story of Poltimore House* (1971. Private)
12 Estate ledgers of: Craddock House, Stover, Escot, Killerton, Poltimore,
    Nutwell Court. *DRO*

CHAPTER FIVE

1   Harold Fletcher, *The Story of the Royal Horticultural Society 1804–1968*
2   William Stearn (ed.), *John Lindley, Gardener, Botanist and Pioneer Orchidist*
    (London 1999)
3   Mea Allen, *The Hookers of Kew* (London 1967)
4   Letters from James Veitch to (Sir) William Hooker July 1840–60. *Kew*
5   Violet Markham, *Paxton and the Bachelor Duke* (London 1935)
6   Kenneth Lemmon, *The Covered Garden* (London 1962)
7   Nathaniel Ward, *The Growth of Gardens in Closely Glazed Cases* (London
    1842)
8   Shirley Heriz-Smith, 'The Veitch Nurseries of Killerton and Exeter'
    Pts 1–2. JGHS 1987–88.
9   Shirley Heriz-Smith, 'William Lobb' JGHS 1995
10 *GM* 1840–42
11 John Veitch's will. *DRO*
12 *Gardener's Magazine*, 1838

CHAPTER SIX

1 Letters from James Veitch to Hooker. *Kew*
2 *GC*, 1842–50
3 *GM*, 1842
4 N. D. G. James, *Trees of Bicton* 1969
5 Adolphus Kent, *Manual of Coniferae* (London 1900)
6 Shirley Heriz-Smith, 'Thomas Lobb' *CG* 1982
7 Shirley Heriz-Smith, 'Lobb Brothers' *CG* 1987
8 Letter from Pince to Hooker. *Kew*
9 Harry Veitch, Reminiscences. *Middlesex Chronicle* July 1913
10 Joseph Hooker, *Himalayan Journals* (London 1854)
11 J. Davies, *Douglas of the Forests* (Edinburgh 1980)
12 Veitch, *Manual of Orchidaceous Plants* (London 1894)
13 J. H. Veitch, *Hortus Veitchii* (Private, 1906)

CHAPTER SEVEN

1 *GC* 1890–63
2 Todd Gray. Elihu Burritt, *A Walk from London to Land's End and Back 1868*
3 E. J. Willson, *West London Nursery Gardens*
4 William Gaunt, *Chelsea* (London 1954)
5 Shirley Heriz-Smith, 'The Veitch Nurseries of Killerton and Exeter' Pts 1–4. *JGHS* 1987–88
6 Letters from James Veitch to Hooker. 1840–60. *Kew*
7 Harold Fletcher, *The Story of the Royal Horticultural Society 1804–1968*
8 *GC* 1859–63
9 Harry Veitch Reminiscences. *GC* 1910
10 Shirley Heriz-Smith, 'Richard Pearce'. *CL*, Mar, 1985
11 Pearce journals. *Kew*
12 J. H. Veitch, *Hortus Veitchii* (Private 1906)

CHAPTER EIGHT

1 John Gould's letters home. Published in the *GC* 1861 *et seq*
2 Shirley Heriz-Smith, 'John Gould'. *CL*, 1987
3 *The Cottage Gardener*, 1866
4 *GC*, 1861–66
5 Rutherford Alcock, *Capital of the Tycoons* (London 1863)
6 Adolphus Kent, *Manual of Coniferae* 1900

7   Steven Spongberg, *A Reunion of Trees* (Harvard USA, 1990)
8   Robert Fortune, *Yedo and Peking* (London 1862)
9   Letter from James Junior to Sir William Hooker, May 1863. *Kew*
10 Letters from John Gould to Joseph Hooker, Dec. 1866. *Kew*
11 John Gould's letters from 2nd trip published in *GC*, 1866 *et seq*

CHAPTER NINE

1   James Veitch's Will
2   William Camp, articles in *GC*, March 1926 *et seq*
3   Charles Darwin, *The Various Contrivances by which Orchids are Fertilised by Insects* (London 1875)
4   Charles Darwin, *The Movements and Habits of Climbing Plants* (London 1875)
5   Veitch, *Manual of Orchidaceous Plants* (London 1887–94)
6   Kenneth Lemmon, *The Covered Garden* (London 1962)
7   *GC*, 1865–70
8   Peter Hayden, *Biddulph Grange* (*NT*, 1989)
9   Letters from James Junior to Sir William Hooker and to Dr Joseph Hooker, 1863–70, *Kew*
10 B. Wynne (ed.) 'The Tuberous Begonia' in *The Gardening World*, 1888
11 Records of Brompton Cemetery. Fulham, London
12 Shirley Heriz-Smith, 'The Veitch Nurseries of Killerton and Exeter' Pts 4–5 *JGHS* 1987–88
13 J. H. Veitch, *Hortus Veitchii* (Private, 1906)

CHAPTER TEN

1   Shirley Heriz-Smith, 'The Veitch Nurseries of Killerton and Exeter' Pts 4–5, *JGHS* 1990
2   Anne Acland, *A Devon Family* (London 1981)
3   J. Caldwell & M. Proctor, *The Grounds and Gardens of the University of Exeter* (Exeter 1969)
4   *Streatham Hall* CL, April 1899
5   F. W. Meyer, *Rock and Water Gardens* (London 1910)
6   B. Elliot, *Victorian Gardens* (London 1990)
7   *Bystock Garden, CL*, April 1881
8   Catalogues of Robert Veitch & Son Exeter and Exminster (Private)
9   Veitch Gardener's memorandum book Exeter, 1895 (Private)
10 Frederick Boyle, *About Orchids* (London 1893)

11 A. Russan & F. Boyle, *The Orchid Seeker* (London 1890)
12 *GC* 1870–1881
13 *The Orchid Review*, 1860–80
14 Merle Reinikka, *A History of Orchids* (Oregon, USA 1995)
15 Veitch, *Manual of Orchidaceous Plants* 1887–94

CHAPTER ELEVEN

1 Charles Maries, 'Rambles of a Plant Collector'. *The Garden*, 1881–94 *et seq*
2 Shirley Heriz-Smith, 'Charles Maries'. *CL* Dec 1986. March 1989
3 *GC*, 1879–90
4 F. Burbidge, *Gardens of the Sun* (London 1880)
5 Shirley Heriz-Smith, 'Western Collectors on Eastern Islands'. *Hortus*, 1988
6 *JRHS* 1880–91
7 L. Ponsonby, *Marianne North* (London 1990)
8 Arthur Swinson & H. F. C. Sander, *The Orchid King* (London, 1970)
9 *Minley Manor. CL* 1899
10 Miriam Rothschild, *The Rothschild Gardens* (London 1996)
11 Charles Curtis' description of Chelsea nursery staff. *JRHS* 1948
12 Henry May, *Seventy Years in Horticulture* (London 1928)
13 J. H. Veitch, *Hortus Veitchii* (Private 1906)
14 Peter Hayden, *Biddulph Grange* (NT 1989)

CHAPTER TWELVE

1 *GC* 1889–1900
2 Veitch Nursery catalogues, Exeter & Chelsea (Private and *LL*)
3 H. J. Veitch, 'The Hybridisation of Orchids'. *JRHS* 1886 vol vii.
4 H. J. Veitch, 'Orchid Culture, Past & Present'. *JRHS* June 1889
5 Letters from Harry Veitch to Thiselton-Dyer. *Kew*
6 'The Late Professor Reichenbach'. *GC* May, 1889 & *The Garden*, 1905
7 Harold Fletcher, *The Story of the Royal Horticultural Society. 1804–1968* (London 1969)
8 Letters between Harry Veitch and Charles Sprague Sargent. *AA*
9 James Herbert Veitch, *A Traveller's Notes* (Private 1896)
10 James Herbert Veitch, 'Traveller's Notes'. *GC* version, March 1891 *et seq*
11 Steven Spongberg, *A Reunion of Trees* (Harvard, USA 1990)
12 *GC*, 1880–1890

13   Shirley Heriz-Smith, 'The Veitch Nurseries of Killerton and Exeter'
     Pts 4–5, JGHS 1990

CHAPTER THIRTEEN

1   S. B. Sutton, *Charles Sprague Sargent and the Arnold Arboretum* (Harvard,
     USA, 1970)
2   Letters from Harry & James Herbert to Sargent, 1899–1900, *AA*
3   Roy Briggs, *A Life of Ernest Wilson* (London 1993)
4   Letters and contract between members of the Veitch family to Wilson,
     1899–1905, *Kew*
5   George Harrow, 'Some Recollections of Coombe Wood'. *The New
     Flora & Silva*, 1931
6   Shirley Heriz-Smith, 'Japan Rooted in Surrey', *CL*, 1990
7   E. H. Wilson, 'Leaves from my Chinese Notebook', *GC*, June, 1905
     et seq
8   E. H. Wilson, *A Naturalist in Western China* (London 1913)
9   E. H. Wilson, *Aristocrats of the Garden* (London 1938)

CHAPTER FOURTEEN

1   Duncan Steward, *The Story of Farnham* (Slough local history library, 1995)
2   Harold Fletcher, *The Story of the Royal Horticultural Society, 1804–1968*
     (London 1969)
3   *GC*, 1900–1923
4   George Harrow, 'Some Recollections of Coombe Wood'. *The New
     Flora & Silva* 1931
5   Letters from James Herbert to Thiselton-Dyer. *Kew*
6   Shirley Heriz-Smith, 'William Purdom, A Westmoreland Planthunter'.
     Hortus, 1996
7   Shirley Heriz-Smith, 'Brightener of British Winters'. *CL*, June 1986
8   Roy Briggs, *A Life of Ernest Wilson* (London 1993)
9   Shirley Heriz-Smith, 'The Veitch Nurseries of Killerton and Exeter'
     Pts 4–5, JGHS 1990
10   Henry May, *Seventy Years in Horticulture* (London 1928)
11   Interview with Sir Harry Veitch. *Daily Mail*, 1920
12   Shirley Heriz-Smith, 'Japan Rooted in Surrey'. *CL*, April 1899
13   Letters from Sir Harry to Sir David Prain 1914 and Sir Thiselton-Dyer,
     1914, *Kew*
14   'Reunion at Chelsea'. *The Times*, May 1958

GENERAL READING

Allen, Mea   *Plants That Changed Our Gardens* (Exeter 1974)

Amherst, A.   *A History of Gardening in England* (London 1910)

Anderson, A.W.   *The Coming of the Flowers* (London 1950)

Bean, W. J.   *Trees and Shrubs Hardy in the British Isles* 3 vols. (London, 1925)

Bean, W. J.   *The Royal Botanic Gardens of Kew* (London 1908)

Best, G.   *Mid-Victorian Britain* (London 1971)

Blanche, H.   *British Botanical and Horticultural Literature Before 1800*

Brander, M.   *The Georgian Gentleman* (London 1973)

Briggs, A.   *The Age of Improvement* (London 1959)

Briggs, A.   *Victorian People* (London 1987)

Brockway, L. H.   *Science and Colonial Expansion* (London 1979)

Campbell-Culver, M.   *The Origins of Plants* (London 2001)

Carter, Tom   *The Victorian Garden* (London 1984)

Clayton-Payne, A.   *Victorian Flower Gardens* (London 1988)

Coats, A. M.   *Flowers and Their Histories* (London 1956)

Coats, A. M.   *Garden Shrubs and Their Histories* (London 1963)

Coats, A. M.   *The Quest For Plants* (London 1969)

Cox, E. H. M.   *Plant Hunting in China* (London 1945)

Curtis, C. H.   *Orchids: Their Description and Cultivation* (London 1950)

Desmond, Ray   *Dictionary of British and Irish Botanists and Horticulturists* (London 1977)

Devon Group (NCCPG)   *The Magic Tree: Devon Garden Plants* (Devon 1989)

Elliot, Brent   *Victorian Gardens* (London 1990)

Fisher, John — *The Origins of Garden Plants* (London 1982)

Fortune, Robert — *Three Years Wandering in the Northern Provinces of China* (London 1847)

George, Dorothy — *London Life in the Eighteenth Century* (London 1865)

Gibbins, Bob — *The Secret Life of Flowers* (London 1990)

Gorer, Richard — *The Growth of Gardens* (London 1978)

Hadfield, Miles — *A History of British Gardening* (London 1990)

Hadfield, Miles — *Pioneers in Gardening* (London 1955)

Hobhouse, P. — *Gardening Through the Ages* (London 1997)

Jacques, David — *Georgian Gardens* (London 1979)

Johnson, Hugh — *The International Book of Trees* (London 1999)

Kingdom-Ward, F. — *The Romance of Plant Hunting* (London 1924)

Lancaster, Roy — *Travels in China, A Plantsman's Paradise* (London 1968)

Lancaster, Roy — *A Plantsman in Nepal* (London 1995)

Laird, Mark — *The Flowering of the Landscape Garden* (Philadelphia USA 1999)

Leapman, M. — *The Ingenious Mr Fairchild* (London 2000)

Lemmon, K. — *The Golden Age of Plant Hunters* (London 1968)

Loudon, J. C. — *Encyclopaedia of Gardening* (London 1834)

Mitchell, Alan — *The Complete Guide to Trees of Britain & Northern Europe* (London 1985)

Morgan, J. and Richards, A. — *A Paradise Out of a Common Field* (London 1990)

Musgrave, T. and W. Gardner — *The Plant Hunters* (London 1998)

Philips, H. — *Mid-Georgian London* (London 1964)

Picard, Liza — *Dr Johnstone's London* (London 2000)

Porter, Roy — *English Society in the Eighteenth Century* (London 1982)

Pugsley, S. (ed) — *Devon Gardens: An Historical Survey* (Stroud 1994)

Rowse, A.L. — *The West in English History* (London 1949)

Sargent, C. S.   *Forest Flora of Japan* (Harvard USA 1894)
Stuart, David   *The Garden Triumphant* (London 1980)
Stuart, David   *Georgian Gardens* (London 1979)
Ward, F. Kingdom   *The Romance of Plant-Hunting* (London 1924)
Waters, Michael   *The Garden in Victorian Literature* (London 1988)
Whittle, Tyler   *The Plant Hunters* (London 1970)

ARTICLES AND PERIODICALS

Botanical Magazine
Country Life
The Cornish Garden
The Garden
Gardener's Chronicle
Garden History Magazine
Gardener's Magazine
Hortus
Illustrated London News
Journal of the Royal Horticultural Society
The Orchid Review

INDEX

Page numbers in *italic* refer to illustrations